THE
BEDFORD
TRIANGLE

'The first casualty when war comes is truth.'

Hiram Johnson
US Senate, 1917

THE
BEDFORD
TRIANGLE

US UNDERCOVER OPERATIONS FROM
ENGLAND IN THE SECOND WORLD WAR

MARTIN W. BOWMAN

First published in 1989 by Patrick Stephens Ltd
First published by Sutton Publishing Limited in 1996

This edition first published in 2009

The History Press
The Mill, Brimscombe Port
Stroud, Gloucestershire, GL5 2QG
www.thehistorypress.co.uk

British Library Cataloguing in Publication Data.
A catalogue record for this book is available from the British Library.

ISBN 978 0 7524 5098 8

Typesetting and origination by The History Press
Printed in Great Britain

CONTENTS

ACKNOWLEDGEMENTS

Many people helped in the preparation of this book, none more so than Connie Richards, a Bedford lady who has been researching the intriguing Miller mystery for many years, and who, along with her husband, Gordon, very kindly allowed me to use their home on several occasions as a base for operations. I am also especially indebted to Carl Bartram and many other researchers, contributors, veterans and fellow authors, some of whom very graciously allowed excerpts of their work to be used in this book. Mike Bailey was his customary altruistic self, permitting me to borrow publications and research material to fill in the gaps I could not, alone, fill. I would also especially like to thank the late Dennis Cottam, a life-long researcher into the Miller legend, for allowing me to quote parts from his extensive library of tapes and interviews. This book would be the poorer without them.

Obtaining photos of the top secret Carpetbagger group did not pose a problem because of the generosity of its members, in particular Sebastian Corricre, who started the ball rolling by providing me with a wealth of material, written and photographic. I am also most grateful to 'Rudy' Rudolph, Wilmer Stapel, Colonel Robert J. Fish (USAF Retd) for their immense contribution of photos and to the late Douglas Walker, who despite the incessant organizational demands of the Carpetbagger reunion, always found time to unearth more material and answer my individual questions.

I am no less grateful to:

John Bailey; Joseph Bodenhamer; Warren Borges; Thompson H. Boyd; William J. Carey (USAF Retd); Art Carnot; Elmer 'Bill' Clarey; Forrest S. Clark; Ron Clarke; Lester Cowling; the late Arthur Davies; Bill Dillon; Colonel Peter D. Dustman (USAF Retd); Professor Marcial and Mrs M. Louisa de Echenique; Roy Ellis-Brown; Don Fairbanks; Brigadier-General Richard E. Fisher (USAF Retd); Royal D. Frey; Peter Frost; Michael L.

Gibson; Ken Godfrey; Gene Goodbread; Chris Gotts; Paul E. Gourd; John W. Guthrie; Cliff and Wendy Hall; Lady Hastings; Mrs Edmund Walton Hill; Harry Holmes; Julius M. Klinkbeil; George T. Johnson; Dave Mayor; Roxanne M. Merritt, Curator, JFK Special Warfare Museum; Frank McDonald; the late William Miskho; Wiley Noble; Erwin Norwood, Lieutenant-Colonel (USAF Retd); John Page; André Pequet; the late Louis Pennow; Nick Pratt; John Reitmeier; Ivon Ressler; Denny Scanlon; Rodman St. Clair; Joseph Staelens; the late Victor Stilwell; Art Talbot; Bernard Tebbutt, Carpetbagger Museum, Harrington; Dale Titler; the late Edgar Townsend; Graham Truscott; Edward J. Twohig; Captain Barney Welch (USAF) and Maurice Whittle.

All of the above, whether they be former Carpetbaggers or English contributors, came forward with rare and exciting photographic material previously tucked away in the recesses of their albums and attic chests. I am most grateful to them all and to the other contributors for their hand of friendship.

PREFACE TO NEW, REVISED EDITION

In 1989, when this book was first published, many files, particularly those concerned with the OSS, political warfare operations, and SOE agent-dropping missions, remained closed. Many files in Britain are still sealed from public view but others, particularly those in the USA concerning Office of Strategic Services (OSS) operations, have been opened thanks to the US Freedom of Information Act. They give the background to some of the Carpetbagger missions which were described in the first edition. I am indebted to Carl Bartram, an OSS researcher in Wellingborough, for kindly making me aware of this new material, and for his help in tracing former members and providing photos, many of which are published here for the first time. Carl's diligent research and correspondence with OSS personnel has led to his appointment as their official UK contact, and in 1995 he hosted the very successful fiftieth anniversary OSS reunion in Northamptonshire. One result was that Carpetbagger and OSS personnel were able to compare notes on their joint operations during the clandestine war, 1942–5. Thanks to Noel Chaffey, the part played by the RAF in Carpetbagger operations from Harrington is revealed publicly for the first time.

During the Second World War at least sixty-one 'safe houses' were used for agent operations, and there were probably more. Many were located in the immediate vicinity of Harrington and Tempsford. Several, like Holmewood Hall, Gaynes Hall, Farm Hall, Sunnyside House and Brock Hall, were used as holding areas for Special Operations Executive (SOE) and OSS agents. The grounds of some of them were used for storage and training, while the real nature of operations at Finedon Hall can now be revealed. Now, all of these country houses have been added to the 'Triangle'. Some were known as Area 'E', Area 'H' and Area 'O', and they were used for American covert operations. Others, like Area 'B', were actually located in the USA, so where were Areas 'A', 'C', 'D', 'G', and possibly others, based? It begs the question: was Milton Ernest Hall one of these? What *really* did go on there and was it connected with the OSS, SOE, Political Warfare Executive (PWE) and codebreaking operations in the Bedford Triangle? The answers to these questions might eventually solve the Glenn Miller mystery too.

In 1992 files released gave details of monitoring operations in 1945 at Farm Hall when ten members of Germany's 'Uranium Club' were 'guests' there. I am most grateful to Professor Marcial and his wife, Mme Louisa de Echenique, for their hospitality and valuable assistance with source material concerning this period in the long history of Farm Hall. Several books published since contain transcripts of the secretly taped Farm Hall recordings, and their nuclear secrets make intriguing reading.

All of these revelations here and elsewhere reinforce the original premise put forward in the first edition of *The Bedford Triangle* that the close proximity of Allied intelligence gathering, political warfare and covert operations concentrated in one area was certainly not coincidental. Hopefully, now that the 'Triangle' has given up a few more of its sinister secrets, a clearer picture of these secret wartime operations has emerged. Undoubtedly, there are more to come. Whether we will be allowed to share in them is another matter.

INTRODUCTION

A dark limousine, its black shiny body and chromium bumpers gleaming in the faint July sunshine, motored along the meandering Bedford to Sharnbrook road on a quiet Sunday afternoon. Turning a bend the driver spotted two brick gateposts to reveal the entrance he was seeking. The car slowed and the chauffeur turned effortlessly into the narrow shingle drive. A few hundred yards further on there stood the baroque towers and solid walls of an imposing English stately home.

The official limousine picked up speed and motored sharply along the driveway, sending clouds of dust into the air and scattering a small fusillade of shingle over the well-manicured lawns. Onlookers could not see the car's occupants. The windows were glazed over with specially darkened glass allowing those inside to see out but preventing any curious people from looking in.

Already, the strains of 'In the Mood' and 'Chattanooga Choo Choo' could be heard from around the back of the hall as the driver turned in to the inner courtyard at the rear. Carefully, he wheeled the car towards the old stables and slowed to a halt. At the double, two tall lean men in dark suits, wearing sunglasses, exited from the rear of the car, slammed the doors and took up position at the front of the vehicle. Quickly, and with only a sideways glance, they held open the right hand door. An unknown silver-grey-haired man emerged. He also sported sunglasses but was dressed in a light coloured suit. The aides ushered the old gentleman into the hall before anyone could get a good look at him.

Inside the hall itself the aides took up their positions as the elderly gentleman went upstairs to a room at the front of the hall where an open window overlooked the scene on the lawns below. It was certainly a sight to stir the blood. The musicians, all dressed in brown American Air Force uniforms with blue SHAEF patches on their shoulders, were waiting for the lead from their band leader, similarly attired but in the uniform of a USAAF major. He stood erect, trombone in hand, at the front of the bandstand. As if taking his cue from the latest arrival at the open window above, he struck up the 'St Louis Blues' march. The packed crowd around the lawns went into raptures. Some who left to answer the call of nature were surprised to be turned away from the hall by the men in suits and barred from going upstairs as they attempted to reach the rest rooms.

Everything had been done to re-create the atmosphere of the heady days of 1944 when Glenn Miller and his Army Air Force Band had temporarily been based at Milton Ernest Hall. He and the band had also used Twinwoods airfield nearby as a launching pad for their musical travels to almost all the heavy bomb groups and fighter squadrons stationed throughout war-torn England.

The band, the band leader and a local audience were gathered but an Englishman who had promised to attend was missing. He had good reason to attend this, the Glenn Miller anniversary concert at Milton Ernest Hall, on a normally peaceful Sunday afternoon in July 1980. During the war he had been batman to Glenn Miller when he had stayed at the hall.

The Glenn Miller orchestra was famous in pre-war America for its distinctive sound, arrived at by mixing some jazz, a large element of swing, and unabashed showmanship characterized by the flapping of their mutes, standing for solos and the choreographed pumping of trombone slides. Miller pursued musical supremacy, demanded perfection and drove his musicians hard. In March 1939 the band was contracted to play for the summer season at the celebrated Glen Island Casino in New Rochelle, New York. They broadcast from the Casino ten times a week, thousands of listeners tuned in and soon the band was a household name. One hit record after another followed, including *Little Brown Jug*, *In the Mood*, *Chattanooga Choo Choo*, *Serenade in Blue*, *I Got a Gal in Kalamazoo* and *Moonlight Serenade*, which became Miller's theme song.

When the band went on the road, each live venue became a sellout. In Hershey, Pennsylvania, the band broke the attendance record set by the Guy Lombardo Orchestra eight years earlier and in Syracuse, New York, it played for the biggest dance audience ever. In December 1939 the band was hired for a three times weekly CBS national radio program sponsored by Chesterfield cigarettes. In the summer of 1940 the results of a poll made the Glenn Miller orchestra the top band in the country with almost double the number of votes of its nearest rival, Tommy Dorsey. Appearances in two Hollywood movies followed.

In 1941 the Glenn Miller band featured in *Sun Valley Serenade* and a year later they appeared in *Orchestra Wives*.

By this time the United States was at war and the draft deprived Miller of most of his established musicians. At age thirty-eight Miller was spared the call up but if he enlisted he could perhaps help the war effort in a musical capacity, possibly by updating military music for the troops. Miller first offered his services to the US Navy, but was turned down so he tried the Army. On 12 August 1942 Miller wrote to Brigadier General Charles D. Young, outlining a desire to enable music to reach servicemen at home and overseas on a fairly regular basis. He argued that this would considerably ease some of the 'difficulties of army life'. Miller's desire to join the armed forces may not have been driven by patriotic reasons entirely. In August 1942 a strike by the musicians' union against the record companies began and it was to last until September 1943, effectively keeping the bands out of the recording studios for a whole year. Although the record companies eventually capitulated, the strike was a severe blow for the Big Bands. Where once Benny Goodman was guaranteed $3,000 a night and Tommy Dorsey was getting $4,000, suddenly one night, the total take was just $700. A wartime 20 per cent amusement tax on nightclub receipts (which continued into peacetime) did not help. Tastes too began to change towards romantic singers who were much in demand for radio performances. In 1943 Frank Sinatra left the Tommy Dorsey band and other vocalists like Perry Como and Eddie Fisher followed. By the end of 1946 eight of the top US bands had disbanded.

Miller reported for induction on 7 October 1942. Eventually, he was named Director of Bands Training for the Army Air Forces Technical Training Command and authorized to organize a band at Yale University, which had become a training area for cadets. The outfit, officially known as the 418th Army Air Forces Band, was activated on 20 March 1943 with permanent station at Yale University.

Yale was not just a training area for cadets. It had links with counter-espionage going back to the days of the War of Independence when three members of the Culpeper spy ring, who graduated in the class of 1773, were established secretly by George Washington to gather intelligence on the British. Unlike the British, the US had no independent intelligence agency for most of its history. Spying was a rather informal affair, confined to the wartime military. With the outbreak of Second World War it became clear that the US needed a large-scale operation and quickly. What better place than academe? Especially since Yale was a hot bed of intrigue and unique secret societies such as the exclusive and infamous 'Skull and Bones' society, whose members are sworn to secrecy for life about the club's activities. The society's origins can be traced back to 1832, when William Russell founded it as retribution for a classmate's having been passed over by Phi Beta Kappa. Many wealthy American families made their money trafficking in drugs. Yale's secretive order of the Skull and Bones was involved in the opium trade and founding family were the Russells. Samuel Russell established Russell and Company in 1823 and acquired opium in Turkey, smuggled it into China and in 1830 established the Perkins Opium syndicate of Boston and Connecticut. During the Opium Wars Russell and Company was at times the only trading house operating in Canton and used the opportunity to develop strong commercial ties and handsome profits. The Skull and Bones cryptic iconography is derived from German University societies. Every year, each society taps a dozen juniors to join their upscale fraternity, where they recount their sexual histories, perform strange rituals, and prepare for a life among the ruling classes. Henry Lewis Stimson, President Theodore Roosevelt's Secretary of War, and Averell Harriman, American Ambassador to Moscow were members.

The majority of leading agents in OSS (Office of Strategic Services), which was founded in 1942 for the acquisition and analysis of intelligence, were provided by Yale. Many of them including Henry Luce owner of *Time-Life*, and his wife Marjorie, Henry Stanley founder of Morgan Stanley, and Captain Charles Black (who later married Shirley Temple) were 'bonesmen' too. In fact so many 'Yalies' joined the OSS that the university's drinking tune, the 'Whiffenpoof Song' became the secret organisation's unofficial song. At the heart of OSS and home to most of Yale's academics was the Research and Analysis branch (R&A) where social scientists, historians, linguists and even literary critics studied friends and enemies, real and potential, present and future. By the end of the war, R&A had gathered 3 million index cards, 300,000 photographs, a million maps, 350,000 foreign serials, 50,000 books, thousands of loose postcards – all indexed and cross-indexed, many of these gathered under the cover of the Yale library. Walter L. Pforzheimer, who helped found the CIA, was educated at Yale, arriving in 1931, then entered the army. Shortly after graduating from Officers Candidate School he was approached by a young officer who asked if he was interested in joining the intelligence community. 'Beats digging ditches,' he thought and became part of the OSS. He had two roles. One was as a liaison officer in the UK; the second was laundering money for the OSS. This was called the Yale Library Project and the money was supposedly being spent on the university's collections. After the war he became the OSS's Legislative Counsel for liaison with Congress and played a major part in writing the bill that brought the CIA into existence in 1947. His father made his fortune in oil but became a significant book collector. For Walter's twenty-first birthday, he gave him a library. It was, said Walter, a shock that shaped his life. He went on to collate a huge selection of intelligence material. When he gave the works to Yale University in 2002, they included more than 15,000 books.

Apart from R&A, OSS comprised four other major categories: Secret Intelligence (SI) was responsible for intelligence gathering. Secret Operations (SO) parachuted agents into the occupied countries. Morale Operations (MO) was involved with propaganda broadcasts to the enemy to undermine his morale. X-2 the counter-intelligence service, which also handled the German Ultra intelligence deciphered at Bletchley Park in Bedfordshire, was dominated by Yale students and Yale alumni such as English Literature professor Norman Holmes Pearson while James Jesus Angleton went on to a legendary career as director of the CIA's counterintelligence staff. Both belonged to the Skull and Bones. Myth says that the society's members form a clique that rules the world. They have promoted one another in enormously successful political and business careers and presided over the creation of the atomic bomb, as well as the CIA. Even today, there is reportedly a 'Bones club' within the CIA, which helps promote the intelligence careers of members of the Yale secret society. A statue of Nathan Hale, which stands in front of the headquarters of the Central Intelligence Agency in Langley, Virginia, is a replica of one on the campus of Yale University.

On 28 July 1943 Glenn Miller's new swinging military band made its debut in the Yale Bowl to a rapturous reception from the cadets. The Miller band continued to play at retreat parades and at review formations on the Yale Green, but really let their hair down performing at dances, open houses, parties and luncheons. On radio Miller's musicians broadcast *I Sustain the Wings*, a series designed to boost Air Force recruitment. The band was such a hit and its appearances at bond drives so successful that Miller began to fear that they might be held stateside instead of being sent overseas to boost troop morale. He need not have concerned himself for the band would go to England but was there an ulterior motive? While at Yale was Miller recruited for OSS propaganda activities and morale operations and even psychological warfare? It would not have been out of the question. OSS operatives included the cream of Hollywood. Actors Sterling Hayden (John Hamilton), William Holden, Broderick Crawford, Julia Child, Charlotte Gower and Hollywood directors, such as John Ford. After the war Ford produced two movies about the OSS called '13 Rue Madeleine' with James Cagney and 'Operation Secret' with Cornel Wilde. They were based in part on the exploits of Colonel Peter Ortiz, one of the most decorated Marine officers of Second World War, who had been a member of OSS since 1943.

OSS and the US intelligence services stopped at nothing that might help the US war effort. They rigged the Norwegian stock exchange. They even enlisted the help of the Mafia and German organizations. In 1941, the security of the port of New York was a matter of great concern, not only to the Third Naval District, but also to the Secretary of the Navy and the President of the United States. Everyone knew that the Mafia controlled the waterfront and Charlie 'Lucky' Luciano, who was serving thirty years in prison for prostitution, was obviously an important man in the underworld. Naval Intelligence was extremely concerned about sabotage and espionage on the New York waterfront. They were equally alarmed at the shipping losses. Between 7 December 1941 and February 1942 the US and its allies had lost seventy-one merchant ships to U-boats and by May 1942 272 ships had been sunk along the Eastern Seaboard Frontier. To secure the New York waterfront a Navy–Mafia alliance was concluded and Operation Underworld was born. As part of the deal, on 12 May 1942 Lucky Luciano was moved from the bleak Clinton Prison at Dannemora near the Canadian border to the more comfortable Great Meadow Prison in New York State.

By December 1942 Lieutenant Commander Charles Radcliffe 'Red' Haffenden and his staff of fifty officers and eighty-one EM and civilian men were working closely with their mob connections. Early in 1943 the Office of Naval Intelligence (ONI) set up a new department called F-Section to collect strategic information which would assist Husky, the allied invasion of Sicily. The mob co-operated and the greater part of the intelligence developed in the Sicilian campaign came from a number of Sicilians associated with Luciano. Haffenden was delighted and even went as far as proposing that Luciano be released. The mobster remained in prison however, but in February 1946, he was given passage to Italy to spend the rest of his life in exile. He died of a heart attack at Naples airport on 26 January 1962.

Officially, Operation Underworld never happened. On 17 May 1946 in an inter-office memorandum, J. Edgar Hoover, the chief of the FBI, wrote on the report, 'This is an amazing and fantastic case. We should get all the facts for it looks rotten to me from several angles... a shocking example of misuse of naval authority in the interests of a hoodlum. It surprises me that they didn't give Luciano the Navy Cross'. On 24 May 1946 after just four months as Commissioner of Marine and Aviation for the city of New York, Haffenden was dismissed.

Towards the end of the war in Operation Sunrise, John Foster Dulles negotiated a separate peace with the German Army in Northern Italy. Six days before VE Day, Operation Sunrise succeeded. Dulles recruited SS General Reinhard Gehlen, head of military intelligence for German forces in the Soviet Union. Gehlen's information was of substantial interest to those planning the Cold War, so he and his organization were enlisted in the good fight against the Soviets. Gehlen became director of the West German intelligence agency on its establishment in 1955. According to an article by John Loftus in the *Boston Globe* (29 May 1984) Dulles, with the assistance of the Vatican, engineered the escape of thousands of Gestapo and SS officers. Among these, it now seems likely, were Josef Mengele, Klaus Barbie and possibly Adolf Eichmann. Ex-filtrated Nazis were free to offer their services to Latin American dictators and drug traffickers, as well as the CIA. As Dulles said, 'For us there are two sorts of people in the world: there are those who are Christians and support free enterprise and there are the others.'

Meanwhile, in the spring of 1944 the AAF orchestra was finally ordered to England. Miller's arrival there can be attributed to General Dwight D. Eisenhower, the Supreme Allied Commander, who wanted Miller and his band for his brainchild, the AEF (Allied Expeditionary Forces) programme. Ike wanted the programme put out on air to the Allied troops who were taking part in the invasion of France and subsequent campaigns. Despite difficulties, Eisenhower's persistence, backed by support from Winston Churchill, finally ensured that the

AEF programme reached the airwaves and the new programme was inaugurated in March 1944. It went out on air for the first time over the BBC transmitter at Start Point, Devon the day after the successful Allied landings in Normandy, 7 June 1944. Miller and the band, which was now known as the American Band of the Supreme Allied Command, arrived at Gourock, Scotland on 28 June and entrained for London where they were immediately caught up in the V-1 flying-bomb blitz on the capital. Almost 5,000 people were killed. Miller persuaded the top brass to move his unit and on 2 July they left their billet at Sloane Court and travelled to Bedford, 50 miles north of London and safe from flying bombs. On the day after the men had vacated Sloane Court, a buzz bomb fell a few feet from the building, blowing away its entire front and leaving the place in ruins. Ever since 1940 Bedford played host to the major recording and broadcasting departments of the BBC and the Music Department and the BBC Symphony Orchestra, among others, had been moved from London to the comparative safety of Bedford.

At first Miller and his executive officer, Lieutenant Don Haynes, were billeted at the American Red Cross Officers' Club in Bedford but later Miller was given a flat in Waterloo Road and the band was billeted in two large detached houses in Ashburnham Road. VIIIth Air Force Service Command Headquarters at Milton Ernest Hall on the banks of the Ouse River about 10 miles north of Bedford carried out the day-to-day administration of the band. In between broadcasts and rehearsals at the Co-Partners Hall the band was taken to the headquarters in trucks for its meals. Captain Bob Seymour, in the Communication Section, recalls:

> It was about the most pleasant place to be during wartime that one can imagine. Our little post, being the closest military establishment, was designated as the payroll location for Glenn and the band. Some of the band members would hang around our place on days off, play poker or softball. Once in a while we'd have parties and invite the local gentry and some of the lonesome girls from Bedford or Cambridge. Captain Miller usually obliged by bringing out a small all-star band to play for dancing, featuring such renowned sidemen as Peanuts Hucko on woodwinds. One night Glenn goosed my hutmate's girlfriend on the dance floor resulting in a minor squabble which had to be pulled apart. Probably too much Scotch from our regular RAF ration. A hard life, indeed! But aside from those times we worked hard and did a good job. We kept them flying.

A small detachment from Miller's AEF band performed for the first time on Saturday evening, 8 July, at a dance for officers of VIIIth Air Force Service Command headquarters at Milton Ernest Hall. On 9 July the Miller band assembled in the Corn Exchange in Bedford for a rehearsal for their first programme, due to be broadcast that night; live on the American Armed Forces (AEF) network. That evening the Corn Exchange was filled to overflowing. Among the audience were some of the biggest names in show-business in America, including Humphrey Bogart and Lieutenant Colonel David Niven, Associate Director of Broadcasting services. Niven reported to Colonel Ed Kirby who had been appointed by SHAEF as Director of Broadcasting services with responsibility for liaison with the BBC. This magical opening performance was followed by hundreds more in England, many of them for troops at American bases throughout East Anglia. The band was so much in demand, especially for radio work, that it became impractical to take the whole unit to every venue. Miller formed sub-sections of the full band to perform different types of music on four radio series. *Strings With Wings* featured a full string section headed by George Ockner; *The Swing Shift*, a seventeen-piece dance band led by Ray McKinley; *Uptown Hall*, a seven-piece jazz ensemble under Mel Powell; and *A Soldier and a Song*, crooner Johnny Desmond accompanied by the full band.

On 15 December 1944 Glenn Miller is supposed to have vacated Milton Ernest Hall suddenly, leaving Twinwoods airfield for Paris. He was never seen again and his sudden disappearance is still something of a mystery. When it was known that Miller would not be returning, his room at the hall and his flat at Bedford were visited by council workmen who cleared out the contents of his lodgings including one of his last records, 'Farewell Blues'. It was as if Glenn Miller had never lived there at all or had even existed.

Miller's disappearance is one of several intriguing episodes in the wartime history of Bedford and its surrounding area. During the Second World War the hall had been the headquarters for the US Army Air Force Service Command but it is not widely known, and many have sought to keep it this way, what other covert activities the hall was put to by the United States military.

From late 1943 Milton Ernest Hall was in the middle of a very intriguing triangle which included many top secret Allied radio and propaganda transmitting stations, political warfare units, undercover British and American units dealing in espionage and subterfuge, as well as the heavy bomber and fighter bases used by the Eighth Air Force First Air Division.

Bletchley Park, Woburn Abbey, Chicksands Priory, North Crawley Grange and Hanslope Park were just a few of the places within the Bedford Triangle that were used by British codebreakers, Secret Intelligence Service (SIS) and the PWE. Why should an area of countryside within a 30 mile radius of Bedford contain so many sites and locations charged with political warfare and covert operations involving espionage, subterfuge and, as we will learn later, clandestine spy-dropping operations?

Certainly, some installations, like Bletchley Park Manor in Buckinghamshire, had been acquired by the British in the late 1930s when war clouds were gathering. The head of the British Government Code and Cypher School (GC and CS) at the outbreak of war was Alastair Denniston, a naval commander. He had already foreseen that expansion of British codebreaking efforts would be extremely important in any future war and had decided that the universities of Oxford and Cambridge would be his best source of personnel. As a result he selected a Victorian country mansion at Bletchley, between both university cities and with good rail links, for the expansion of the GC and CS.

The move from central London to north Buckinghamshire was made in August 1939. At the same time the school was officially renamed Government Communications Headquarters. Bletchley was codenamed Station X and the perimeter of Bletchley Park was patrolled by men of the RAF Regiment.

Bletchley was to be successful in breaking the German *Enigma* codes. The *Ultra* codebreaking effort became so large that several other units had to be set up, first in country houses in the area and later in large centres on the outskirts of London. Centres were set up at Gayhurst Manor, 8 miles north of Bletchley and at Wavendon Manor, 3 miles to the north-east. The centres were dispersed to safeguard *Ultra* from the risk of enemy action should one of the centres be bombed and put out of action. Wrens arriving at 'Station X' from London for the soul-destroying but vital job of cypher machine operators found themselves despatched to often pleasant surroundings such as Aspley Guise, Woburn Sands and to a beautiful Tudor house at Crawley Grange, 5 miles north of Wavendon. Houses in Aspley Guise were not just full of bombed-out evacuees from London. Many, known as 'Hush Hush' houses, were home for the cryptanalysts and mathematicians who worked at Bletchley Park and for propagandists who worked at Woburn Abbey, home of the Government's political propaganda unit of the PWE. All described themselves to local people as 'working for the Foreign Office'.

Doreen Page, who before the war had been a travel courier, was employed by the Foreign Office as a civilian linguist in the Naval Section, working closely with the Wrens. She recalls:

> I believe there were about 10,000 people working at Bletchley. I was billeted as a 'guinea pig' (so-called because our landladies received just one guinea a week for our keep!) with a family in Newport Pagnell. We were bussed in and out to and from Bletchley by the official transport coaches day and night. I actually worked alternate weeks on day or evening shift most of the time.

Meanwhile, in 1939, the RAF had also set up a listening post at Chicksands Priory, which stands in several hundred acres of ground just west of Shefford, for the purpose of intercepting enemy radio traffic and encoded messages. It is reported that the RAF personnel at Chicksands were instrumental in breaking German codes and permitting the Allies to take advantage of the resulting intelligence information. Much of this, of course, was handled at Bletchley Park Manor.

Late in 1940 Chicksands Priory received the unwelcome attentions of the Luftwaffe, which bombed the facility but only lightly damaged the priory. Chicksands' other role was in the field of communication. Much of the British radio traffic to support the Allied invasion of North Africa in November 1942 originated from the priory. Chicksands was never short of wireless telegraphy operators because the RAF Radio Communications School was stationed nearby at RAF Henlow.

In addition to the intelligence and propagandist centres and radio communications centres in Buckinghamshire and Bedfordshire there was also a sprinkling of airfields like Tempsford, Cheddington, Harrington and Chelveston, located within easy reach. These airfields were used, amid great secrecy, first by the British secret services and later, jointly by the American OSS, to mount propaganda leaflet raids and to send secret agents into the very heart of German-occupied Europe.

British spy-dropping operations were carried out under the auspices of SOE, which had its beginnings in the dark days of May 1940. Winston Churchill, on assuming the office of Prime Minister and Minister of Defence, aimed to restore British confidence after the military setbacks leading to the resignation of his predecessor Neville Chamberlain, and his first priority was to ascertain from his chiefs of staff whether Britain could fight on alone after the recent collapse of France.

Air Chief Marshal Sir Arthur Harris, Chief of Bomber Command, in particular, was adamant that Germany could only be put out of the war by the calculated and relentless destruction of her industrial and economic might from the air. Britain's military chiefs were united in one respect. They suggested that the only other way Hitler could be brought down was from within. The Allies had to sow the seeds of discontent and ferment rebellion in the subjugated nations of occupied Europe and Germany itself. This romantic ideal immediately appealed to the swashbuckling Churchill. In July 1940 Dr Hugh Dalton, the Minister of Economic Warfare, was placed in charge of sabotage and subversion and given the job of setting up a new organization called SOE. Churchill's directive to Dalton was to 'Set Europe Ablaze'.

The staid and correct military men in the regular branches of the armed services tartly referred to the SOE 'outcasts' as 'The Cloak and Dagger Mob'. In their naïvety the conventional staff officers overlooked the fact that these 'agents provocateurs' were in fact brave, highly trained professional killers, armed to carry out a very dirty form of subversive warfare involving assassination, murder, manipulation and sabotage among an implacable enemy whose Gestapo was a feared and ruthless foe.

Despite antagonism from the chiefs of staff and Air Marshal Harris in particular, under the direction of the far-sighted Brigadier Colin McVeagh Gubbins, SOE would grow from humble beginnings in June 1940 (when its headquarters was a small suite of offices at No. 64 Baker Street, London), to a peak of its achievements on D-Day, 6 June 1944. Harris opposed the allocation of valuable aircraft to the infant SOE because it represented a diversion away from the main bomber offensive. Therefore, the aircraft which did find their way to SOE were small in number and not all of them were entirely adequate for special operations.

SOE was responsible for the co-ordination of Resistance operations with Allied strategical requirements in enemy-occupied countries of

Europe. The French Resistance was among the leading contenders for arms and equipment. There were four distinct types of French Resistance activity, as identified by M.R.D. Foot, the noted historian: intelligence gathering; running escape and evasion lines; killing Germans; and lastly, political subversion.* Political subversion existed in France itself and was directed against the Vichy régime. Although all of these activities were closely monitored and assisted by secret organizations in London and Algiers (which provided money while further aid and comfort was provided by the PWE and, later, by the American OSS), their roots were planted in secret outposts scattered throughout the rolling countryside of Bedfordshire and Buckinghamshire.

For the purpose of this story the apex of the Bedford Triangle begins at Harrington. Its eastern side is at Tempsford while its western side includes Woburn Sands and Bletchley. Although much has been revealed about the *Enigma* code-breaking operation at Bletchley in recent years, the wartime secrecy surrounding SOE and OSS, and even some of the operations mounted from Tempsford and Harrington, is still covered by the Official Secrets Act.

Now, at long last, the triangle is beginning to give up some of its secrets, and conclusions about the disappearance of certain aircraft and their occupants can therefore be drawn.

---

* *Organisation and Conduct of Guerrilla Warfare* M.R.D. Foot (Purnell, 1973)

PROLOGUE
Douglas D. Walker

The big ash tree bent to the cold English spring wind, as it had forty
years before when the Spitfire fighter plane had ripped through it,
cartwheeled into the finance hut and slammed into the ground in front
of us. Douglas D. Walker, from Tacoma, Wisconsin, felt the years peeling
back to that day in 1945:

The time for going back to England with my wife Jackie to visit the
Air Force base from which I had flown in the Second World War had
arrived. I had retired from a business career and had plenty of time;
our sons had grown and left home; our relatives in Scotland had
offered their hospitality and our youngest had offered to house sit.

There were no longer the excuses that had surfaced whenever we
had discussed the trip. We both felt fine and, to put the icing on the
cake, the fortieth anniversary of VE Day in Europe was coming up
on May 8th. It was hard to believe, but the young airman was now a
greying retiree and the war was a distant forty years in the past.

May 8th was sunny, but brisk. We mixed with a crowd lining
Buckingham Palace Road and waved at Queen Elizabeth and Prince
Philip as they drove past on their way to Westminster Abbey for a
special service commemorating VE Day.

Three ladies in the crowd with pronounced 'cockney' accents talked
with us. They had heard our American voices. They asked if I had
been in England in the Second World War. I said, 'Yes, in the 8th Air
Force.' We reminisced about those dark days. They told us about the
terror they had experienced night after night during the 'Blitz' as the
Nazi planes attacked the docks and ships in the Thames River and
bombed their homes to rubble. One said, 'Luv, we was glad to see the
war come to an end forty years ago.' My wife and I solemnly echoed
the sentiment.

I remembered the original VE Day forty years before. It had been a joyous celebration as the men on our airbase had welcomed the end of the war in Europe with relieved abandon, shooting pistols and flares into the skies. And why not? There was an immense sense of relief that we would no longer have to face death in those same skies, as we had mission after mission. We – the lucky ones – would soon be going home to our loved ones. Our dead comrades would not. After the first moments of joy, we grieved for them.

Later, while visiting Winston Churchill's underground war Cabinet offices on Whitehall Street, now open to the public as a museum, we saw Walter Cronkite getting ready to participate in a special BBC VE Day commemorative TV broadcast to America. We paused in awe in front of Winston Churchill's desk where he had broadcast many of his radio speeches during the Second World War, including his famous, 'We shall fight them on the beaches, we shall fight them in the streets. . . .'

I remember seeing the great Prime Minister drive by when I was on leave in London one weekend in 1944. His bulldog look was no sham; his defiant rhetoric and adamant stance rallied his people to do their part to help earn ultimate allied victory when, early in the war, it looked like England was doomed to annihilation, as she faced the Nazi war machine alone after the fall of France.

After taking in the sights of London, we rented a car and drove towards Northamptonshire in the 'Midlands' section of England. I wanted to see what remained of my old airbase. I had a strong desire to return to this place, which played such an important part in my young life in the Second World War.

Forty years ago, like thousands of other young men, I was based in England as an aircrewman on a B–24 Liberator in the 8th Air Force. I was stationed near Kettering in Northamptonshire, not far from the city of Leicester, about 80 miles north-west of London.

There were many 8th Air Force bases in this section of England. On any given morning, the sky over Northamptonshire would be filled with many hundreds of B–24s and B–17s circling and assembling into units for that day's bombing attacks on Germany. (More than 26,000 8th Air Force aircrewmen died in the skies over France and Germany in the Second World War.)

My outfit was the 492nd Bomb Group, flying out of Harrington Air Force base. We did not fly normal daylight bombing missions; we flew black Liberators on clandestine missions at night – dropping teams of radio-equipped spies into France and Germany as well as munitions and supplies to underground Resistance forces in France, Denmark and Norway. We bore the nickname Carpetbaggers.

In the spring of 1945, one of our crews parachuted a group of sixteen American commandos of Norwegian descent into the Jaevsjo Lake area of Norway, along with ten tons of explosives and supplies. Jaevsjo Lake is located near the Swedish–Norwegian border. These commandos were a special arm of the OSS (the forerunner of the CIA) and, joining up with a small group of Norwegian Resistance fighters, they proceeded to blow up rail lines and bridges, cutting the main north–south railway lines. Outnumbered ten to one, the commando force completed their missions and managed to outrun their Nazi pursuers in a demanding 50 mile ski chase into the mountains. They successfully evaded the Nazi patrols until the end of the war.

Two of our aircrews from Harrington crashed during the first four attempts to land additional commandos and supplies in the mountainous Jaevsjo Lake area, killing sixteen aircrewmen and ten commandos. These crashes were due to the exceptionally severe weather conditions in the Norwegian mountains in early 1945. Our crew was one of the lucky ones – we had to turn back on a mission to this area during that period after encountering blinding blizzards and heavy icing conditions.

As I drove along looking at the rolling, mist-shrouded landscape I had known so well from the air forty years previously, I began to remember faces of long-forgotten friends, as well as incidents I had tucked away in my 'memory bank' and now recalled with exact detail. I turned to my wife and told her about a sunny morning in February 1945 when I was strolling to the mess hall with a few friends to have lunch. We had noticed an English Spitfire fighter plane landing on the runway nearby (this did not surprise us – many English pilots landed at our base to purchase American cigarettes and candy bars). The pilot hopped out, strolled in our direction and stopped to chat with us. He was a member of the Free Polish Air Force and was just finishing his training. We invited him to join us for lunch. During lunch we learned how, as a child, he had fled from the Germans when they had invaded his country and how he had waited impatiently to be old enough to join the Free Polish Air Force so that he could 'fight Messerschmitts'.

As we parted company, he told us to watch him – he was going to perform a 'fly over' and show us some 'fancy flying'. We watched as he skilfully threw his Spitfire into a series of aerobatics, until, in horror, we saw him dip too low to the ground: a wing ripped through a nearby tree, then the plane smashed into the finance hut and dug a hole into the ground near us.

We ran to help him, but there was nothing we could do. We watched helplessly as he was pronounced dead by the medics. Fortunately, the loss of life was not greater; the two men normally in the finance hut were in the mess hall when the accident happened.

I also remembered a happier time when I had travelled to Aberdeen, Scotland on a three-day pass to see my grandparents, whom I had not seen since I was four. I recalled how their eyes had lit up when I had unpacked five pounds of sugar, a large tin of Spam and three pounds of butter – through the courtesy of a friendly mess sergeant. They hadn't seen food like that since wartime rationing started in 1940.

My base had been located at Harrington, a one-pub hamlet about 5 miles from the town of Kettering. Because I didn't think I could locate the place without help, I followed my wife's suggestion and stopped at the police station in Kettering. I didn't think that the young sergeant on duty would be able to help me as it was obvious he wasn't even born when the war was on. However, surprisingly, he knew all about the history of the airfield and was able to give me exact directions. He regretfully pointed out that I wouldn't see much evidence of the airbase. Seems they had torn it down after the war to resume farming operations. However, he said we might see some pieces of the original concrete runway.

As we drove, the weather turned nasty. A cold north-east wind was blowing and premature dusk was setting on. We drove over single-track roads surrounded by rolling farmlands and very little sign of habitation. Finally, we reached the general area described by the police sergeant. It was in the midst of hundreds of acres of farmland. I could see no familiar traces of the airbase, not even any pieces of the old concrete runway. I was beginning to feel despondent.

The contrast was even more sombre, comparing this pastoral scene with one forty years previously, when the area had been a bustling beehive of activity, with more than a thousand men and dozens of airplanes creating a busy and vital aerodrome.

It was now darker. I started to turn the car around to leave when I noticed an old stone farmhouse in the distance. I decided to talk with the inhabitants to see if they could help me find some remnants of the base.

Two fat geese snapped at me as I left the car to knock on the door. There was no response to my knocking. I backed the car up to leave, just barely missing the geese, when I noticed a big man approaching the car with a dog at his heels. He was dressed in work clothes and boots.

I stopped, opened my window and began to explain that I was an American who had been stationed at Harrington air base during the Second World War and had returned to try to find the place. Halfway through my explanation he gave a big friendly smile, and when I had finished, swept his hand towards the farmhouse and invited us in. He said, 'Any 8th Air Force man is welcome here. Come on in with your fine lady and I'll give you all the information you need.' He cheerily introduced himself as John Hunt. My falling spirits took a quick upturn.

We followed him into the farmhouse, which we later learned was over 300 years old. His wife Angela proved to be an attractive and intelligent mother of two girls, who hadn't heard my knocking because she was bathing the children.

Jackie and I sat down in their living room in front of a cheery gas burner to get rid of the May chill, as Mr Hunt took out an illustrated book on the history of the RAF and US Air Force operations in Northamptonshire. He pointed to a picture of a black Liberator taking off from Harrington with a nearby farmhouse in the background. I recognized the farmhouse as one that had stood across the street from our quarters. He indicated that it was still there. There was an accompanying article about the operations of our base and about our clandestine missions during the war.

John admitted that even though he had been only a few months old at the start of the war, he had become a 'buff' concerning air operations in the Second World War and knew all about the operations of the 8th Air Force bases in the vicinity, including a special interest in Harrington due to its proximity to his farm. I had found the right man at last.

John said that he had become familiar with Harrington Air Force base in the late fifties when he used to ride a motorbike on the old runways. He remembered the government removing the Nissen hut barracks and 200 acres of concrete runway, tarmacs and revetments to turn the acreage back into farming.

He also remembered the demolition of the control tower complex. 'But', he said, 'your old brick administration building is still standing, together with a mess hall.' I felt better. At least I would get to see something of the old base.

John was also familiar with other 8th Air Force bases in the vicinity, such as a nearby B–17 base at Grafton Underwood. We later drove there to see a marble monument honouring the men of the

384th Bombardment Group, which flew from that base. The 384th enjoyed a singular achievement: they dropped the first US Air Force bombs on Germany in 1942 and the last bombs in 1945.

I remembered this base. They were only 3 miles from us. One morning there was a tremendous blast which shook our quarters. We rushed out to see a plume of black smoke rising into the sky in the direction of Grafton Underwood airbase. Later, we learned that a B-17 fully loaded with fuel and 500 lb bombs had crashed on take-off, killing all ten of the crew and injuring crews on two other bombers awaiting take-off. In all, the 384th lost more than 1,600 young aircrew flyers in two years of operations against Germany.

John offered to show my wife and me what remained of the Harrington air force base if we would return the next morning. We readily accepted and drove to Kettering and stayed at the Royal Hotel for the night. The back of the menu in the hotel dining room featured a copy of a letter written by Charles Dickens to his wife in London while a guest at the hotel in 1835.

The next morning was cold and drizzly. The wind whipped up suddenly, but I didn't mind a bit. Finally, after forty long years, I was about to return to the wartime scenes of my youth, along with the girl who had patiently waited for me to come back.

As we drove through the first of several open gates, John waved to a man watching us from the front yard of a modern farmhouse. He explained that this man was the farm manager for the owner, the late Sir Gerald Glover. I asked how he achieved the knighthood and learned that he received the honour as a result of his wartime services, 'in the same type of clandestine spying as you chaps, but on the British side of things'. John went on to explain that Sir Gerald had purchased the majority of the 800–acre airbase after the war to conduct farming operations.

We drove deeper into the farm pastures over rutted and muddy roads. Now and then we would ride over concrete surfaces and John would point out old revetments where bombs were stored – or fuel dumps – or airplane tarmacs and portions of old service roads. Most of the decaying installations in the area were overgrown with weeds and bushes.

Finally, we came to the crest of a long hill and John pointed across planted fields to a copse of trees about 2 miles away in the distance. He explained that the main runway had run from where we were standing to these trees. Of course, no concrete remained, but I needed no concrete under my feet – I suddenly visualized that 2-mile long runway in my mind as it existed forty years ago. I saw no crops – just a ribbon of white concrete, a black Liberator and eight anxious young men as we roared down the runway in the darkness on our way to drop fully loaded canisters of munitions, guns and supplies to the Norwegian underground; or to parachute a team of spies into Germany.

John interrupted my reverie to ask if we would now like to see the old administration building and S–2 Group Intelligence hut. I asked where they were located and he pointed across the farmland to a deep gully about a half-mile away.

John explained that a contractor specializing in earthmoving and water drilling had bought a piece of the airbase which had contained the only buildings left standing from the original Second World War construction.

Before we visited the contractor's property, John drove me to the Harrington pub. It wasn't open at that time of the morning, but it was fun to see it looking the same, still retaining its old-fashioned thatched roof. It brought back fun-filled memories for me of 'bicycle missions' to the pub to hoist a few pints of 'bitter'. Of course, the trip back to our quarters on a wobbly bicycle in the dark saw quite a few of us plunging into the ditches alongside the road, laughing all the way.

As we approached the contractor's home, the buildings came into view. I felt a real excitement as I recognized the brick administration building which had contained the commanding officer's office, the post office, the map room, and Operations room where I had reported many times to learn the details of our missions.

As we toured through the building, now converted to stables, workshops and storage rooms, Mr J.B. Tebbutt, the contractor, told me that when he had purchased the building there was a large poster in the Operations room with the names of all the aircrew members who had served at the base, their aircraft designations and the names of those who did not make it back from their missions. I excitedly asked him where it was, only to learn that one of his men had burned it up by accident when cleaning out the building.

We went outside and I asked my wife to snap my picture with the only other building in the background – a Nissen hut formerly used as an officers' canteen – now a decaying storage building.

Mr Tebbutt said that our commanding officer had been back several times over the years. In fact, he had been there a few months ago and had told Mr Tebbutt that a stone memorial was being planned for installation on the site as a perpetual reminder of what had gone on there during the war and to honour those men who had given their lives. I was very glad to hear this. [The memorial, designed by Douglas and Jacqueline Walker and based on a concept by R. Wallace Clarke, was dedicated in 1987.]

When we turned to go, Mr Tebbutt said that his uncle had worked at the base all during the war and had told him about a Spitfire that had hit a tree and then careened into the finance hut, killing the Polish pilot. He pointed to a large ash tree about fifty yards away and said, 'That's the tree.'

At that moment, I saw it all over again. The Polish flyer – the crashing Spitfire – the ambulance. I told Mr Tebbutt that I had stood almost in this same spot and watched it happen forty years ago. He was surprised, but pleased that I could verify the details.

He pointed out a low concrete foundation and slab half hidden by weeds and said, 'That's where the finance hut was located. We know it was because we found an old safe in the building when we bought the property. We've since torn the Nissen hut down.' Then he mused, 'You know, we're still digging up pieces of that Spitfire from time to time.'

As we drove away, I took one look in the direction of the now obliterated runway – wearing a mantle of trees and lush farm crops – and, for one last time, imagined the distant roar of a black Liberator lumbering down the runway, shattering the quiet of the night with pulsating engines.

1

THE CARPETBAGGER PROJECT

The major USAAF effort to supply the Resistance movements and secret armies in Europe began in the summer of 1943 under the codename 'Carpetbagger', which someone had lifted from the annals of the American Civil War. At first the Americans had been as unprepared for Resistance support as the British had been in 1940. OSS was introduced to supplement SOE operations and by 1942 was functioning very effectively under the dynamic leadership of Colonel (later General) William 'Wild Bill' Donovan. In September 1942 the joint Anglo-American SOE-SO was formed and the Americans began participating in the planning of operations in many north-west European countries.

Eventually, OSS consisted of five major categories: Secret Intelligence (SI), responsible for intelligence gathering; Secret Operations (SO), the parachuting of agents into occupied countries; Morale Operations (MO), which involved propaganda broadcasts to the enemy to undermine his morale; and 'X–2', the counter-intelligence service.* A Research and Analysis (R and A) Branch provided analysis of bomb damage and its repercussions on the German economy.

Unlike SOE, which came under the aegis of the British Government, authority for the Carpetbagger Project came from the American Joint Chiefs of Staff. It was they who directed that OSS would be the US Agency charged with sabotage and with the 'Organization and Conduct of Guerilla Warfare'. In a cable dated 26 August 1943, from the Commanding General ETOUSA (European Theater of Operations USA), to the War Department, these directives were approved and three days later in a letter to Donovan the OSS was directed to work out with G–2 and G–3, ETOUSA, 'the composition of Staffs for Army and Army group HQ and to proceed

---

* *Piercing the Reich* Joseph E. Persico (Ballantine Books, 1979)

with the organization and training of Jedburgh teams for the purpose of co-ordinating activities behind the enemy lines.'

Hundreds of Jedburgh teams were to be dropped into France just prior to and after the Allied invasion of Normandy. These teams consisted of three members, usually English, French and American. Most Jedburgh teams were dropped into areas well in advance of the allied invasion forces in order to provide a general staff for the local Resistance wherever they landed. They also organized sabotage and the disruption of enemy supplies and harried the retreat of enemy troops. Jedburgh teams usually remained in the field until overrun by the advancing Allied forces.

At first, Carpetbagger operations would be mounted from the English Midlands. Later in the war, missions were extended to include Scandinavia when a team headed by Bernt Balchen, the famous arctic explorer, mounted operations from Leuchars in Scotland. First, the 'Sonnie' project, as it was called, was so successful that ultimately, 3,016 passengers were evacuated, including 965 American internees. In July 1944 Carpetbagger crews were involved in the 'Ball Project' (so named because of the removal of the ball turret from the B–24), and carried out supply drops to the Norwegian underground.*

Initially, personnel for the Carpetbagger unit were drawn from the 4th and 22nd Squadrons of the 479th Anti-Submarine Group, which had been disbanded in August 1943. They were selected because of their experience in long navigational patrols at night. For almost three months, operating from an aerodrome at Dunkeswell, Devon, these two squadrons, flying Consolidated B–24D Liberator aircraft, had carried out anti-submarine sweeps over the Bay of Biscay, flying lone patrols of between ten and twelve hours' duration, looking for German U-boats. Their record was a good one. On one occasion they had taken on formations of twelve Ju–88s and had won through. They had even been fired upon by anti-aircraft batteries along the Spanish coast.

In October 1943 Anti-Submarine Command was disbanded and the task of keeping the Atlantic sealanes free of U-boats passed exclusively to the US Navy and RAF Coastal Command. On 26 October the ground section of the 22nd Anti-Submarine Squadron left Dunkeswell by motor convoy for Alconbury. They overnighted

---

* *The B–24 Liberator 1939–45* Martin W. Bowman (PSL, 1989)

at Yettingdon and arrived at Station 102 the next morning. Meanwhile, the air echelon had flown north from Devon but bad weather prevented them from landing at the Huntingdonshire base. They were forced to land at other airfields over a wide area and many were fogged in for a week. Ground crews in the 4th Anti-Submarine Squadron had better luck, leaving Dunkeswell on 1 November by train and road. At Alconbury the 4th and 22nd joined the men and machines of the 482nd (Pathfinder) Group.

At first the ex-anti-submarine group crews did not know what their new role would be, although the later change in squadron designation from 'anti-submarine' to 'bombardment' made them draw the wrong conclusions. Existing squadrons in the 482nd were carrying out pathfinder missions but the two new squadrons took on a curious demeanour when their B–24D Liberators were painted black. It was an appropriate choice of colour because the new commanding officer, Lieutenant-Colonel Clifford J. Heflin, was still in the dark.

Not until 24 October 1943 did Heflin learn what the new duties of his former 22nd Anti-submarine Squadron and of the 4th would be. On this date Heflin, his deputy, Major Robert W. Fish and Lieutenants Robert D. Sullivan and Akers, were summoned to attend a meeting at Bovingdon. They were met by Colonel Williamson, A–3 of VIII Bomber Command, Group Captain (later Air Vice-Marshal) E.H. 'Mouse' Fielden from RAF Tempsford, Colonel Oliver of 8th Air Force and Colonel Joseph F. Haskell and Major Brooks of OSS, London. While the Americans were new to the sabotage game, Fielden and the RAF Special Duty squadrons in complete contrast, were old hands. Fielden was a former Captain of the King's Flight and had taken command of No. 138 Squadron in August 1941. RAF clandestine air operations on behalf of SOE had begun in August 1940 and by mid-1941 was operating with a handful of Lysander single-engined army co-operation aircraft and Whitley bombers. The Lysanders and later Hudsons, were used in the dangerous task of flying out SOE agents who had finished their spell of duty in France, or who were on the run from the Gestapo. Escaping RAF airmen were also plucked to safety on occasions. Altogether, the Lysanders delivered 304 agents to France and exfiltrated 410 to Britain for the loss of thirteen aircraft and six pilots.

War-weary Whitley and Wellington bombers and later Halifax, Stirling and Hudson aircraft, were used for long-range parachute operations. By February 1942 138 Squadron had been joined in special duty operations by No. 161 Squadron and both squadrons began operations from Tempsford in the spring of 1942. Their hard-won experience and techniques were made available to the USAAF.

Williamson explained that the former anti-submarine squadrons had been assigned duties as 'sabotage' squadrons. Amazed at this development, Heflin and his junior officers listened attentively as they were briefed in turn by the OSS officers and the British Group Captain about their involvement in a new operation with the cover name 'Carpetbagger Project'. For the most part, Heflin's squadrons would come under Special Operations. OSS would direct operations and arrange details of reception grounds (working in close co-operation with SOE who would specify the contents of the containers and packages to be delivered).

SO–SOE anticipated that the strength of Resistance groups on D–Day would be about 160,000. The continual problem that this posed to the Allied high command was their leadership, communications and supplies. The Resistance forces had to be organized into well-disciplined units, controlled by an effective system of communications and be capable of carrying out military operations such as attacks on enemy installations, disruption of enemy road and rail systems and hindering the deployment of enemy troop and tank movements.

In France this aim was a commander's nightmare. The Free French operated under a command network of no fewer than a dozen *délégués militaires régionaux* (DMRs) who were able to request arms drops, via radio contact with SOE, from the Allied air forces. The Resistance movements were also divided between the *Front National* and the Communist-directed *Franc-tireurs et Partisans* (FTP).*

The situation was made even more intriguing by political infighting between the Allies. In London General Charles de Gaulle claimed to represent France and therefore argued that all operations in his country should come under his direction.** Initially, the British and American governments opposed this on political grounds. They also mistrusted the apparent lack of security, justifiably on occasions, at Free French Headquarters. All this led SOE to establish an 'independent French' (or 'F') section headed by Colonel Maurice Buckmaster (which by June 1944 was operating 50

---

* *Triumph of the Resistance* M.R.D. Foot (Purnell, 1973)
** *Helping the Resistance* Major General R.H. Barry (Purnell, 1973)

réseaux in France). Understandably, de Gaulle was unhappy about this arrangement, which persisted until 1944 when in preparation for D-Day, he formed the FFI (*Forces Françaises de l'Intérieur*).

It was proposed that the SO (Special Operations) Branch of the OSS undertake the delivery of supplies to Resistance groups in a plan co-ordinated with the SOE. Heflin's crews would air drop the Jedburgh teams, supplies and small arms, light automatic weapons, munitions, explosives, demolition and incendiary equipment. Generally speaking, pinpoints suitable for dropping a certain number of containers or packages would be proposed by SO. It was envisaged that no more than three squadrons of aircraft would be needed to supply the Resistance groups in occupied Europe.

At first approval was given only for supplying Resistance groups on a limited scale, for previous British experience had shown that considerable time would be needed to train crews for this type of operation. Lieutenant Wilmer L. Stapel, pilot of one of the original twelve B–24Ds commanded by Colonel Heflin that arrived at Dunkeswell in early August 1943, recalls:

> After numerous briefings and stern warnings about ever discussing our clandestine operation, with a constant threat of court martial, if we ever disclosed anything at any time, one more prerequisite remained to be done before our crews would be turned loose over the continent of Europe. Each pilot, navigator and bombardier had to fly two combat missions each, with a combat ready crew. Since the USAAF had none, we were sent to the RAF squadrons at Tempsford to fly with their crews.

As has already been mentioned, both Nos. 138 and 161 Squadrons were stationed at the airfield, located just to the north of Sandy in Bedfordshire. To maintain security, Tempsford was known simply as 'Gibraltar Farm' to civilians and servicemen alike. Seemingly, its only link with civilization was with the main London to Edinburgh railway which runs parallel to the base and which is bounded on the west side by the Great North Road. The Special Duty squadrons at Tempsford had amassed a wealth of experience on varied cloak-and-dagger missions to the Low Countries and France and as far afield as Austria, Norway, Poland and Czechoslovakia. The assassination of SS–*Obergruppenführer* Reinhard Heydrich, the Nazi *Reichsprotektor* of Bohemia and Moravia, was carried out on 27 May 1942 by Czech agents who had taken off from Tempsford. Heydrich was mortally wounded and died on 4 June 1942.

MI6 and SOE agents departing from and arriving at Tempsford were held at staging areas at Tempsford and Hasells Halls, and at Farm Hall, an unimposing mansion on West Street in Godmanchester. In 1942–3 Farm Hall (Special Training School No. 61) was used by six members of the Gunnerside team, whose mission was to destroy the German heavy water plant at Vermork in Norway, near the region of Telemark close to the electricity-generating area and nitrate plant at Rjukan. It was known that German scientists were working towards developing an atomic bomb and it was crucial therefore towards developing an atomic bomb and it was crucial therefore to deprive them of heavy water, which was needed to slow down the process of atomic fission. Thirty-four commandos of the First Airborne Division had taken off from Scotland on 19 November 1942 in two gliders to sabotage the plant but the attempt had ended in disaster when one of the towing aircraft crashed into a mountainside in Norway and both gliders crashed. All the surviving commandos were captured and shot.

For three months the Gunnerside team trained at Farm Hall, practising the demolition of simulated heavy water concentration cells. One member of the team, Knut Haukelid, described the Hall thus:

> It was a station for people who were going to Europe on secret errands and who had to wait for planes. The place was very closely guarded. A number of servicewomen kept the house in order, cooked the meals and gave the boys some social life . . . But if we asked the FANYs [First Air Nursing Yeomanry] about our comrades who had gone out before us, they became dumb and knew nothing.*

According to Arnold Kramish in his book *The Griffin*:

> Farm Hall was not just a staging area for agents going out; it was an interrogation centre for agents and their captives coming in. Every room in the house, and some of the garden trees, was wired with microphones and there was a listening post in an isolated room.

---

* *The Griffin* Arnold Kramish (Macmillan, London)

In the early 1990s, floorboards were removed and revealed underfloor bugging devices in 'finely crafted containers, like pencil boxes, with wires in them . . . Loyalties were automatically questioned, and the wiring gave information sometimes not elicited through interrogation'. Kramish states that the bugging devices had been put there on the orders of Lieutenant Commander Eric Welsh, a Royal Navy intelligence officer in SOE. Professor R.V. Jones, in his book *Most Secret War*, says that he asked for microphones to be placed there in 1945 before the arrival of ten German nuclear physicists (of which more later).*

On 16 February 1943 the Gunnerside team, led by Lieutenant Joachim Rönneberg, took off from Tempsford and parachuted into Norway where they rendezvoused with four men of the *Rype* (Grouse) advance scouting party which had been dropped on 18 October 1942 to reconnoitre the area. The sabotage team made its way to Rjukan and during the night of 27/28 February blew up the heavy water concentration cells without any casualties. In the event, the Germans were able to repair the damage and make the plant operational again but production of heavy water was denied them for a critical few months and a stock of about 350 kilograms of heavy water was lost.**

Tempsford, therefore, provided an ideal training school for the eager young American aircrews. The Special Duty Squadrons' ability to exfiltrate secret agents and escaping aircrews from Occupied Europe did not go unnoticed either. During 1943 no fewer than 157 pick-up operations,† of which 111 were successful, were attempted by Lysander pilots of 161 Squadron. During operations from Tempsford and the forward base at Tangmere 138 Squadron made over 2,500 sorties and dropped almost 1,000 agents in occupied Europe for the loss of seventy aircraft.

The first Americans to arrive at the Tempsford 'academy' were Robert W. Fish (now Lieutenant-Colonel), Robert D. Sullivan (now Captain) and the Group Intelligence Officer and one crew, captained by Lieutenant-Colonel Robert L. Boone of the 406th Squadron.

---

* *Most Secret War: British Scientific Intelligence 1939–1945* Professor R.V. Jones (Hamish Hamilton, 1978)
** Introduction by David Cassidy in *Hitler's Uranium Club; The Secret Recordings at Farm Hall* by Jeremy Bernstein (American Institute of Physics)
† *Moon Squadron* Jerrard Tickell (Hodder, 1960)

Altogether, the party of American officers spent two months at the top secret Bedfordshire airfield. The American officers and crews found the training routine very demanding and completely different to anything they had been used to. In order that accurate drops could be made, pilots would have to get down to within 400–600 ft off the ground and reduce their flying speed to 130 mph or less. The low speed reduced the chances of damage to parachutes, as the shock is much less at the slower speed. The pilots, navigators and bombardiers each made two operational flights with RAF crews in the Halifax. The first flight involving an American trainee was made on 3/4 November but it ended disastrously when the 138 Squadron Halifax in which Captain James E. Estes was flying struck high ground in fog at Marcoles-les-Eaux. Only the tail gunner survived the crash. By 7 November, numerous training flights had been made and only the lack of suitably modified Liberators was preventing American crews from flying their own missions.

Converting to nocturnal special duty specification from daylight long-range bomber configuration was enough to tax even the most hardened of ground crew personnel. Ball turrets had to be removed and replaced with cargo hatches, nicknamed 'Joe Holes', through which the secret agents or 'Joes' dropped. A static line was installed for them and to facilitate bale outs, the hole had a metal shroud inside the opening. If the Liberator did not have a ball turret, a hole was made there. Plywood was used to cover the floors and blackout curtains graced the waist windows and navigator's compartment, while blister side windows had to be installed to give the pilots greater visibility. Later models had their nose turrets removed. A 'greenhouse' was fashioned instead to allow the bombardier a good view of the drop zone and to enable him to carry out pilotage for the navigator. Suppressors or flame dampers were fitted to the engine exhausts to stifle the tell-tale blue exhaust flames. Machine-guns located on both sides of the waist were removed, leaving only the top and rear turrets for protection. In flight the entire aircraft would be blacked out except for a small light in the navigator's compartment.

Oxygen equipment would not be needed at the low levels flown and was removed. A variety of special navigational equipment and radar aids had to be installed. The air crews learned that during the non-moon period, flights at night would be made with the use of *Rebecca* and an absolute radio altimeter. By means of all this equipment, the percentage of accuracy on a drop could be even greater than with ordinary visual pilotage.

Rebecca was a British radar directional, air to ground device which was originally fitted to aircraft in the RAF Special Duties squadrons. It was used to record impulses or 'blips' on a grid and directed the navigator to the ground operator. By varying the intensity or frequency of the blip, the ground operator (whose set was known as *Eureka O*) could transmit a signal letter to the aircraft. These signals could be activated from up to seventy miles away to enable the aircraft crew to pin-point its drop zone. *Eureka* sets, which weighed up to 100 lb, were parachuted in to Resistance groups. However, many Joes and Resistance radio-operators, not wishing to lug the set, which was heavy, or run the risk of being caught with it in their possession, refused to use it.*

While training flights continued Sullivan made a study of Intelligence techniques and Fish surveyed the entire operational procedure. On 9 November King George VI and Queen Elizabeth visited Tempsford. Six American crews were among those who were introduced to the royal party and the following day Major Joyce, the 8th Air Force Security Officer, and Captain Stearns of the OSS arrived to obtain information and to assess progress made thus far. On 11 November Lieutenant Cross, a bombardier, failed to return when the Halifax in which he was flying was lost on a sortie to France.

These early training flights in which the Americans flew with their brother officers and men of the RAF squadrons were proving quite an education, in more than one sense of the word, as Wilmer Stapel recalls:

My first introduction flight was with a Flight Sergeant and his crew on the night of 15 November in a Halifax bomber. I rode the co-pilot position. The mission consisted of cargo and 'Joes' that we were to drop somewhere east of Paris. The weather was not favourable and although we reached the drop area, we were unable to complete the drop. On our way homeward we arrived at an area where we were in and out of cloud. Before the navigator could pinpoint our position, the enemy did.

We were showered with a barrage of flak before the pilot could take evasive action. No. 3 engine was hit and put out of

* *Flight Most Secret* Gibb McCall (Kimber, 1981)

commission. The cockpit lights were put out by the intense firing from the ground and several anti-aircraft shells burst on my side of the plane directly behind my seat. Fragments of shrapnel scattered throughout the cockpit, striking the pilot, flight engineer and radio operator.

The pilot skilfully manoeuvred the aircraft out of ack-ack range and an assessment was made of the damage and injured. While the pilot and other crew members were given first aid treatment for their wounds (none were real serious), I was asked to fly the aircraft: my one and only experience in flying a Halifax. The pilot returned to the cockpit and managed to fly the plane back to Tempsford without further incident. During all of the action I had remained unscathed. Only after landing and at the crew debriefing was it noted that some of the shrapnel had torn a couple of holes in the back of my flight jacket.

I went to bed and tried to sleep. The RAF sergeant's crew were sent on recuperation leave while the aircraft went to the hangar to have the battle damage repaired. The sergeant and his crew were lost on the very next mission after returning from leave.

On 22 November Heflin and Fish attended a meeting in London, where it was decided to use the air echelon of the 22nd Anti-Submarine Squadron and the ground echelon of the 4th Anti-Submarine Squadron to form two new squadrons, the 36th and 406th Bomb Squadrons, commanded by Fish and Heflin respectively. The two men learned that as of 11 November the two squadrons had been assigned to the First Bomb Division (equipped with B–17s!) although their activation would not officially be published until 4 December. Though the Liberators were still not ready for night operations it was decided that for the next operational moon period (December), the squadrons would again operate from Tempsford but would use their own aircraft.

Six new crews were brought in from the States. One of them was led by the pilot, Lieutenant William G. McKee. Charles D. Fairbanks, the crew's original ball turret gunner, recalls:

Our crew of ten were put on two B–17s (five on each) and flown by Ferry Command to England via Bangor and Newfoundland at night. I crawled up in a cargo hold in the forward bomb bay and tried to sleep. Even in our sheepskin coats it was cold. We were also on oxygen.

When it got daylight I discovered that the cargo rack I was sleeping in was retained by one bomb shackle. One little malfunction and I could have been dropped into the north Atlantic!

We arrived at Nutts Corner in Northern Ireland. It was difficult to find because the runway had been painted to blend in with the countryside. In Belfast we boarded a steamer and sailed to Liverpool. We were fed and driven in trucks to the Combat Crew Replacement Centre at Stone after dark. None of us were familiar with the blackout and we had to hold hands to make sure we found our way from the barracks to the mess hall. Next morning we could not find the mess hall because we did not know where we had been the night before!

We were processed and several days later we were taken to Alconbury where we and five other crews were assigned to the 36th and 406th Squadrons. Our ten-man crew was trimmed down to four officers and four enlisted men. Two of them, Pasvantis and Dickenson, were sent to other outfits. I was the ball gunner but since the Carpetbaggers had no ball turret, they moved me back to the tail. Later we learned that Dickenson had been killed. He had been standing in the bomb bay with his arm wrapped around a bomb when the bombs were salvoed. He went out the bomb bay doors without a parachute.

At Alconbury we were assigned 'C' for *Charlie*, a B–24D Liberator painted dull matt black. The 'C' and the serial number were about the only markings on it. There were no large emblems on the wings. Later, about halfway through our tour we were given B–24Js with the nose and ball turrets out. They were painted a real glossy black. It was said that when the searchlights hit them at night the people on the ground could not see them as well as the matt black.

McKee's crew went through indoctrination procedures at Harrington and prepared for their training flights from Tempsford. Wilmer Stapel, meanwhile, flew his second mission from the Bedfordshire airfield on the night of 10 December:

The aircraft was very sluggish and slow on take-off. We barely got airborne before the end of the runway. The climb-out was just as bad and at about 1,000 ft the RAF pilot decided to abort the flight and return for a landing. He ordered us all into our crash positions. I found out that mine was directly behind the cockpit bulkhead.

I couldn't see what was going on but from the sound of the engines winding up, it sounded as if he had temporarily lost control of the aircraft. We began a tight spiral and proceeded down. The next thing we heard was the thumping of this heavy aircraft as it bounced on the ground. We bumped a couple of times and then the aircraft stopped. The crew immediately disembarked and I followed them. We were on the airfield but off the runway. End of mission!

On 14 December Lieutenant-Colonel Heflin relinquished command of the 406th to Captain Robert Boone and was assigned to the parent 482nd Group as Air Executive – Special Project. Major Fish became Operations Officer and command of the 36th Squadron passed to Captain Rodman St. Clair, who since 5 December had been in charge of the latest group of American trainees seconded to Tempsford. There, training missions had continued with the odd hiccup. On 17 December Lieutenant Glenn C. Nesbitt and his crew had to bale out of their Liberator in bad weather over England after a mission with the RAF over France. The bad weather grew worse and three days later the American crews returned to Alconbury without completing any further missions.

The 36th and 406th Squadrons spent their first Christmas at Alconbury playing host to a group of English children, giving them candy and gum rations that the officers and enlisted men had contributed to for several weeks. For children living under wartime austerity conditions for four years, the Yuletide festivities were a time of great excitement. For the men it was a welcome break from the perils and stress of Carpetbagger flying. It was amazing to see hard-bitten crew-chiefs handling the little children, catering for their every whim. One of the First Sergeants was even seen riding a little blond boy around on the handlebars of his GI bicycle. When the ice-creams were served, many of the little ones were very excited as only some of the older ones had ever seen ice-cream before.

Two days later the festive spirit had truly disappeared with the sobering reality of the first loss of a complete crew. The Liberator, flown by Captain Robert L. Williams, Operations Officer of the 36th Squadron, ran into very bad weather during a cross-country navigational training flight and crashed into the side of a hill on the south coast with the loss of all eight crew.

Wilmer Stapel, meanwhile, was anxiously anticipating his second mandatory mission with the RAF after the original one had been aborted on the night of 10 December:

After two harrowing experiences with my RAF cohorts and another mission to go before my crew was declared combat ready, I strongly suggested to Colonel Heflin that I preferred to do the piloting myself. If I was destined to 'buy the farm' I'd prefer that it be at my hands if I had to go. Colonel Heflin said he would use my crew and I could be the co-pilot on the next mission. This is how it happened that Colonel Heflin, with my crew, flew the first combat mission on the night of 4 January 1944. The flight was into France and was successful. The total flight time was seven hours and no enemy was engaged.

Despite the veil of secrecy surrounding the new unit there was still little to be secretive about at Alconbury, since few men knew very many details about the Carpetbagger Project. The newspapers gave hints, if one knew which articles to read, and could read between the lines. The *Daily Express* of Saturday, 15 January 1944, carried an inconspicuous item datelined Geneva. Under the headline, 'Patriots Wreck Railways', it was reported:

> French patriots last night attacked the German-held Annecy railway depot and blew up several locomotives. At Romilly, in Savoy, patriots stopped a train, forced the passengers to alight, then sent the train rushing uncontrolled along the line until it overturned.
>
> In Belgium, patriots complying with directions given to them by the Allied Command, carried out forty-two acts of sabotage in one week on the railway tracks in the province of Hainault. They stopped trains and started them without drivers, placed bombs on the tracks, unbolted rails, destroyed signal boxes and put pumping stations out of action.

The following day, the *Sunday Graphic*, in a brief item, referred cryptically to '"Secret Airmen" whose work is a close secret and will make amazing reading after the war'.

The Germans already knew of course. Don Fairbanks recalls:

> One night we really got a shock. We would listen to music coming from Germany. One night 'Lord Haw Haw' welcomed us to Europe. He named our squadron CO and read out our squadron numbers and said the Luftwaffe was waiting for us to come over to the mainland. We were

green troops and this really got to us. We were really concerned about our safety and security on the base and all those things you think of when you're a nineteen-year-old.

At Alconbury the flight line was becoming overcrowded with Carpetbagger aircraft trying to operate alongside the Pathfinder aircraft of the 482nd and vice versa. Fresh moves and promotions were put into effect in late January and early February 1944 which were designed to increase operational efficiency. A new base at Harrington, just west of Kettering and only 35 miles from the packing and storage depot at Holme in Huntingdonshire, was under consideration. Until it was ready for occupation it was decided to transfer several of the Carpetbagger aircraft eastwards to RAF Watton in Norfolk, where the 328th Service Group would provide an administrative headquarters.

On 7 February movement of some of the Liberators and their crews to Watton began. The Norfolk base was thought to be, in some ways, an ideal location for a month's winter sojourn until Harrington was ready for American occupancy. The 3rd SAD (Strategic Air Depot) was already based at Watton and its role of Liberator repair and modification would greatly assist the Carpetbagger outfit. The 406th Bomb Squadron began the movement while seven crews and six Liberators were left behind to continue operations with the 36th Squadron. Skeleton ground sections and some combat crew also remained behind at Alconbury. In the midst of all this operational upheaval, on 10 February, King George VI and Queen Elizabeth visited Alconbury. During their tour of the base they took time to inspect one of the Pathfinder aircraft and also Captain Wagstad's crew standing beside their black-painted B–24. Sadly, Wagsted and his crew would die one month later on 3 March, when their B–24, together with another in the 36th Bomb Squadron, was lost on a Carpetbagger sortie.

By 17 February the move to Watton was complete. However, the Norfolk base was not matching up to early expectations. Watton had been constructed before the war as a permanent RAF base with purpose-built hangars, mess halls and barracks. However, no room could be found for the Carpetbagger contingent so they had to put up with life on the mud-flats on which tented accommodation had been erected.

Out of nowhere, clothes racks, shelves and packing box entrances sprang into existence. Each tent had a supply of firewood (scrounged from the local area) to last a long, cold winter. Don Fairbanks recalls:

Each tent was set up for six men. In my tent there were four men from one crew and two of us from our crew. We walked into the tent after one mission and there were six guys in it we had never seen before. We went to the First Sergeant and told him our belongings had gone. We were told that a crew had been shot down and our stuff had gone into storage with their stuff. He said we could draw our stuff from supply and go back and explain to the guys in the tent but we weren't to upset them. It turned out that these guys in our tent were all cooks and bakers and this was why the First Sergeant didn't want us to upset them! They were worth more to us as friends then enemies! Two did leave and we got to know the rest very well. After this we all ate like kings living off steaks and real eggs instead of powdered.

During the time the squadrons spent there, a few air raid alerts sounded. It was during one of these that in one of the Ordnance Sections, the order went out to sleep with helmets on! All in all, the men made the best of it in the short stay in the Watton mud-flats. The hiking to the main road with boots and hiding them in the bushes, putting on another pair carried along. The most difficult part of it all was finding the right bush in the dark, with a belly full of beer.

The big problem at Watton was that only grass runways with pierced steel planking (PSP) were available. These proved totally unsuitable, as Don Fairbanks recalls:

We could not operate loaded B–24s so we TDY'ed back to Alconbury for our missions during the full moon, then back to Watton. At Alconbury the four EM from our crew bunked in an abandoned mess hall. It was better than the tents at Watton. Prior to our arrival one crew had made up their bunks, went on a mission and had got shot down. Another crew was brought in to replace them. They made up their bunks, went out that night and also got shot down. We came in with two other crews and on hearing the story nobody would sleep in those four 'unlucky' beds. People slept on the floor first.

Although the Project was now scattered hither and thither, on paper at least, the Carpetbaggers existed as a functional unit. On 27 February the group was officially relieved of its assignment to the 482nd and the 1st Bomb Division. Headquarters, 328th Service Group, was designated as the acting Group HQ following a message signed by General James E. Doolittle. Higher headquarters passed to VIII Air Force Composite Command, based at Cheddington.

The first side of the triangle was taking shape.

2

AREA OF DOUBT

Composite Command, which was commanded by 48-year-old Brigadier General Edmund W. Hill, controlled a mixed bag of units in the Bedfordshire, Buckinghamshire and Northamptonshire areas which apart from the Carpetbaggers included a Radio Counter Measures Group and the Night Leaflet Squadron at Cheddington. It was to Cheddington, in February 1944 that Headquarters, Composite Command, moved after first being located in Northern Ireland and from February 1943 to January 1944 at Bushy Park, Teddington in Middlesex. Composite Command was also responsible for all 8th Air Force Combat Crew Replacement Centres (CCRC) and the 12th CCRC was based at Cheddington.

The Night Leaflet Squadron, the Radio Counter Measures Squadron and the Carpetbaggers all had one thing in common; they all flew black B–24s. The Americans had soon realized the importance of propaganda and morale-boosting leaflet missions and first began leaflet, or 'Nickel' operations from Chelveston in 1943. Dropping propaganda leaflets was not new, for the practice had been part of British 'gunboat diplomacy' for many years throughout the Empire, warning warring tribes before their forts were to be bombed by RAF biplanes. In September 1943 the 422nd Bomb Squadron, part of the 305th Bomb Group flying B–17s on operational daylight missions, was taken off combat status and re-trained for night operations.

The squadron flew its first 'Nickeling' sortie on the night of 7/8 October 1943. At first the leaflets were thrown out in bundles by hand. Later, they were sealed in cardboard boxes and thrown out of the bomb bays of their war-weary B–17s. Eventually, an enterprising armament officer in the 42nd developed a leaflet bomb which was fused to burst at about 1,500 ft and shower the countryside below with up to 80,000 leaflets. Each aircraft carried up to a dozen leaflet bombs, which were first dropped in quantity during April 1944. That month the 422nd extended its operations to as far afield as Norway.

In June 1944 the 422nd Squadron moved to Cheddington airbase and became the 858th Bomb Squadron. On D-Day aircraft from this Squadron dropped leaflets on French villages warning the inhabitants that bombers would blast districts with access roads leading to the bridgehead. That summer leaflet dropping increased and on some nights the 858th could despatch five B–17s to as many as 25 different targets. In July the old B–17s and early B–17G type Fortresses were replaced by Liberator B–24s and Js and Squadron strength would almost double by the end of the year. In August 1944 the Night Leaflet Squadron was re-designated and 406th Bomb Squadron and operations included scattering leaflets over Germany for the first time.

In March 1945 The Night Leaflet Squadron moved to Harrington and flew its last Nickeling mission from there on the night of 31 May 1945. Fortunately, only three aircraft were lost to enemy action and accidents during the Squadron's leaflet dropping career but Colonel Aber, the Commanding Officer, was killed by a fragment from an Allied flak burst over Holland in March 1945. By this time the Squadron had earned the dubious honour of having dropped almost 4,000 tons of propaganda leaflets on 319 missions. The shooting was over, the Night Leaflet Squadron moved to Germany in July and flew missions for the OSS until October 1945.

Dropping propaganda leaflets at night was one method whereby SOE and OSS could deliver messages to the peoples of the occupied countries and at the same time try to sow seeds of discontent among the occupying forces. Another method was by radio broadcast. This was carried out on many occasions from Chicksands Priory near Shefford. Following the Luftwaffe blitz on London, Chicksands played host to the BBC (British Broadcasting Corporation) which was evacuated to the Bedford area and broadcasts made from the Priory contained coded messages to Resistance groups and secret armies in occupied France and the Low Countries. Any listener to the foreign-language broadcasts of the BBC must have wondered why valuable airtime was taken up merely to inform 'Marie' that 'Her Uncle Paul remembered to wear his goloshes.'

Meanwhile, in January 1944 a Radio Counter Measures Detachment, which also came under the control of Composite Command, had been formed and designated as the 803rd Bomb Squadron (Provisional). For a time during its wartime career the RCM Squadron was based at Cheddington and Alconbury. Initially, its crews were trained by the RAF, who also supplied the Carpet and Mandrel jamming equipment for their B–17 Flying Fortresses. By mid-May training had been completed and about ten American crews and their B–17s joined their RAF counterparts at RAF Oulton in Norfolk for night missions over Europe.

It will now be evident that Composite Command controlled several units designed to deceive, confuse and thwart the enemy. Another important US command was also located in Bedfordshire and at first glance despite its close proximity, seems to have had little in common with Composite Command. From 1 August 1943 Air Force Service Command (then known as Advanced Air Service Headquarters and later, HQ, Strategic Air Depot Area until February 1944) was based at Milton Ernest Hall in the village of the same name, located four and a half miles north-west of Bedford. Throughout the war it was responsible for servicing bomber and fighter units of the 8th Air Force.

Advanced Air Service Headquarters controlled four Strategic Air Depots in Britain. The 1st SAD was already established at Honington, near Bury St Edmunds, Suffolk. Until the second depot close by at Little Staughton could come into operation, stores at nearby Thurleigh, home of the 306th Heavy Bombardment Group equipped with B–17s, were used for Flying Fortress parts. (Thurleigh is located only two miles to the south of Milton Ernest.) It will be remembered that the 3rd SAD was based at Watton, Norfolk, while the 4th SAD occupied a site near the 8th Air Force fighter base at Wattisham, Suffolk and after D-Day a fifth and final Strategic Air Depot was established at Merville, in north-western France near the Franco-Belgian border.

Many English stately homes have a very colourful past and are often 'haunted'. Milton Ernest Hall is no exception. It has been dogged by disappointment and tragedy right from the date of its very construction. Lime Avenue, which leads to the south front, is said to be haunted after a Victorian horse-drawn carriage, containing a woman occupant, crashed, killing her and her driver. (In recent years, the owner-occupier, Mr Harmar-Brown, was found dead in the grounds and his wife died twelve months later.)

William Butterfield, the celebrated Victorian architect, designed the house for his brother-in-law, Benjamin Starey, a local landowner. Construction began in the summer of 1854. The stonework was laid by London masons, quarried two miles away at Pavenham and brought to the site by boat down the Ouse which flows immediately below the house. Butterfield's attempts to reconcile Gothic church architecture with the practical demands of a country house were remarkably successful but they also cost his patron so much that by the time the house was completed, in 1856, he was unable to afford to live in the splendours he had commissioned!

Milton Ernest Hall was owned by Captain Starey who lived there with his family before the war. When war came in 1939 the Starey family chose to live at Home Farm on the estate nearby. When the Americans came looking for a suitable headquarters for 8th Advanced Air Service Command in February 1943, they selected the Hall, now vacant.

Connie Richards, who was born at Twinwoods and who as a schoolgirl used to play regularly with Captain Starey's children, John and Betsy, recalls the arrival of the Americans at Milton Ernest Hall:

> The old men of the village were standing around the pubs, hands up to their mouths, 'The Yanks are coming, have you heard?' 'I suppose you've heard them old Yankees are coming,' and similar comments punctuated their games of darts, skittles or pints of beer. 'They'll be after our women – they are all oversexed.' The men seemed despondent.
>
> As the weeks passed, we noticed a great change. The big house [Milton Ernest Hall] where I used to play was surrounded with barbed wire. 'No Admittance' signs hung about and there were two new guard posts. First came the GI trucks and jeeps, then we started seeing the Americans themselves, good looking men in uniforms. 'What will life be like now,' I thought. 'Maybe I'll marry one of them when I grow up and go to live in America. They were good to us then, as we were the 'Chewing Gum Kids.' One of the Americans used to come to my home for dinner and my mother did washing for them. My father worked on the aerodrome at Twinwoods, which was used by the RAF as a Beaufighter base.

At first, local people in and around the Milton Ernest area had no reason to believe that the old Hall was anything more than what it appeared to be, the headquarters for US Service Command. However, people such as Connie Richards, who were bussed to dances at Milton Ernest Hall, were always escorted into and off the premises. Connie Richards and others were surprised at the number of machine-gun posts, barbed wire and sentries in evidence in the grounds and approaches. On numerous occasions khaki-coloured staff cars with blacked-out windows were seen to drive in and out of the estate.

Altogether, six MPs guarded the main entrance to the Hall. Two of these stood opposite the main gates on the other side of the Sharnbrook Road looking down the driveway to the Hall while two faced the main road. The others were stationed on the approach to the Hall. At the other entrance, near the barracks, there stood two sentries while inside the wall there was an MP hut. Even the river was guarded by up to three MPs with a machine-gun pit, and children were prevented from swimming up to the hall in that direction.

The sentries were guarding what was after all an organization designed to oversee and co-ordinate activities at the advanced supply and repair (from August 1943, Strategic Air) depots in the ETO (European Theater of Operations). Obviously, Service Command was very important to bombing operations in that it helped provide the very parts that kept the bombers airborne, but if the headquarters had been put out of action the command would still have had the necessary communications and back-up bases to keep up the flow of parts to the bases.

Even if the Germans had known about Milton Ernest Hall it would have been a very low priority target compared to say, the various Bomb Division headquarters such as Elveden Hall, near Thetford or the 8th AF Bomber Command headquarters at High Wycombe. It is pertinent to note that at Elvedon Hall, where General Curtis E. LeMay had his headquarters for a time, security, when compared to Milton Ernest Hall, was negligible! Louis Pennow, a weather officer at Elveden, recalls, 'There were about ten MPs and one officer. They guarded the doors and courtyard but there was only one sentry on the main gate. Mostly, the MPs were concerned with blackout precautions.' By comparison then, Milton Ernest Hall was a veritable 'Fort Knox' although official records do not mention any SOE or OSS involvement, nor any covert activities which may have been undertaken by the wartime occupants of Milton Ernest Hall.

A local electrician was called in to install red and green lightbulbs above doorways in some of the rooms. As the war progressed several locals became increasingly curious about some of the activities going on at Milton Ernest. In the six acres of land surrounding the Hall the Americans had constructed several brick and corrugated metal huts. The delightful brick summer house with a thatched roof near the river now housed radio transmitters, concealed from view by curtains over the windows. However, radio aerials nearby were very evident. Service Command had no need of radios; land lines (with scramblers) and teletape machines were standard on American bases and were used by 8th Bomber Command headquarters to pass classified operational information to divisional, wing and bomb group assignments. The transmitters could only have been used for contacting personnel many hundreds of miles distant, where land lines or teletape machines were either unavailable or impractical – such as occupied Europe. Passing the summer house one day a local Police Constable was intrigued when he overheard operators speaking in German!

A great many people who worked at Milton Ernest Hall were not on the wartime roster which lists only 22 people. This appears to be contradictory because there were nineteen girl stenographers alone who worked at the Hall. However, these and other British personnel such as Victor Stillwell, a British civilian batman who worked at Milton Ernest Hall from 1943 to early 1945, could have been classed as 'temporary staff'. Stillwell recalls:

> Some of the officers were up at Twinwoods. Some of the people who were at Milton Ernest used to do the writing and the arranging. They were not in the military. They were more like the Civil Service. . . . We used to be picked up at Bedford station in a coach and were taken to the Hall. Those that worked there were dropped off at the bottom while others [like Stillwell] were dropped off at the house. At night they used to collect us and take us back. We could not walk in and out as we liked. We were checked in and checked out.

The bussing arrangements seem identical to those performed every day at Bletchley Park.

British civilians were not the only ones who were barred from certain parts of Milton Ernest Hall. Don Upchurch, a sergeant in the 306th Bomb Group at nearby Thurleigh airbase, often used to drive his commanding officer, Colonel Stanko, to Milton Ernest village. Their route often took them past the Hall gates. When Upchurch enquired about the imposing Hall his commanding officer quickly dismissed it with the terse reply, 'That place is out of bounds to air force personnel.'

Milton Ernest Hall is in a very low-lying, secluded spot in what was, during the Second World War, thick woodland. It was therefore very difficult to spot from the air and many of the huts were deliberately built among the lime trees. When air raids did sound, 'No one,' according to Stillwell, 'took much notice. I expect that at that time the Germans would like to have known about the base and got any information possible.'

Did Milton Ernest Hall have a secondary role which would explain the tight security and veil of secrecy surrounding it? During the Second World War hundreds of English stately homes, many of them in Bedfordshire, Northamptonshire and Buckinghamshire, were taken over, first by the British War Office and later, by the American OSS and other clandestine services, for use as training centres, communications posts, operations rooms and headquarter buildings. The allies had to conjure up a believable tale about each house, while at the same time not provoking attention and possible rumour from locals and servicemen alike which could ultimately alert the German counter-intelligence service. At first glance these palatial residences often appeared to be what they were, but behind the façade of ancient brick, stone and tile, were important nerve centres for the RAF, US Air Force and the special forces.

Many more were taken over by the British and US special forces' units who were engaged in sabotage, spying, political warfare, propaganda, subterfuge and decoding and communications activities. The French, Polish and Scandinavian special units also used hidden accommodation in stately English homes and castles away from prying eyes in woodland, parks and rolling countryside. At many locations the allies went to great lengths to disguise the fact that covert activities were going on within their historic portals. It was a requirement which would have taxed even the most imaginative peacetime estate agent. However, the allies had specialists in every department and the wartime 'estate agents' came up with bogus, but believable, schemes which convinced almost all and sundry. Those that were privy to the schemes did nothing to dispel rumours in the local pub that the military had taken over yet another country house for use as a 'hospital' or 'headquarter building'.

Finedon Hall, near Wellingborough, is an excellent example of the lengths that were sometimes taken to protect an installation's identity. A French wartime brochure described Finedon Hall as a 'Centre de Technologie Scientifique'. It said:

> The centre was founded by General de Gaulle to undertake tropical research work, such as the cure of diseases, exploitation of natural resources by the natives [and] at first . . . was only open to disabled

soldiers of the Allied armies who wished to learn a new trade. Now boys also are being admitted in order to be trained with the wounded soldiers to assist in the work of reconstruction after the war. . . . Directors, teachers, apprentices, boys and disabled soldiers of every nationality and class form one big happy family, whose dominating feature is an atmosphere of liberty, goodwill and friendship.

However, Finedon Hall was also home for French Army Joes and Jedburgh teams which left on the short journeys by road to Harrington and Tempsford, from where they were flown to be parachuted into their homeland to assist the FFI and bring hope to millions of their countrymen and women. It was also used in experiments with gases.

It is usually assumed that SOE and OSS Jedburgh teams and Joes left their offices in Baker Street or their secret houses in London and were driven directly to the RAF airfield at Tempsford, or to Station 179, Harrington, a USAAF base, where they were flown across the Channel or North Sea in Halifaxes, Stirlings and Liberators and dropped over the occupied countries. In fact, there were a number of 'holding stations' and agent training schools, which, for the purposes of this book, were scattered throughout Bedfordshire, Buckinghamshire, Cambridgeshire and Northamptonshire. In his book *Piercing the Reich* (published in 1979), the author, Joseph Persico, makes references to two secret locations called, 'Area O' and 'Area F', either or both of which offered an OSS staging facility. In *Piercing the Reich* Persico makes several references to 'Area F', describing it as a 'walled estate outside of London where OSS agents trained. Agent schooling operations were carried out there including burglary, bribery and blackmail. The course was designed to last two months. Students learned to operate radios, communicate in code, read maps. . . .' It would now seem that this refers to a holding area at a Ruislip manor house which was used by 'F Section' (see Chapter One), the independent French section, one of several 'country' sections operated by SOE. (There are others: XVII, a station for sabotage, was at Brickendonbury Manor, between Hertford and Hoddeston, Hertfordshire, for example.)*

From the recent release of previously secret OSS files it is now known that 'Area F' was the Congressional Country Club outside

---

* *SOE: The Special Operations Executive 1940–46* M.R.D. Foot (BBC, 1984)

Washington DC. ('Area B' was Camp David.) 'Area F' was responsible for training the Norwegian Special Operations Group, a branch of the Office of Strategic Services, which had formed about June 1943. Most of the 100 or so men – all volunteers – came from the 99th Infantry Battalion, a ski battalion stationed at Camp Hale, Colorado which was taken over by the OSS as a special training area for Operational Groups (OGs). Consisting mostly of men of Scandinavian ancestry, some were seamen from the Norwegian merchant marine who had lost their ships in the early part of the war. Every man had a knowledge of the Norwegian language and some proficiency in skiing. They were told very little about the mission they volunteered for, except that they could expect to be parachuted behind enemy lines in Norway.

For several months, the NORSO group, commanded by Captain Larsen, was given intensive training in guerilla warfare at various camps surrounding Washington. The training was conducted by extremely competent instructors, all experts in the various phases of guerrilla fighting. Training included amphibious landings at night in canoes and rubber rafts from simulated submarines off Martha's Vineyard, Massachusetts.

Late in 1943 the group was sent overseas to England and was stationed at 'Area E', one of several covert and sinister-sounding 'area' locations used by US forces in the Midlands. 'Area E' was in fact the code-name for Brock Hall, an English mansion house at Weedon, close to Daventry in Northamptonshire, conveniently located just a few miles from 'Area T', Harrington, the departure airfield for airborne operations in occupied Europe. Originally, Brock Hall belonged to SOE; it was No. 1 Training School, commanded by Colonel A.T. Thornton, but in 1943, after its cover had been revealed by an agent and a bombing raid attempted by the Luftwaffe, it was turned over to the OSS. The new commander was Lieutenant Colonel Serge Obolensky, a Russian prince, born Serge Obolensky-Beledinsky-Meletsky in 1898, who had escaped the Bolsheviks in 1918. While at Brock Hall the NORSO group received parachute training at Ringway, the British Airborne Division's training base on the outskirts of Manchester.

After D-Day, various units of the group were parachuted into different sections of France still occupied by the Germans. Working with the French Resistance forces behind enemy lines, their job was to prevent the retreating Germans from blowing road and railway bridges and to keep them open for the advancing allied armies. One such mission, Operation *Donald*, to Brittany on 5 August 1944, involved thirty-four NORSO personnel, led by Obolensky (Codename 'Milton') and thirty-six containers, carried in three RAF Stirling aircraft of 620 Squadron. Their task was to link up with Jedburgh team 'Chadbourne', then advance to the 32 metre high, 140 metre long Morlaix railway viaduct and prevent its destruction until relieved by the advancing ground forces.

Geoff Murray and crew in Stirling 'W', Derek De Rome and crew in Stirling 'Y' and Ross Bunce and crew in Stirling 'X', took off from their base at RAF Fairford at 15.00 hours and flew to Harrington, forty-five minutes away. Noel Chaffey RAAF, air gunner in de Rome's crew, recalls:

> Upon arrival at Harrington we were confronted with cameras of the *Stars and Stripes* magazine led by Captain John Ford and a team of nine. The re-fuelling of the three Stirlings by the Americans caused some fun when 'our' fuel trucker pulled away before finishing. Frank Pearman, our flight engineer, was doused with 100 octane gas. 'Pepé Le Phew' had nothing on Frank for the rest of the operation. We had a meal of roast pork and raw cabbage and a wonderful selection of ice-cream. Briefing was another change: no 'ten-shun!' – it was done whilst the officers and men were preparing their paratroop equipment and dressing, cigars all alight, and much chatter.
>
> Cameras were still turning when the US 'paras' loaded up into the trucks to go out to fill up the three Stirlings. We sure looked good. Cameras repositioned and kept turning as each 'stick' filed into their strange craft, to drop out of a bottomless bath-tub set in the floor! Ross Bunce and his crew had the worst luck. They had engine failure and didn't leave Harrington.

Derek De Rome and crew with their stick were first off. Frank Pearman recalls:

> While crossing the sea on the way to our DZ, some of the 'paras' came up front to look out of the astrodome and flight deck. One asked, 'Where are your fighter escort?' 'Oh,' I replied, 'they don't come in too close but they're out there somewhere.' We reached our DZ and all was prepared at the jumping position at the back of the Stirling and we continued to circle the area. Difficult weather conditions allowed only brief glimpses of the ground but no reception fires or lights. After three or four circles and no further reception, we decided to return

to Harrington, much to the distress of the paras and especially our man in charge [Obolensky]. Even when we returned to Harrington he was trying his best to take them back, although by now it was almost sun-up. Operations were never done in daylight except in extreme circumstances. We flew back to Fairford without delivering our load.

Ken Beck, Murray's navigator, adds: 'We took off from Harrington at 23.45 in 'W-Willie' and took eleven paratroops. Time airbourne, 4hrs 20 minutes. 'Gee' was working well that night although we were in fog and cloud but confident of our position so the stick jumped "blind". Great chaps, and determined to go.' (The NORSO unit successfully prevented the Germans from destroying the area's infrastructure and assisted local resistance groups with the 'Hilary' Jedburgh team. All eleven men returned to England at 1920 hrs on 19 August.)

After the liberation of France, the NORSO group units returned to England. A few months later, more than half of the group was shipped back to the USA for special jungle training for the Far East, and later worked with OSS units in China. The remainder, selected mostly for their skiing ability and proficiency in Norwegian, went into vigorous training in Scotland under their new commanding officer, Major William E. Colby. Their assigned mission was to cut the north–south railway lines in northern Norway which the Germans were using to bring troops back from their defeat in Finland.

Piercing the Reich also mentions an 'Area O': ' . . . when they were ready, the luckier agents out of OSS London waited to depart from the splendid isolation of Area O, the lovely manor house outside London. The house, in a lush green park, was operated by British enlisted personnel and girls from the countryside who worked in the kitchen and dining room. The staff had been screened by MI5 . . .'. The description could fit any number of manor houses used by the special forces in Britain and further correspondence with Persico, who in turn passed on my request to William J. Casey, wartime chief of OSS and later, the CIA, produced a letter (from Casey) which confirmed that 'Milton Hall was used to train Jedburghs,' which, it will be recalled, were three-man teams – two officers and one enlisted man – who were dropped behind the German lines just prior to and after D-Day to take command of Resistance groups and secret armies. (Jedburghs were flown out of Harrington in 1944.)

Milton Hall is situated near the A1 just a few miles west of Peterborough. Another veiled clue to its wartime use can be found in the official records of the Carpetbaggers. Among the letters of thanks and commendations the Carpetbaggers received was a letter addressed to Major Fish on 2 March 1944 from a British major at Milton Hall. It reads:

> . . . This is to tell you how much we appreciate the hard work and co-operation which you and your squadron put into the show last night. What you were able to do for us was of very great value to our people and there is no doubt that, from our point of view, the job, with its unavoidable limitations, was very well worth doing. Several of your guests of last night have told me that they would go anywhere with your fellows and I can assure you that they are not 'shooting a line'.

The 'guests' referred to in the letter are 'Joes' (later Jedburgh teams were also dropped) who were airlifted by the Carpetbaggers the night before to occupied France. The location of Milton Hall meant that agents could be transported safely and secretly across to Harrington or to Tempsford, which was also easy striking distance, a few miles further south along the A1. Sergeant Maurice Whittle, a member of a Jedburgh team at Milton Hall, says that airfields other than Tempsford and Harrington were used for embarkation of Joes and Jedburghs: 'All Jedburgh teams were at Milton for the stages of training. A large number would go from Tempsford, although my team went into France from White Waltham airfield in Berkshire.'

Casey went on to say that he did not know whether Milton Hall was designated as 'Area O' or 'Area F'. The late William Casey could perhaps be forgiven for the confusion. Even now it is difficult to determine who worked for whom in the covert organizations. For instance, 'exactly who did and did not belong to SOE are questions so intricate and difficult' that M.R.D. Foot made no attempt to answer them.* (It now seems that 'Area O' was in fact Sunnyside House at Kingsthorpe near Boughton, just to the north of Northampton. A holding area, it was used by or as many as twenty-five OSS/SOE agents at a time. Operatives arrived from London accompanied by their operations officers.) On a hill two miles from Bicester is Pounden Hall, which in the Second World War was used as a 'Y' Station but it might just as easily have relayed coded radio messages to London

---

* *The Special Operations Executive 1940–46* M.R.D. Foot (BBC Books, 1984)

from both SOE and OSS agents. Another SOE training school was established at Gaynes Hall, at Perry village beside Graffam Water (Diddington reservoir), now a private residence in an area which has become Littlehay Prison, but other groups may have trained there. 'Area H', an OSS training school, was located at Holmewood Hall, a large country house 8 miles south of Peterborough, whose grounds were also used as a massive packing station by US forces for supplying both Harrington and Tempsford. At various times some 200 million rounds of ammunition, 10,000 skis and thousands of containers were stored in its large expanse away from prying eyes. German prisoners of war from Ramsey Prison, Cambridgeshire were used to help load the supplies and containers for onward transportation to Tempsford and Harrington.

As has already been stated, the secrecy maintained at both Harrington and Tempsford, and at other special operations' bases, was of paramount importance if SOE–OSS operations were not to be compromised by enemy spies and their intelligence gatherers. It will now be realized that communications centres, political warfare establishments, propaganda outlets and SOE–OSS facilities as well as secret airfields, abounded throughout Bedfordshire and Buckinghamshire in the Second World War. The 'Bedford Triangle' is therefore formed. Taking Harrington as the apex the first side descends to Tempsford in the east, across to the secret communications sites at Bletchley Park Manor and Brock Hall, to the west, and back up to Harrington. In between are a veritable 'nest of vipers', including Chicksands, Woburn, and Milton Ernest Hall, right in the centre of covert activity. We can now safely assume that it was not connected with OSS–SOE activity but if it was merely the HQ for the US Service Command, why all the secrecy and high security?

Officially, Chief of Composite Command, Brigadier-General Edmund W. Hill, who had overall command of several specialized units including the Carpetbaggers and the Night Leaflet Squadron, had his headquarters at Cheddington. However, the General was a frequent visitor to the Milton Ernest Hall Operations Room which was located in the large former dining room overlooking the lawns at the rear. The bay windows were covered by wooden shutters to prevent access to the maps and charts scattered on the tables inside. Service Command hardly needed an Operations Room and even if it had, why did Composite Command need to be represented?

PSP (Pierced Steel Planking) had been laid in the very long grassy field opposite Milton Ernest Hall permitting single-engined liaison aircraft such as a Norseman or Grasshopper to land and take off. General Hill was a rated pilot and he could quickly and easily make visits to Milton Ernest Hall from Cheddington in an aircraft. A bailey bridge had been erected across the river to permit easy access to and from the Hall.

Connie Richards knew an American called James E. 'Scotty' McPhail, who was a photographer at the Hall and who worked in a caravan which stood next to the bailey bridge. The caravan was used by McPhail to develop camera film shot by photo-reconnaissance aircraft, probably of intended Jedburgh landing grounds in France. After evaluation by Hill and his intelligence staff, the photos would have been flown out to Harrington. The Carpetbaggers needed up-to-date photos of possible dropping grounds in France and the occupied countries.

General Hill continued to use Milton Ernest Hall until late 1944 when he was named Commanding General, AAF Units, Installations and Activities in Russia. In the meanwhile General Charles E. Goodrich, chief of 8th Air Service Command at the Milton Ernest post, often resided a mile away at The Bury, a lovely château at Pavenham. Hill's presence at Milton Ernest Hall begs the question, was Milton Ernest a link in the chain of the entire Allied clandestine war effort? Either would certainly explain why there was such tight security in and around the Hall. It would also partly explain the need for a radio transmitter and why a company of British MPs were stationed at The Grange, a large town house on the Sharnbrook Road (and only a few hundred yards from Milton Ernest Hall) which backed onto Twinwoods airfield.

What is certain is that in July 1944 Captain (later Major) Glenn Miller, one of America's most famous musicians, took up temporary residence at Milton Ernest Hall.

3

CIRCLE OF DECEPTION

Glenn Miller's arrival in England can be attributed to Gen. Dwight D. Eisenhower, the Supreme Allied Commander, who had originally asked for the bandleader in May 1944. Specifically, Miller and his band were needed for Eisenhower's brainchild, the AEF (Allied Expeditionary Forces) programme, which he wanted put out on air to the American, British and Canadian troops taking part in the invasion of France and during their subsequent campaigns.

The new service, which depended on co-operation from the BBC, was vital, to Eisenhower's way of thinking, for morale purposes as well as acting as a medium for SHAEF to pass on instructions to the soldiers, sailors and airmen of the United Nations at the battlefronts. Unfortunately, relations between the military command and the BBC were often less than cordial. Early in 1944 Eisenhower gave Brigadier-General Ray W. Barker, chief of SHAEF G–1 Division (Personnel), the unenviable task of handling discussions between SHAEF and the BBC.

Colonel Ed Kirby was appointed by SHAEF as Director of Broadcasting Services with responsibility for liaison with the BBC. David Niven, the British movie idol, who had starred in several Hollywood films before and during the war, was promoted from Major to Lieutenant-Colonel and became Associate Director. Niven's responsibilities included ironing out difficulties arising from what programmes should be broadcast by the BBC and AFN (Armed Forces Network). In effect he became Glenn Miller's commanding officer.

General Eisenhower's persistence, backed by support from Winston Churchill, finally ensured that the new service reached the airwaves. The AEF programme was inaugurated in March 1944 and went on the air for the first time over the BBC transmitter at Start Point, Devon the day after the successful Allied landings in Normandy, on 7 June, D-Day + 1.

Meanwhile, Miller and his assembled bandsmen were *en route*. The party arrived at Gourock, Scotland on 28 June and immediately entrained for London. At this time Londoners were experiencing daily attacks by German V–1 rockets which were landing over a widespread area in and around the capital. The raids were particularly disconcerting to the new arrivals and Miller wasted no time in asking for a safer place to broadcast. He got his wish immediately, not least because SHAEF could ill afford to have a live broadcast interrupted by the sound of an exploding V–1; it would have confirmed to the listening German monitors that their vengeance weapons were finding their targets. On Sunday 2 July Miller and the AEF band left their billet at Sloane Court and travelled to Bedford.

Why Bedford? Before the war the BBC had planned for an evacuation of its major recording and broadcasting departments to other parts of the country in the event of enemy air attack on London so that regular broadcasting could continue uninterrupted. After Bristol was bombed during the series of 'Baedeker raids' in 1940, the Music Department and the BBC Symphony Orchestra, among others, were moved to the comparative safety of Bedford. The town afforded a good rail link to London and was able to house the 500 artists and staff attached to the BBC. Performances recorded in the Bedford studios were sent to London by landline and hit the airways via Broadcasting House.

Charles Davies, a photographer employed by the *Bedfordshire Times* during the war years, recalls:

> Broadcasts were made daily from five studios. These were used by the BBC for performances overseas and especially for the land forces in Europe. There were many people at the time who did not know that the broadcasts were coming from Bedford, not even the US personnel at the East Anglian bases, for they were supposed to be 'hush-hush' at that time. We were never allowed to state where the broadcasts were coming from.
>
> Many famous celebrities came to the town, particularly from the entertainment industry. Famous stars, both American and British, were making their tours of the factories and the battlefronts. Such names as Gracie Fields, Bea Lillie, Bing Crosby, Bob Hope, and many others were to be heard in concerts from the Corn Exchange which was the principal studio in town, but most of these were sent out only on the American network.

The American Forces Network, which had been operating in Britain using low-powered transmitters over localized areas where American troops were concentrated, provided American programmes including Armed Forces Radio Service recordings from Hollywood. Bedfordshire held such concentrations of American troops: thousands of airmen in the heavy bomb groups, fighter squadrons and composite units. It is almost certain that at least one localized transmitter was in the area.

A small group from Glenn Miller's AEF Band performed for the first time on Saturday evening, 8 July, at a dance for officers of 8th Air Force Service Command at Milton Ernest Hall. On this and several other occasions, Miller did not lead the band himself. Locals well remember small groups of his musicians who would play to selected audiences in and around Bedford. Next morning, 9 July, the whole band assembled in the Corn Exchange in Bedford for a rehearsal for their first programme, due to be broadcast that night, live on the AEF network.

Charles Davies describes that memorable evening:

Besides Glenn and his band there were a number of the biggest names in showbusiness in America including Humphrey Bogart, David Niven and many others. When the lights went up it was a big surprise to me to find that they were seated on each side of me. It was a cold, dark night and the hall was filled to overflowing with US Air Force officers and men and a sprinkling of US sailors, all in their neat blue uniforms. I had received instructions as to when I was to take my pictures for at that time we were having to use the old-type big flash bulbs which, until they coated them, used to explode with a terrific bang on contact; this the broadcast people wished to avoid, to make the broadcast a success.

As the red light came on there was a hushed silence over the great audience as the strains of 'Moonlight Serenade', Glenn's signature tune, floated through the air. The rest of the evening was sheer magic as the band went through the whole gamut of the melodies that they had made so popular; and so it was until the end when at the close of the broadcast everyone stood and gave Glenn and his musicians one of the greatest welcomes that they could have wished, with loud cheering and whistles urging them to continue. It went on until the light faded and then the scene was pandemonium for the crowd just went wild. I was an old newspaperman and had seen many occasions like this but none so spontaneous and generous to this great and talented composer and band leader. This was tops in my experience.

At first Miller and his executive officer, Lieutenant Don Haynes, were billeted at the American Red Cross Officers' Club in Bedford. However, Milton Ernest Hall carried out the day-to-day administration of the band and was responsible for feeding them and giving them medical attention. The band were billeted in two large detached houses in Ashburnham Road. During most of its sojourn in Bedford the band was taken out to Milton Ernest in trucks for its meals in between broadcasts and rehearsals at the Co-Partners Hall in Bedford.

Charles Davies recalls:

Glenn's flat in Waterloo Road was only a stone's throw from the official HQ. What went on was nobody's business now, for at that time everyone lived from day to day. They were dangerous days in which we all lived so whatever they did is to be excused all these years after.

I knew clubs where the Americans were charged an extortionate fee for membership but where they could drink all and every day and night if they wanted to. The clubs even had an air of respectability for 'hostesses' were kept there for the Americans. These girls would induce these young fellows to drink all kinds of beverages. One bottle of scotch to six bottles of blackberry cordial which could be bought on the black market – talk about a racket. This went on unhindered by any police, military or civil, for they were all mixed up in it.

It has to be remembered at this time that the members of the band had a lot of rehearsing to do but they also had a lot of leisure time on their hands. This they spent in their own way for there was hardly anyone who did not offer their hospitality of different sorts for a bottle of something when you could neither buy beer or cigarettes. It often gained them access to the household with so many menfolk away on active service or war work in some factory miles away.

I knew the assistant to the Mayor of that time who was also his entertainment manager. Naturally, he had a lot to do with Glenn Miller and his band for at that time it was all 'fiddles' of short commodities such as cigarettes and drink, which the Americans used to help out, unofficially of course, and there were many parties at various private houses for Americans and their girlfriends so drink was a must. This was where the Americans would be so generous for they seemed able to get it when no-one else could. In this Glenn was no exception for they often had private parties away from any official receptions for which the mayor was allowed a generous allowance for entertainment purposes, although he never attended these private parties.

Miller often overnighted in rooms at Milton Ernest Hall and was a frequent visitor to the 'Club Castle' (Officers' Club) located in the grounds near the enlisted men's barracks. He also made appearances at the large dance hall which had been built near the club. Victor Stillwell was batman to Glenn Miller during his sojourns at Milton Ernest Hall and got to know him well. He recalls:

Glenn spent about four months at Milton Ernest Hall. The longest time he spent at the house was when Bing Crosby came [on 29 August 1944]. Miller lived in the huts in the grounds for about a month until we shifted back into the house. He was always willing to explain anything. He mixed with everyone and wanted to be with his officers. He was just an ordinary man. He talked to us on the same level. I never saw him in a temper.

In return for the hospitality shown by General Goodrich and his officers at 8th AF Service Command, Miller agreed to play a concert on the back lawn of the Hall on the afternoon of 16 July. It was a great success, with 1,600 officers and men present. A few weeks later, on the evening of Saturday 22 July, a small group from the band played during a dance function for the men at Milton Ernest. The dance was held in a large hut, which had been built for recreation purposes near the enlisted men's barracks and the Club Castle.

Local people were also invited. Among them was Connie Richards:

I was invited with three of my friends, including Margery Surridge (16) and Max Kalker, her boyfriend (whom she later married), an American cook at Milton Ernest Hall. I wore a green dress with a soldier painted on the pocket, a pleated skirt and a pair of navy blue suede shoes I'd borrowed. Max Kalker introduced me to Glenn Miller and also to Broderick Crawford, the film star. The haunting tunes like 'Perfidia' and 'Moonlight Serenade' and many others were played that night. Some we danced to, others we just stood and listened. Miller spoke to us and he was very nice. He talked of a music score he was about to write or was writing. He was with a lot of people that night and it was a night to remember.

I was at 'Scotty' McPhail's caravan with Jimmy and some friends a few nights after the dance. A single-engined plane landed in the field behind the headquarters. Two men got into it. One man I saw was at the dance. McPhail said it was Colonel Norman Baessell, General Goodrich's executive officer. I'm sure the other was Glenn Miller.

(All efforts to trace McPhail have proved fruitless and Max Kalkner has refused to return to the Hall or even discuss what went on there.)

On 24 July the theme of AF Service Command was maintained when Glenn Miller and his band flew from Twinwoods in six B–17s to the 3rd SAD at Wattisham (Heacham) in Suffolk to give a concert there. It was the first in a series of flying visits Miller and his band made to bomber and fighter bases in eastern England and as far afield as Gloucestershire. All the flights were made from Twinwoods airfield in either B–17 or B–24 Liberator aircraft or C–47 Dakotas.

So, wartime Bedford became synonymous with movie stars, musicians and bandleaders. Such a preponderance of musical personalities in such a small area was no coincidence. Apart from helping to build up the morale of Allied troops, they were also employed for Allied broadcasts aimed at the German people and her armed forces. These broadcasts were the perfect vehicle for passing on a great deal of 'disinformation' to the unwary listener, especially if he thought the music was coming from inside Germany.

The use of music as a medium for passing messages goes back to the First World War, although the method then employed bears scant resemblance to the technological advances of the Second World War. In 1916 Courtenay de Rysbach, a British subject with a naturalized Austrian father, was arrested for passing information to the German spy service. The British MI5 discovered that de Rysbach, a music hall artist, was passing secret information written in invisible ink on innocent-looking sheets of music.*

When Germany invaded Poland on Friday 1 September 1939 Woburn Abbey, to the east of Bletchley and situated only 43 miles from London, became, by prior arrangement in the event of war, CHQ (Country Headquarters) for the British propaganda service. Actually, the large stable wing and the riding school were used by PWE. The flats above the stables provided sleeping accommodation

---

* *The British Secret Service* Richard Deacon (Muller)

for which no charge was made by the Duke of Bedford. However, the Duke stipulated that 'he would not have to set eyes upon, let alone encounter, any of his unwanted guests. The fact that they were there at all was because his grace preferred temporary civil servants to a mob of children evacuated from the London slums.'*

The PID (Political Intelligence Department) and the 'white' leaflet production team were also based at Woburn. Early in 1942 a great many staff, and in particular those connected with work for the BBC, returned to London. Hence the decision that PWE's HQ should be located on the three upper floors of Bush House (the BBC's European services HQ in the Aldwych).*

Black propaganda (secret broadcasting) and the production of white leaflets remained at Woburn. PWE retained possession of the riding school, which provided office accommodation for the staff administering the small clandestine broadcasting teams, now known as Research units (RUs), whose members lived and worked in a dozen or more private houses in the Woburn District. Whaddon Hall, a few miles west of Bletchley Park, a recording centre at Wavendon Tower and the Old Rectory at Toddington, a village about 4 miles south of Woburn, were all used by PWE. 'The Rookery' at Aspley Guise, a few miles from Woburn, was used by Sefton Delmer, head of the 'black' propaganda service, and 'Dawn Edge' at Aspley Guise was staffed with German émigré political groups who were anti-Hitler. Eventually, many of them were employed by the BBC.*

The establishment of short wave and medium wave transmitting stations in Britain was one of PWE's greatest achievements. Some of the stations attempted to give the illusion that they were broadcasting from inside Germany. By February 1942 sixteen stations were recording material for broadcasting at a common recording centre in the Woburn area, outside the control of the BBC and classified 'Most Secret'. American 7.5 kW transmitters were installed at Gawcott, 2 miles south of Buckingham. A similar one was sited at Potsgrove, close to Milton Bryant and not far from Woburn Abbey. The recording disks used were of American manufacture.*

Before 'disinformation' could be imparted to the enemy, the British had to capture their audience. Any station, especially today, must broadcast music which will appeal to the potential listener. The

* *The Black Game* Ellic Howe (Michael Joseph, 1982)

British were particularly successful in their attempts to demoralize U-boat crews. The German Propaganda Ministry would not permit American jazz to be broadcast in Germany. However, the U-boat crews and thousands of young Germans serving in the Wehrmacht in occupied Europe greatly enjoyed it. Many popular German recordings reached Woburn from Stockholm and programmes containing 'American jazz with the German flavour' were broadcast from England over 'Grey' transmitters (relying on the listeners' gullibility or commonsense to establish where they were being broadcast from). German refugees and even U-boat PoWs, carefully screened, were used.*

A representative of the American Foreign Information Service (FIS) had inspected the set-up at Woburn in September 1941. (The FIS was then part of Colonel William G. Donovan's new Office of the Co-Ordinator of Information, which President Roosevelt transferred to the American Chiefs of Staff in 1942.)*

It was only natural that the Americans, on entering the war, should exploit the possibilities of propaganda warfare. Following Pearl Harbor, when America became fully committed to the war in Europe, the theme of the special agent with a musical background was featured in Hollywood movies such as *My Favorite Spy*, a pleasing comedy about a band leader who is drafted into the army on his wedding day and ends up the target for assassins. Made in 1942 and produced by Buster Keaton, it starred Kay Kyser who, like Miller, was a professional band leader during the 1940s. In Britain George Formby played a British band leader inadvertently tapping out coded messages to the Germans with his baton in *Let George Do It*.

US broadcasts to Europe were transmitted from the American Broadcasting Station In Europe (ABSIE) in London. ABSIE was controlled by the Overseas Branch of the Office of War Information, a civilian propaganda outlet for the American Government. As in the case of the British, the Americans had to first capture and then seduce their radio audience. Geoffrey Butcher has written:

> Entertainment too played a vital role in these broadcasts, and ABSIE's 'pride and joy' (to quote *Time* magazine) was its music programmes, and among American stars who broadcast were Bing Crosby and

* *The Black Game* Ellic Howe (Michael Joseph, 1982)

Dinah Shore, introducing their songs and putting over 'the message' by reading from phonetic German scripts.*

The first recording session was held at the HMV studio, Abbey Road, St John's Wood in London, on 30 October 1944. Following its success Glenn Miller and his band recorded a series of transcriptions for half-hour weekly broadcasts beamed at the German Army. These were broadcast over ABSIE on the 'Wehrmacht Hour'. Many of the programme announcements and some of the vocals were in German. The first programme was aired on 8 November 1944.

Though the British and American propaganda operations were under the civilian control of the Political Warfare Executive and Overseas Branch of the Office of War Information (OWI) respectively, by October 1944 OWI work in Europe had become integrated into the Psychological Warfare Division. This functioned as part of military intelligence under General Eisenhower and the US Chiefs of Staff (SHAEF).

The history of PWD can be traced back to November 1942 when the 'Torch' landings took place in French North Africa. There, Allied political warfare work was largely dominated by the Americans who considered that propaganda warfare was an integral part of the Armed Services and not a new service in itself. At Algiers, General Eisenhower established a Psychological Warfare Section, soon to become the Psychological Warfare Branch of Allied Force HQ under the command of Colonel Charles B. Hazeltine, an ex-US cavalry officer. Soon after D-Day, PWD, now commanded by Gen. Robert McClure and still composed of predominantly American staff, was operating as part of SHAEF in France.**

Was Glenn Miller working for the Psychological Warfare Division? He had fulfilled Eisenhower's first objective of helping to improve the morale of the US forces using the medium of the AEF programme. Then had come the propaganda broadcasts. Miller was certainly feeling the strain and he was smoking more and more heavily. His demeanour was obvious to all who came into contact with him. Miller often visited the Officers' Key Club, run by Norman and Stella Knowlton in Bedford High Street. On one occasion Mr Laws, who

---

* *Next To A Letter From Home* Geoffrey Butcher (Mainstream, 1966)
** *The Black Game* Ellic Howe (Michael Joseph, 1982)

ran Russell & Bromleys' shoe shop below the club, witnessed two GIs who, bumping into the Major outside the club, greeted him with the customary 'Hi Glenn'. Miller flared up and rebuked them for calling him Glenn. 'You address me as "Major Miller",' he told them tersely. On another occasion, inside the club, he flared up again when a GI failed to salute him. These incidents were out of character for a man who never lost his temper.

Was Miller, ideally placed in the very heart of it all in Bedfordshire, employed by the Psychological Warfare Division for 'black' propaganda operations and was it this that was affecting his health and state of mind?

4

JEDBURGHS AND 'JOES'

Meanwhile, life in rural Bedfordshire, Buckinghamshire and Northamptonshire, outwardly at least, was carrying on much as normal, or as normal as a wartime economy would permit. Farmers ploughed the arable soil and reared livestock to help keep the populace fed. Few glanced skywards at the sound of aircraft engines any more because by early 1944 the area was inundated with American bomb groups. It came as something of a surprise therefore, when the local farm workers in wheat fields around Harrington witnessed a new sight and sound, as curiously black-painted Liberators circled the airfield.

Early in March 1944 Wellington crews of 84 OTU (Operational Training Unit) of the RAF had been informed that they would be vacating the base at Harrington (which had been built by American engineering battalions) because it was needed to accommodate the Carpetbaggers. The black Liberators had continued to fly night operations from Watton and Alconbury during each moon period.

A complex chain of organization now linked the Carpetbagger and SOE airfields, the London headquarters and underground hideouts all over Europe. Local Resistance leaders selected the reception fields, usually farmlands or sports grounds, and sent their requests for drops by secret radio or by pigeon to 77 Baker Street, an obscure building in a drab London street. There the reception fields were given codenames, Christian names such as *Bob, Percy Red, Luke*, and numbered 1 to 300; trade names such as *carpenter, lawyer* and *salesman* (appropriately because Carpetbagger means 'an opportunist travelling salesman'), equine names such as *rump, bridle* and *saddle*.

It is perhaps pertinent at this stage to detail the sequence of events early in 1944 which led to a Joe boarding a Carpetbagger Liberator at Harrington for a flight into enemy-occupied territory.

Requests for supplies or personnel came from the field itself, or they might have started as a result of planning by a Country Section at OSS, London (a number of Country Sections in OSS Headquarters,

Baker Street directed Resistance activities in France, Belgium, Norway and Denmark, etc.)

The operational priority of a mission was determined by the Chief of Special Operations (American) and the Chief of Special Operations Executive (British), London. The pinpoint section of Air Operations plotted the pinpoint on an operational map and worked out the latitude and longitude of the location. The pinpoint was then taken and given to the Eighth Air Force, where the suitability of the terrain and the strength of enemy forces were taken into consideration.

If the Eighth Air Force approved the pinpoint, the Air Operations Section would be notified and they in turn then notified the Country Section concerned with the approval and of the number assigned to the mission. The Air Ministry was also informed of the pinpoint and would cancel the Carpetbagger operation if it should clash with other operations that night. Often, photographic reconnaissance aircraft would skirt and photograph the field and surrounding landmarks to facilitate identification.

At 17.00 hours in the Conference Room at Air Operations Headquarters, via the scrambler telephone, a list of approved targets would be sent to Captain Sullivan, the S–2 at Harrington. During the evening Sullivan would plot the targets on a large operational map covering the wall in the office of the Deputy Group Commander, Lieutenant-Colonel Fish. The map was in a scale of 1 to 500,000, or about 10 miles to the inch. It showed topographical features such as elevations, rivers and forests. Any areas where 'Special Operations' flights were prohibited, were clearly indicated on the map.

When the field was approved, another coloured flag blossomed on the map, marked with the dates when underground men would be standing by to receive drops. The comparative priority of the missions would be shown by bits of coloured paper, attached to the pins. British or SOE targets proposed for the same night would also be plotted with distinctive tabs.

If a Maquis leader sent to London a call for supplies or arms, a Liberator was loaded with metal canisters and wicker panniers containing sten guns, ammunition and sundry supplies. These would all be in readiness at Harrington, having been brought there from the storage facility at nearby Holme. An operational order would be made out and placed in a pool of approved operations.

At about 09.00 hours the following morning the weather officer at Harrington would advise Colonel Heflin, or his deputy, of weather conditions anticipated in the target areas and at that time it would be decided where it would be practicable to send Carpetbagger aircraft. Heflin or his Deputy then selected the list of targets for the night, considering the priority of requests for material in the field, the reception record of the particular ground, the possibilities of any enemy opposition, the distribution of desired missions and the availability of aircraft and crews. The list of selected missions was then telephoned to the London Conference Room by Captain Sullivan. If London had no practical changes to suggest, the list was in effect for that night.

Meanwhile, the agent, or Resistance group in the field, would have been advised of the period in which reception committees should be prepared to stand by and of the codephrase they should listen for on the BBC news broadcasts. The codenames used were pre-arranged and were called 'Crack Signals'. The day-to-day priority of approved missions was approved by Colonel Heflin and communicated to London headquarters each morning. Headquarters then advised the Country Section concerned of the missions proposed for the day and it arranged for the transmission of the appropriate 'Crack Signal' in the BBC News broadcast. When the signal was received in the field the reception committee proceeded to the dropping ground at the proper time and prepared to receive the Carpetbagger delivery.

At around 11.00 hours, the squadron commanders, Majors St Clair, Boone, McManus and Dickerson, would be called in for a meeting before the map with tabs pinpointing the targets for the night. Together, they would select targets for their crews, balancing the difficult with the not so difficult, the distant with the near, so that each squadron finally had about the same work load. Any disagreement among the squadron commanders would be decided by the toss of a coin, or Colonel Heflin would have the casting vote.

At about 12.00 hours, the navigators of the crews received their targets from their squadron navigator, who had already received his list from Major Tresemer, the group navigator, who had been advised of the targets by Sullivan. In the meantime, the S–2 officers would have been gathering briefing data and preparing maps and special instructions. At 15.00 hours, each crew navigator turned in his flight plan to his squadron navigator, who collected them and took all of them to the group navigator. The flight plans and courses would then be checked and if necessary changes would be made. A take-off time schedule was made up and posted.

Also at 15.00 hours, S–2 officers would begin meeting with the officers of each operational crew. Crew maps would be checked for location of target (latitude, longitude and terrain feature). Each crew would be briefed separately by an S–2 officer and they would have the opportunity to study the large-scale 1 to 50,000 or 1 to 80,000 S–2 map. The crew's target maps were on a scale of 1 to 250,000, or about 5 miles to the inch.

At 16.30 hours a final briefing session would be held for all crew members. A weather officer displayed the weather map and gave a complete explanation for each target area, stressing expectations *en route* and the home base on the return flight. Then Captain Sullivan would give any special information which may affect the crew. Lieutenant-Colonel Fish would add general flying and dropping instructions and finally, Major Tresemer would give out instructions on the route to be followed while over England, and the point and altitude for crossing the English coast. He ended by giving the men a 'time check', on which all crew watches were synchronized.

Already that afternoon the enlisted crew members would have been briefed as neccessary on the course, type of reception signal, the code recognition letters for the target and so on. The radio operators would be given a radio 'flimsy' just before take-off detailing all signal information, code letters, the ground challenge and reply letter, colours of the day for flare signals over England, the navigational radio beacons and direction finder stations in England, a list of the airfield signals and other navigational information, including the night's bomber code used in communication between bombers and home stations.

If necessary, the group communications Officer, Captain Silkenbaken, would brief the radio operators on special information. Dispatchers, when the aircraft carried special packages or personnel to be dropped, were briefed by the group armament officer, Captain Cunningham, who was chief dispatcher for the Group.

During the day, if the opportunity presented itself, the crews would give their Liberator a pre-flight inspection. A half-hour test flight would be made with each B–24 scheduled for a mission, in order to test all the equipment. Crews ate two and a half hours before take-off time and would arrive at their crew rooms, located in Squadron Operations, about two hours before the take-off itself. There the navigator would receive up-to-date weather reports on a weather card. Using the new information he would then turn in a revised flight plan and estimated time of arrival. The pilot, meanwhile, would receive kits containing rations of candy and chewing gum, flares, purses and emergency packets for distribution to the rest of his crew.

With all preparations nearing completion, it only remained for the Joes to arrive. The Joes were a varied lot. American, British, Canadian and other allied officers, young men, pretty girls and old gentlemen. At times the agent was American and at times a national of the country he was being dropped in. They would have left their OSS and SOE safe houses for the journey to Harrington about six hours before they were due to take off.

Typically, the time set for departure from London was 17.00 hours. A quarter of an hour beforehand a uniformed captain of the US Marine Corps, carrying a heavy suitcase, walked up the steps of an inconspicuous, shabby, private house in a London back street and rang the bell. The officer, Captain Howard Grell, wore two rows of brightly coloured Belgian ribbons from the First World War. His job for the night, as conducting officer, was to give final instructions and say goodbye to an American and a British agent. In a matter of hours these agents were to leave by aircraft and parachute for sabotage in plain clothes near to the Swiss border, in German-occupied France.

Captain Grell's ring was answered by a small white-haired man, who also wore First World War ribbons on the lapel of his blue civilian suit. Inside, the house was bare, cramped and drab. There were no rugs on the uncovered floors. The only furniture was utilitarian cheap board tables and uncomfortable chairs without paint. The house was not now a place for living. It was a place where agents, brought to London, could be interviewed with security, by officers from SOE–SO headquarters.

A number of people stood about, some in uniform, but the greater number in civilian clothes. There were three or four women among the men. They talked quietly, in small groups, obviously waiting to say goodbye to two of their own. On the second floor, Captain Grell called for 'Le Breton' and led the American agent into the lonely room. The room was entirely bare of furniture and the only decoration was a notice in red crayon thumbtacked over the fireplace: 'Restaurant Celesta on Queen Street is out of bounds for students.'

Captain Grell smiled and said, 'I have a little present for you from the colonel.' From his trouser pocket, the conducting officer brought out, unboxed, a pair of plain, heavy gold cufflinks. He handed them to 'Le Breton' who looked at them, embarrassed, obviously pleased. 'Gosh, thanks. I never thought I'd have something like this.'

'It's little enough,' Grell nodded, 'they make a nice souvenir – they might even be useful. In France, even today, they are worth 7,000 francs. That's about $140. If you should get into trouble, get arrested, the police might take your money but overlook these. A good bribe for a guard.'

'Yes, but what about my commission, Captain?'

Le Breton, the agent wireless operator, was a good-looking eighteen-year-old American boy. His hair, slightly long, was thick and truly brown. He was wearing a cheap, brown suit and a brown pullover. Le Breton was of French parentage and had enlisted in the US Navy from his New England textile town. In 1943 he found himself taking the Navy course for radiomen in the mid-west. There he was picked up by the OSS, which was seeking radiomen with language qualifications.

Volunteering for dangerous duty in enemy country, Le Breton went through the OSS communication and target schools near Washington. Late in 1943 he reached England, where his training as a W/T operator, parachutist and agent was continued. Now he was ready for the field. Tonight, in company with a British captain called 'André', he was going to the field by parachute route, to act as W/T operator in an SOE–SO Jedburgh sabotage circuit.

Le Breton was relaxed and wholly at ease. He was obviously untroubled by the obvious dangers his mission presented. His only concern was the status of his application for a Navy commission.

'We are doing what we can,' Grell told him. 'You know these things are hard to do. They take a long time. I can promise you we will try like hell and we'll let you know by radio the minute we hear. Let's get going, it's almost five o'clock.'

The London goodbyes were swift. In the narrow, crowded hallway on the ground floor, the British colonel in charge of sabotage operations in France urged André and Le Breton not to hurry things. 'Lie low and take your time until you know you are unsuspected. Then give them Hell!'

The Colonel saluted and shook hands. Le Breton and André shook hands around the circle of other agents. André kissed, ardently, one of the girls. Grell, looking at his watch, said tentatively, 'It's after five.' The white-haired civilian with the war ribbons opened the door. He saluted, 'Good luck gentlemen.'

Unescorted, Le Breton, André and Grell left the house and got into an American car painted in British Army fashion and driven by a uniformed British woman driver. The journey to Harrington took a little more than two hours. During it, Grell, sitting in the back between the two agents, talked casually of this and that, sometimes in English and sometimes in French.

'The programme,' he said, 'is that we eat as soon as we reach the airfield. After that you get dressed. It will take an hour or more. The 'plane leaves at 10.35.'

André said, 'I got married one month ago, today.'

André was a French Canadian from Montreal. He was short, slight, wiry, excited but unalarmed. As an enlisted man with the Canadian Army at Kiska, commissioned a captain in the British Army, he was bound for German-occupied France as lieutenant to the organizer of the well-established Jedburgh circuit for which Le Breton was to be W/T operator. The good-looking girl he had just kissed goodbye was his wife.

'I met her in one of the training schools,' he said. 'I was at parachute school with her. She was the first girl I met there.'

The car motored along the Great North Road and headed for Harrington. Immediately after the meal the agents were driven to a three-roomed Nissen hut for the long process of dressing. The men under the care of the French officer took over one room, Grell's charges another. The third room was occupied by two security officers, one a very tall civilian, the other a very short Army officer. The pair were called variously, 'Sherlock Holmes and Watson' and 'Mutt and Jeff'.

First in the dressing ritual was the security check, the agents appearing separately before 'Mutt and Jeff' who searched clothing with meticulous care for evidence that would be incriminating if uncovered by the Gestapo. This evidence included such scraps of paper as London bus tickets or theatre stubs. It is possible that a second and equally important function of the security examination was to make sure that no hitherto unsuspected 'double agent' took with him into France written material of value to the enemy.

The security check completed for his two men, Grell took charge. First, he sealed in manila envelopes marked with the agents' names, all personal belongings such as English money, pocket books and personal papers and letters. These envelopes, he told them without irony, would be available when called for at the London headquarters.

Next, seating Le Breton in a chair close to his, the conducting officer opened his suitcase and speaking in a quiet tone, began to explain certain items of equipment as he handed them over. Money came first. In a white cloth belt, to be worn under the coat like a life preserver, was the considerable bulk of 100,000 francs, in notes of various denominations.

'This is quite a lot of money,' Grell said seriously. 'It amounts to $2,000 or £500 sterling. We are not going to ask you for an accounting of this money, Le Breton. It is yours to spend as you like. I should, however, give you one warning. Be careful how you spend it. The quickest way to get yourself into trouble with the police will be to live beyond your means. What would you think in your home town in America, if a strange young man who was supposed to be a farmer began to flash $100 bills in the local lunch room? You'd think there was something fishy and you would want to know what was up. The same will be true for you in France. Don't make yourself conspicuous by spending too much money.'

Personal papers followed. Each of these papers was necessary to any security of existence in enemy-occupied territory and each had been prepared with meticulous care to meet existing laws and to fit the identity that Le Breton was to assume in the field. These papers in Le Breton's case included an identity card (*carte d'identité*), ration card (*carte d'alimentation et carte de vêtement*), census card (*certificat de recensement*), occupation card (*certificat de travail*), certificate of residence (*certificat de domicile*) and a birth certificate (*certificat de naissance*).

When Le Breton had indicated that he understood his personal papers and he had stowed them about his person, Grell produced and handed over a large leather wallet. 'You can put enough small denomination franc notes in this wallet to last you for a time after your arrival in the field. Actually, the wallet hides the sheet of silk carrying the code you are to use for W/T messages in the field. Remember that while the wallet will pass casual examination, it won't stand a real search. I advise you to hide it with your radio set.'

A package of about 12 in x 6 in x 2 in contained the crystals for Le Breton's radio set. 'You carry this in the front of your jump suit,' said Grell. 'These jump suits are roomy enough to carry a baby grand piano!'

The conducting officer produced capsules, both blue and white, requiring Le Breton to sign for their receipt. He explained that the blue capsules were benzadrine sulphate to be taken for overcoming fatigue. The white capsules, on the other hand, were knock-out drops, capable of producing a quick state of unconsciousness which would last for at least six hours. A third capsule given to agents was the 'L' pill which was laced with cyanide and encased in rubber. To kill him or herself, the agent had to bite into it. The rubber casing otherwise allowed the Joe to swallow it harmlessly.

'They are useful, these pills, but don't get them mixed up in your mind,' Grell advised. 'The results might be embarrassing!'

Finally, Le Breton was supplied with a .45 calibre automatic pistol and a small .32 calibre revolver with a two inch barrel. Both weapons were loaded there and then. In regard to the revolver, Grell warned that it would be effective only at very close range. He also warned it had no safety catch and would fire with the slightest pressure on the trigger. 'That's all as far as the equipment is concerned,' concluded Grell. 'You might as well get dressed now while I give André his stuff.'

The dressing process was lengthy. Le Breton took off his shoes so that rubber heel pads could be inserted and so that his ankles would be bandaged against injury in jumping. This service was performed by a young man in khaki overall and peaked cap, who introduced himself as the 'dispatcher'. The key man in the business of dropping Joes and supplies, he was also known as the waist gunner in ordinary circumstances. Dispatchers underwent special training to prepare them for their special kind of mission. So that they understood the procedure of jumping, they were required to complete two low-level jumps before going out on their first operational flight.

'I'm the boy who tells you to jump and when,' said the sergeant dispatcher, in a low, southern drawl. 'This is my fourteenth trip over yonder, so I've done it before. Haven't ever jumped myself and I don't reckon I ever will,' he grinned. 'I'd jump quick though, if they told me I was over Athens, Georgia. I'd jump without a 'chute to get back to Athens.'

The jump suit, known as the 'camouflaged strip-tease', followed. This garment, a coverall of heavy canvas, was mottled dark green and brown. When worn, it hung loose. Baggy folds, resembling more than anything else, the dress of an underwater diver minus the belt and helmet. There were many pockets. Into these Le Breton slipped his revolver, compass, a knife for freeing himself if he should land in a tree, a French-made torch with two extra batteries, a tin of RAF emergency rations and a small flask of rum.

A spade with handle, which fitted into a back pocket, was removed on order of Captain Grell, who said that Le Breton's reception committee would take care of burying his jump paraphernalia. In order to cushion the Joe's fall, a spongy rubber cushion was placed in the seat of the suit. A rubber jump helmet and goggles and leather gauntlets completed the outfit.

On the afternoon of his mission, the dispatcher would have been briefed by Captain Roy Cunningham, the armament officer. It was then that the dispatcher learned of the type of packages he would drop that night. The armament and ordnance sections would have combined to see that supplies and agents would be put onto the B–24s. Containers, loaded with guns, ammunition, food and medical supplies, would be loaded by the ordnance section. Cunningham's men would step in to load packages, 'Nickels' (propaganda leaflets) and Joes. The propaganda value of dropping Nickels was secondary, since they were unloaded some distance from the target points in order to give the enemy the false notion that dropping leaflets was the prime purpose of the sortie.

Supplying the underground with its own particular brand of produce perhaps caused the storage point for the loads to be designated as the 'farm'. In any event, the packages, leaflets and parachutes were kept near the perimeter, in well-concealed Nissen huts. Here, the loading crews checked the packages and parachute packs before they were taken out to the Liberators.

The line armament and ordnance crews had a particularly demanding job in loading the aircraft. Each job demanded its own load and the loads had to be carefully checked to make sure that the correct equipment went to the right aircraft. In addition, each Liberator had to be fitted with straps and lines to which the packages would be attached. Loading hundreds of packages, whose weight varied from 50 lb to 150 lb, made for hard work throughout the afternoon and sometimes after supper, for the armament section crew. Containers were loaded on board by the ordnance crew and it went on throughout the afternoon.

After hours of checking and working, sweating out the loading of several aircraft, one word sometimes went out to the farm and bomb dump at Harrington. The word was 'scrub'.

However, this particular mission was going ahead and the dispatcher would be informed that his aircraft would be carrying Joes. He would be coached in the procedure for dropping both packages and Joes. 'Running-in', 'Action Stations', and 'Go' were the three phrases used in 'dispatching' the Joes from the Liberator. To some of the dispatchers carrying Joes was an onerous task but others volunteered for it. They enjoyed fitting and 'handling' the Joes.

The sergeant dispatcher called for assistance in adjusting the British-type parachute to be worn by the American agent. With the suit zipped up, the job was made more difficult because of the awkward bulges caused by the scores of articles stored in the suit. Help was supplied by the American Marine Corps sergeant, who took his work seriously. He adjusted each strap with meticulous care and tested the release mechanism more than once. A good fit was accomplished only after a tug-of-war and the expenditure of much energy and sweat, by both the fitters and the man being fitted. The fitting was accompanied by the steady run of conversation. If a French Joe was being prepared, an interpreter would stand nearby to translate instructions and requests. Fitters sometimes tried out their French on the Joes and they sometimes volunteered instructions in their own language.

In the end the American Marines Corps sergeant expressed satisfaction by patting Le Breton on the back. 'This is one of our best 'chutes. It opens quick and easy.'

'Yeah!' the agent was good-naturedly sarcastic. 'I know all about that stuff!'

By this time the room resembled that of a bride changing for the wedding. In addition to the two agents and Grell were the liaison officer, the dispatcher, the parachute adjuster, the pilot of the Liberator making the trip and Colonel Heflin.

The pilot was saying to André, whose parachute was still being fitted, 'When you get on the ground, tell your reception committee that we'll try to make two more runs to drop packages. The first will come about eight minutes after you're in. If it's safe, we'll circle and make another.'

To Le Breton the conducting Officer was saying earnestly, 'You must remember the message. It's important. I can't let you take a thing like that with you in writing. Too dangerous. Repeat the message to me.'

For the first time, Le Breton looked slightly bewildered. He stammered, trying to reply. In a corner, Colonel Heflin was talking about his boys and their jobs. 'This work is harder than bombing, trickier. You're not following a formation, you are on your own. It takes a lot of training and flying ability to hit a target and pinpoint it on the nose. The best pilots for the job are those who have been on anti-submarine patrol. We've got them here. Good boys.'

Colonel Heflin spoke from experience. As a pilot he had made more than sixteen operational trips dropping agents and containers to Resistance groups, ranging from Norway to the Swiss border. He admitted the danger involved. 'We've lost six planes so far,' he said slowly, 'but a lot of those aren't gone for good. We know that they got down safely and that the Underground is bringing them out.'

In the Colonel's mind, the most disquietening thing about flying an operation was not the enemy flak or fighters. 'What gets me,' he confessed, 'is crossing the Channel in fog or cloud, on instruments, knowing that the stuff around you is lousy with aircraft but not being able to see a thing. When you are dealing with flak or fighter, you have so much to do that you haven't got time to be scared. When you're waiting for a collision in this type of weather, there isn't a thing to do but sit and sweat.'

As the time for take-off approached, the Joes shook hands all round. Some of the men outwardly took the flight as a lark and attempted a few lunging waltz steps. Others just sat more quietly, smoking and saying little. On the whole, however, the atmosphere was not appreciably different from that of a routine practice flight.

At precisely 22.15 Lieutenant Reardon gave the signal for departure. 'Let's go.' The procession straggled out into the cold, damp twilight, Le Breton and André moving awkwardly in their bulky jump suits and parachute harnesses. Grell was still talking to the American agent. 'You're sure that you have the message right? Repeat it to me.'

The trip to the aircraft was made in the same car which had brought the men from London. It swiftly circled the field on a broad runway. At the dispersal point the Liberator with a big black 'D' on its side, engines idle, was waiting. Its crew, in coveralls and Mae Wests, stood by its side. Out of its element, the bomber appeared fat, clumsy and ungraceful.

'We're loaded to the ears,' said the pilot, pointing to the bomb bay. 'Twelve containers to get rid of at another ground after we drop the 'bodies'. We've got a tail wind though, they say. The trip out should take less than three hours. We're due back here at 5.20 am.'

One of the Liberator crew drew Grell to one side, pointing at Le Breton. 'How old is that guy? He looks like a kid.'

Grell smiled. 'He's eighteen, just. How old are you?'

The crewman shook his head. 'I'm nearly twenty, but that's different. Eighteen, by God.'

Le Breton shook hands with Grell. The two agents climbed into the bomber through the 'Joe hole' in the bottom of the fuselage. It was the same hole through which, approximately three hours later, they would jump into the darkness over France. The pilot again glanced at his watch. To his crew he said conversationally, 'Well, let's go.' He nodded to Grell. 'See you for breakfast.'

Standing to one side, Grell watched the Liberator's twin Wasps burst into life until all four propellers were turning. As the bomber jerked forward and swung onto the runway, André and Le Breton waved from the open waist window. André called out something unintelligible. Grell saluted.

From the balcony of the control tower, on the west side of the airfield, the conducting officer watched the Liberator take off. It was almost dark. The lights of the flarepath made a road in the middle distance. The west wind was colder, if possible, than ever. It almost blew away the sound of the Liberator's engines. At last, however, it became more insistent, growing louder. The bright lights in the wingtips wobbled and moved. The bomber took off almost opposite the control tower, with a roar that was deafening and then was gone. Grell looked at his watch. It was 22.36. In the heart of occupied Europe, underground groups would be scanning the night sky, anxiously waiting for the arrival of supplies or for men and women agents who could bring them the latest detailed information and instructions which would aid them in acts of sabotage against the enemy.

It would not be until the aircraft returned, several hours later, and the interrogation forms were filled in, that the armament and ordnance sections would know whether the mission had been marked 'complete' or 'non-complete'.

5

BLACK SHEEP IN
WOLVES' CLOTHING

On the night of 2/3 March 1944 the mission was marked 'non-complete' when Lieutenant Frank C. McDonald and crew in the 36th Squadron failed to return. Their Liberator was hit at low altitude by flak guns mounted on railway wagons, and crashed at Fienvillers. They were too low to bail out so McDonald decided to ride the aircraft down. Sergeant Norman R. Gellerman, flight engineer, was killed in the ensuing crash. Lieutenant Thomas H. Kendall, navigator, Lieutenant Edward F. Shevlin, bombardier, and T/Sgt Warren L. Ross, radio operator, scrambled out of the left side of the Liberator while McDonald, Lieutenant Fred C. Kelly, co-pilot, and S/Sgt Leroy S. Goswick, dispatcher, exited from the right. S/Sgt Edward H. DeCoste, tail gunner, managed to get out through the tail as this section had been snapped off in the crash. He later managed to contact the French Underground but during his time on the run Germans in civilian clothes captured him and for a time treated him as a spy. Finally, DeCoste convinced them he was an American airman and he was sent to the prisoner of war camp at Stalag IV at Gross Tychow, Pomerania on the Baltic coast. On 6 February 1945 DeCoste and his fellow prisoners were forced on a 'death march' of 600 miles in eighty-four days, suffering near-starvation and abuse until freed by the Russians on 2 May 1945.*

Lieutenant Fred C. Kelly was taken in by the French Resistance after three days on the run. The Resistance checked him out and arranged a journey south. At one point the American was led down the main street of a village, conspicuous in his flying clothes. In a Paris underground railway station, Kelly, lagging behind his guide, had the seat of his trousers caught in the train doors as they closed.

---

* *Home By Christmas* Martin W. Bowman (PSL Ltd, 1987)

Instinctively, he shouted 'Whoa there' in English. Everyone in the compartment looked up in amazement but no one raised the alarm. Travelling by road and by train Kelly eventually reached the *Zone Interdite* along the Spanish border. He had a close escape at one point when a *gendarme* asked where he was going. His identity card said he was a blacksmith so Kelly said he was 'going to work'. The *gendarme* laughed and waved him on. Kelly spent an uncomfortably cold night in a sheepfold.

Next morning a woman took him in, fed him and arranged for a guide to escort him over the mountains into neutral Spain. Having crossed safely into Spain, the guide, a little eccentric and rather drunk, decided to take Kelly on a little sightseeing trip 3 miles out of their way to see a marker stone indicating the Franco-Spanish border! The detour was not to his liking but Kelly eventually returned to England on 1 June 1944.

Meanwhile, on 3/4 March 1944, the night following McDonald's shooting down, two more crews in the 36th Squadron failed to return from Carpetbaggers sorties. Lieutenant Wade A. Carpenter crashed at Humbercourt after being hit by flak at low altitude. All nine crew survived but Lieutenant William D. Rees, bombardier, who was trapped under the wreckage, later had to have both legs amputated and he died from shock. Captain Gerald S. Wagstad's Liberator is believed to have gone down in the Channel off the coast of France.

Wilmer Stapel, a veteran of fifteen Carpetbagger missions and now a captain, was allocated the same target the following night to discover what had caused the loss of Carpenter's and Wagstad's crews. He also had a personal reason for the trip. Lieutenant Glenn C. Nesbitt, his original bombardier, had volunteered as a replacement to fly with Wade Carpenter's crew and had failed to return. By 5 March Stapel's crew had undergone several changes:

My co-pilot, Lieutenant Hal M. Harrison, now had his own crew and had been replaced by Lieutenant Russel C. Rovers. Rovers had been a member of the RCAF and had just recently been transferred to the USAAF. Since Lieutenant Hubert A. Bowman, my new bombardier, had not yet checked in, Major Charles Teer, the Group Bombardier, volunteered to fly with me this night.

We crossed the enemy coast as planned without any trouble and had settled down on course to the drop area which was south-east of Brussels. About fifteen minutes inbound after crossing the enemy coast, all hell broke loose. Our aircraft was bathed in the brightness and glare of searchlights. The ack-ack guns were accurate. I could hear the thumps as the shells found their target and the aircraft would give a shudder as if it were trying to shake off the hits. Our altitude at this time was 2,500 ft. We were in the middle of a gigantic ambush by the enemy gun emplacements. I immediately started evasive action and my gunners had the presence of mind to start firing at the searchlights as best they could. I dove, pulled up, twisted, turned, skidded and tried any other manoeuvre that might cause the enemy's guns to miss their target. Our bizarre, unpredictable, erratic and unconventional flight path must have been something to behold. The enemy gunners must have felt certain they had shot us down. They didn't.

At one point in our flight to escape their fire, a shout from Major Teer was given just in the nick of time to prevent us clobbering a water tower directly in front of us. A lift of the wing and a slight turn solved that immediate problem. We were, as one has no doubt surmised by now, buzzing our way further into Belgium. We ran out of the action as rapidly as it had begun. The aircraft was still manoeuvrable and all four engines were still churning away, so we proceeded to the drop area. As I dropped my wing flaps and started my drop run, we were greeted with more small arms fire. I poured the coal to the engines, cleaned up the aircraft and requested Lieutenant Milton S. Popkin, my navigator, to give me the most direct heading to get out of the country. I took up the heading given me, dropped to buzzing altitude, firewalled the engines and out we came. There were other aircraft coming into Belgium as we were hastily going out. Their presence had the enemy guns concentrating on them. That, plus the fact that we were so low that by the time they heard us coming we were gone, saved us.

During crew debriefing our intelligence personnel insisted that we must have been lost and confused because there were no enemy gun emplacements in that entire area. It was days later that the new flak maps were distributed to our organization. The new maps showed that the Germans had moved into the area hundreds of guns and ack-ack units. The Germans were prepared for our Allied invasion. Later on the morning of 6 March, the entire crew wandered out to our aircraft. There was a large gaping hole in the left wing that seemed large enough for a man to crawl through. Most of the left aileron was shot away, as was the left vertical tail stabilizer and rudder. There were numerous flak holes scattered the length and breadth of the fuselage. The excessive power placed on the engines meant that they had to be changed.

On 25 March echelons began leaving Alconbury for Harrington. Three days later the black Liberators took off from Alconbury for the last time and flew to their new airbase. Of course the customary rumours and speculation as to their purpose quickly became favourite gossip at bars in pubs at nearby Clipston, Maidwell and Oxenden. Security was tight and the true nature of the work carried out by the secret squadrons was never known locally. People just thought that the aircraft were painted black for night bombing missions. On 29 March, group personnel arrived from Alconbury and the remaining sections and crews at Watton arrived on 1 April. The new base seemed altogether beautiful after Watton and the Nissen huts were the last word in luxury after having to live in tents throughout the winter. The Carpetbaggers now began to take on a more unified look and three days later General Orders No. 4, HQ 8th Air Force Composite Command officially assigned the 36th and 406th Squadrons to the 801st Bomb Group (H). Everyone was pleased that they now had their own base from which to mount operations.

On the night of 5/6 April the 801st dispatched 17 Liberators on the inaugural Carpetbagger mission flown from Harrington. Lieutenant William W. Nicoll and his crew in the 406th Squadron, who were flying their first mission, failed to return. Their orders were to drop a Joe over France. At the last minute numbers one and four engines on the Liberator needed adjustment and take-off was delayed until 22.00 hours. The Joe breathed a sigh of relief and Nicoll and his seven-man crew took off without further mishap. They set course for their target many miles to the south of the Loire. At 1,200 ft they went onto automatic pilot while outside an overcast began to develop over the Channel. Nicoll turned the automatic pilot off and dropped to 500 ft above the waves.

Approaching the coast of France one hour out Nicoll and his co-pilot, Lieutenant A.W. Kalbfleisch, brought the nose up and increased speed to 190 mph. Twenty minutes later all hell broke loose as enemy flak guns bracketed the sky around them. Tom Davis, the bombardier, yelled over the interphone, 'Hard Right!' The warning came too late. A burst of flak shot away the B–24's tail, killing Ralph Kittrell, the rear gunner. Almost immediately, the nose took a direct hit. Davis's voice again bellowed over the interphone, 'Get Out, Get Out' but William G. Harris, the navigator, was silent.

By now the Liberator was enveloped in a fiery inferno and down to only 300 ft. Nicoll ordered the survivors out as Kalbfleisch turned on the automatic pilot and sounded the fire alarm. He stepped into the radio compartment but there was no sign of Warren A. Brewer, the radio operator. He could see that Richard Bindel, the engineer, was having difficulty finding his parachute. Kalbfleisch, his hair and eyebrows singed and with the fur collar on his jacket burned off, made his way to the bomb bay. Nicoll was standing on the catwalk putting on his parachute. The bomb bay doors would not fully open so Kalbfleisch ducked under the catwalk and as the Liberator began tipping over, he stepped through the hole and immediately pulled his ripcord. Luckily, the parachute did not get caught on the aircraft.

The next thing Kalbfleisch knew was that he was on the ground. A moment later, the burning Liberator crashed a few yards away from him. In the distance he could hear guttural shouts and sporadic gunfire. He tried to run but his ankle had been injured in the landing. Somehow, he managed to get his parachute harness off and stagger to a nearby stream. He threw his Mae West into the water, then the Liberator's fuel tanks exploded, sending him five feet across the other side of the stream. The sky was illuminated in a brilliant white glow and in this artificial light, dazed as he was, Kalbfleisch was able to make out his surroundings quite clearly. Their Liberator had crashed beside a German radio station surrounded by anti-aircraft guns. In the sky above he could make out the unmistakable shaps of four Liberators. One of them took a flak hit in one of the engines.

Despite his injured ankle Kalbfleisch staggered away from the scene of death and destruction. Progress was slow and he was not helped by the cross-patches of barbed wire, ditches and streams. He carried on until three o'clock in the morning, when, utterly exhausted, he climbed into a pile of faggots intending to rest up for a while. Cold quickly enveloped his body and his ankle began to hurt badly. Kalbfleisch decided his best bet was to carry on but his ankle gave way. He eventually had to crawl, determined to reach a nearby house and get help.

He came upon a row of houses and after surveying the quiet scene for a short while, struck out for the nearest one. A dog rushed out but Kalbfleisch calmed him before knocking hard on the door. No one stirred. Suddenly, a window opened above him and a man's voice said, '*Attendez*' (wait). The Frenchman appeared at the door and ushered Kalbfleisch in. He built a fire and brought wine while his wife prepared some eggs.

That night Kalbfleisch slept at the house. The next morning another Frenchman appeared and using an English-French dictionary, explained that he would take the American airman to a German-speaking truck driver who could drive him to the Pyrenees. Kalbfleisch was given civilian clothes and a blue patterned scarf. He was warned not to speak to anyone who did not wear the same patterned scarf as his.

After treatment to his ankle by a local doctor, Kalbfleisch was moved to another house in the vicinity. He was delighted to discover that Joe Porter, the waist gunner and dispatcher on the crew was there. Porter told Kalbfleisch that he had baled out and had been shot at by Germans firing machine-guns.

Both airmen were informed by the French that five of their crew had been killed outright and were not permitted a proper burial by the Germans. A French Catholic curate had therefore risked his life by carrying out a secret burial service over the common grave of the fallen American crew. The eighth man aboard, who was an American agent, baled out. He landed in a tree and his chest was crushed in the fall. The Germans found him and removed him from the branches but they made no effort to aid him. For two days he was left unattended on the ground. An officer questioned him each day but the Joe refused to give him any information. On the morning of 8 April the Joe was taken to the Château de la Rochelle where he still refused to talk. The German officer took out his Luger pistol and shot him through the head.

Kalbfleisch and Porter were hidden in a haystack. At night the doctor returned and drove them in his car to another town where he deposited them with a wealthy Frenchwoman whose house was large and prosperous looking. It transpired that she was a member of the secret French Intelligence Service and it was her job to transmit information about German activities to London. Ironically, she had three times pinpointed the position of the flak guns which had shot down Kalbfleisch's Liberator but the information had not been acted upon.

Kalbfleisch and Porter remained at their host's house for over a month. Preparations were made to move them and ID passes were forged, showing that they were workers on authorized leave from the Renault factory in Paris. Meanwhile, the Germans were openly advertising a 25,000 franc reward for information leading to the capture of Kalbfleisch and Porter. However, the French people, out of their four years of experience, had come to understand the worthlessness of German currency and German promises and no one ever came forward to claim the reward.

In the early days of their stay with the Frenchwoman, many plans were put forward for their escape. The original plan was to contact a Royal Navy motor torpedo boat, which made regular runs to the French coast. This plan had to be discarded before it had developed very far because the MTB service was stopped. Then it was planned to move the two men to the Pyrenees but this plan was deemed impracticable because the Germans were gathered in strength along the entire route which Porter and Kalbfleisch would have to cross. Another plan was to move the men into Switzerland but they themselves vetoed this idea since they did not relish the thought of being interned for the duration.

In all this planning, a French officer, who had travelled to the house from Geneva, took an active part. It became his responsibility to make other arrangements, which would be practical. In the meantime, Kalbfleisch and Porter led more or less uneventful lives. They were forced to remain hidden for the most part but they had a comfortable room of their own and enough to eat. At 23.00 hours each night, which was the customary time for the Gestapo to make their visits, the two men would adjourn to a chicken coop in the back yard where they would hide until the Gestapo had left. The only time the two Americans appeared in public was on Sundays, when, dressed in civilian suits, they were allowed to saunter in the garden, accompanied by specially invited ladies. To the casual observer, they were simply Sunday visitors.

Inevitably, restlessness set in. The two men were anxious to get going and at least attempt to return to England. They decided that travelling to the Pyrenees and crossing into Spain was the most practical approach and they were determined to begin their journey as soon as possible. The French captain told them that if they could learn French in two weeks, he would take them to the Pyrenees. Kalbfleisch and Porter took him at his word but decided that the French captain had made the proposal simply to keep them occupied. After the first fortnight, they had stopped using the chicken coop at night. For use in any future emergency, they dug out a large deep pit, which they camouflaged imaginatively. During the course of their digging, they also took time to bury 400 quarts of their host's very best champagne, which she wanted to hide from the Germans. She was very generous to the two Americans and they had ample opportunity to discover that it was an excellent vintage!

As the weeks passed, a Mustang pilot joined them at the house. When D-Day arrived there was great excitement and a new determination on the part of the Americans to return to their units. Shortly after D-Day, Allied bombers blasted targets nearby but missed a camouflaged German airfield. Kalbfleisch and Porter were even more determined to return home and pinpoint the target the bombers had missed.

Eventually, two Frenchmen arrived from the Normandy Front who could guide them to the Allied lines. The Frenchmen were very happy about the invasion, carried 'invasion money' and spent much of the time toasting the Americans with 'Bonne Santé'. The party of five set off for Caen but got off to a bad start when they walked right into a German munitions camp. They managed to bluff their way out of trouble and at a further ID check later in their journey and arrived in the town amid heavy shelling.

At first they stayed in a house in Caen already overcrowded with refugees and with a 1,000 lb bomb lodged in the ceiling, before being moved to another house a few doors away. The sky seemed constantly filled with Allied aircraft. In one week they experienced a major attack by Typhoons and another by Marauders, besides scattered, smaller raids. Bombs dropped nearby and one blew in the windows. Kalbfleisch, standing in the middle of a downstairs room, saw a blown-in door hurtling towards him. He moved away in the nick of time!

To make matters worse, the Germans chose this house to station a dummy Tiger tank outside to serve as a decoy for the Allied bombers. However, everyone had to stay put. A B–17 pilot and five British joined them, making a total of nine men in the house. On 4 July the Americans celebrated with a little wine. In the cramped conditions, tempers flared and relations between the Americans and the British deteriorated. In addition, the B–17 pilot was beginning to get jumpy and unpredictable.

One day two SS soldiers appeared over the backyard wall with Lugers in their hands. The British spotted them and yelled. The Fortress pilot made a bolt for the toilet and locked himself in. Kalbfleisch, Porter and the Mustang pilot were asleep. The SS soldiers entered the house, gathered up whatever appeared edible or saleable and then made a tour of the house. They thrust open the door where the three Americans were sleeping.

Kalbfleisch was awake by now but decided it best to simulate a discreet slumber. One of the stormtroopers barked a command in German which the American ignored. Getting no response, the SS soldier kicked Kalbfleisch vigorously. He stirred drowsily and murmured a few unintelligible words. The stormtrooper made a scornful remark, probably reflecting on these decadent French who sleep their lives away, and left abruptly.

A few days after this incident the men were moved to another house, located on the western edge of Caen, not far from the river which marked the outskirts of town. They had been there for only a short time when the sky was filled with a massive aerial bombardment. British troops moved up and the German defenders began firing machine-guns on the eastern bank. One day a Frenchman who attempted to cross the river to the British side in a boat was cut to pieces by the German guns.

For days British tanks replied by shelling the German machine-gun posts. Typhoon fighter-bombers roared overhead and at last a barrage of artillery fire developed from the west bank, lasting a day and a night. The Americans huddled miserably in their shelter, not daring to leave while the shells screamed through the air and shrapnel ricocheted from walls all about them. When the firing died down Kalbfleisch sought out and finally convinced their French guide that they had to leave this hot spot. When they returned they discovered that SS troops had turned up at the house and had taken the other men away for questioning. On the way they had been asked if they were English. Porter had replied, 'Hell, no!' Apparently, the remark went unnoticed and after a short while they were released from the German headquarters.

Kalbfleisch and the others headed out of Caen but had not got very far when they realized that the position was hopeless. They returned to Caen and ran straight into SS Panzer troops. They asked permission to stay in a house nearby and, surprisingly, were granted it. Then they realized that the house acted as a buffer for British shells. The French guide left saying that he would return the following morning. The men spent an uncomfortable night in the house and were there all the next morning. The guide did not return so the men set off on their own. They were stopped several times but eventually they found their way back to the Frenchman's home they had left several weeks before. They were sick, hungry and weak.

The men rested up at the house, putting up with some Germans who descended on them and billeted themselves with the Americans, before setting out again with two other French guides for the American lines. They stopped off at a town where they met their next contact, a Frenchman called 'André' who could speak a little broken English. The town had been heavily bombed by Allied aircraft and André would look out over the ruined buildings from his window, shake his head sadly and say, 'All this crash'. This phrase became his nickname. Although he was almost the 'Lord Mayor', André was an ordinary genial Frenchman and offered his guests warm hospitality. He loved to serve wine, saying in uneven English, 'Like hell we drink; we drink like hell!'

André made arrangements for the four Americans to reach the American lines. They were given a course to follow, necessary provisions, arms, and at the last minute, Porter found a baby thrust into his arms. The purpose of the baby was to provide an excuse for the journey, in case the men should be stopped for questioning. They walked for a long time before finally reaching their next contact in the hills. There the Americans learned that 'All that crash' André been arrested by the Germans and was being tortured. The Americans knew that he would never talk, no matter what tortures were carried out to his body.

That afternoon the French contact man walked the four American airmen towards the American lines. He led them along a road and through a minefield, where the only Germans they saw were dead ones. They continued walking and finally the guide said, 'You can now sing "Yankee Doodle"!' But the Americans, after four months in occupied France, could not believe they were actually safe at last. They did not dare sing yet but the Frenchman broke into a lusty rendition of the 'Marseillaise' and finally, the Americans began singing too! That was they way they were when they found the first American patrol, marching along the road, Porter wearing a German helmet, which he had appropriated along the way.

Kalbfleisch, Porter and the two pilots were taken in jeeps to Field Headquarters. All the way back they were handed cigarettes and sweets by GIs whom they passed. It was as if they were entering the promised land! Kalbfleisch and Porter were soon back at Harrington detailing their story to an interested party of Carpetbagger personnel.

The 5/6 April mission had ended in disaster for Lieutenant William W. Nicoll and four of his crew. It was also a personal setback for OSS in London who had lost possibly one of their best operatives when the unidentified Joe was murdered by the Gestapo three days later. Had they been captured alive, the American Liberator crew would have been treated as prisoners of war. The poor Joe was not.

A lull in operations from Harrington followed, punctuated only on the nights of 10/11 April, when 23 Liberators were dispatched and on 11/12 April when a dozen B–24s flew sorties over Europe. Both missions were flown without loss and the group had good reason to be pleased. It meant that their cargoes of Joes and supplies to the Resistance had been delivered, it was hoped, into friendly hands. Like their colleagues in the 8th Air Force, if a malfunction meant an early abort, then the Carpetbagger crews could bring their cargoes home. However, too many aborts could cause a few eyebrows to be raised back on base. On 16 April Major St Clair had the distasteful task of participating in the court martial of one of the pilots in his squadron who, it was determined, had made too many aborts without mechanical problems being diagnosed. He compounded his problems later by going AWOL.

On 23 April Lieutenant Colonel Heflin, with Lieutenant-Colonel Gable of OSS, flew in a B–24 to Algiers. The purpose of the mission was to show the Algiers Squadron, then being set up for Carpetbagger missions to southern Europe, a modified B–24 and also to discuss ways of co-ordinating operations from OSS London and Algiers. Heflin was back at Harrington in time to greet Brigadier-General Edmund Hill, Commanding General, 8th Air Force Composite Command, who inspected the Carpetbaggers on 27 April.

During Heflin's absence the Carpetbaggers had dispatched 23 Liberator sorties without loss. Then, on the night of 27/28 April one aircraft out of the 21 dispatched failed to return to Harrington. First Lieutenant George W. Ambrose and his crew in the 36th Bomb Squadron had taken off in *The Worry Bird* for a mission to target 'Lackey 3a' in France. First reports of what had happened to Ambrose and his crew filtered through via OSS HQ at Baker Street. All had gone well until they neared the French village of St Cyr de Valorges in the Tarare area near Lyons. One Liberator had already dropped its cargo in the drop area when Ambrose arrived. He made three descending circles. The B–24 was very low when one of the crew, Sergeant James C. Mooney, who was on his first mission that night, fell through the Joe Hole while pushing out a package and 'chute. He held on to the 'chute and landed, breaking his back. Mooney was taken in by a Frenchwoman but the French said later that they had no option but to hand him over to the Germans. (Mooney survived the war.)

The drop area consisted of a clearing surrounded by high hills, and as *The Worry Bird* banked in descending circles, on the third circle a wing struck a hillside. The French reception committee, which was already gathering up the load dropped by the first Liberator, saw the aircraft crash just 500 metres away from them. Five of the crew, including Ambrose, were killed, but Sergeant George Henderson, tail gunner and Staff Sergeant James J. Heddleston, radio operator survived. Heddleston owes his life to the fact that he was going towards the tail of the aircraft to retrieve an object at the time. He was jolted halfway through the camera hatch and then back into the aircraft, when it struck the ground and bounced and crashed again. Heddleston was catapulted into the undergrowth. Meanwhile, Henderson was hurled from the tail to the bomb bay by the force of the crash.

After the initial shock Henderson climbed out of the wreckage and saw Heddleston, who was struggling in a maze of cables. With Henderson's help, Heddleston extricated himself and the two men, despite their bruises and the severe cuts to the head Heddleston had sustained, began running away from the scene of the crash. They had not gone more than twenty-five yards when *The Worry Bird* exploded, showering the two men with sparks and debris.

For a mile and a half they ran at random, motivated by fear and shock. Then they stopped. Calmly now, they sat on the ground and began to plan, determined to evade capture by the Germans and to escape to England. From their emergency kits, they drew compasses and set themselves a heading for the south-east, where the Pyrenees and Spain lay. Then, having rested for a short while, they began walking in the direction they had set for themselves. Progress was slow because they kept to woods and out-of-the-way places. They walked until about 08.30 hours, when they stopped in a wood to hide out and rest. Later, they discovered that the Germans had blocked off all roads within a radius of 10 miles from the crashed Liberator and that Dornier 210s and Junkers Ju–88s were reconnoitring the area for the men who had escaped from the crash.

Henderson and Heddleston remained in the woods for three hours. They walked up to the top of a hill nearby, where they looked down upon a group of houses. For a time there was a lot of activity around the houses but when the way seemed clear they decided to approach one of the houses, which was set apart from the others. Sergeant Heddleston was by now very weak from his wounds and had difficulty walking. Henderson went on to the house alone, holding his flying wings in his outstretched hand.

The farming people who lived in the house knew about the 'plane crash and as soon as they saw Henderson's wings, they understood immediately who he was. Immediately, the man of the house went with Henderson to the hiding place where they got Heddleston and helped him to the house. The two men were given water to wash their wounds and Henderson, using a knife sterilized in cognac, removed four pieces of steel from the back of Heddleston's head. He patched the skin together with adhesive tape from his First Aid box. Then the two American airmen returned to their hiding place in the wood and slept while the farmer stood guard.

That afternoon they were awakened by the farmer. Handing them field glasses he pointed down into the valley. They Germans had come to haul away the aircraft wreckage and from where they were standing, Henderson and Heddleston could see a platoon of German soldiers load the unrecognizable remains of their Liberator into two lorries and drive away. (The Germans did not retrieve all the wreckage because the Maquis had managed to collect some parts, including a plate from a piece of radio equipment, which they sent to England for recognition purposes. From this, OSS managed to verify the aircraft's serial number, 42–40997, and piece together the fate of the crew.)

The French farmer became nervous at the presence of the German soldiers and he told Henderson and Heddleston that they would do well to leave rapidly and at once. The two men thanked him for his help and set off, travelling for the rest of the afternoon. At a stream they were able to fill their water bottles. They did not cover much ground because it was hilly country and their legs were so cut and swollen, they could only cover 200 yards at a time. After about five hours they had only managed to travel about a mile and a half. Utterly exhausted, they laid up under some trees and rested, keeping a watchful eye on the road.

At 18.00 hours they started out again across an open field. They progressed slowly for about an hour, came to a stream, which they jumped with difficulty, and at last saw a farmhouse. The two men approached the house but a small boy was the only inhabitant. He managed to convey that his mother would be back soon. About half an hour later the mother returned. She acted in a friendly manner, fed the two Americans and allowed them to sleep for the night in the hay gathered in her barn.

Next morning the two men woke early. The woman gave them breakfast and pointed out a direction for them to follow. They thanked her for the help she had given them and set out again for open country. They came across railway lines, rusty with disuse and decided to follow them because the steep banks on either side provided good cover. The railway lines led to a tunnel, emerging, to their astonishment, in the centre of a small town. Realizing that it would be suspicious to turn suddenly and retrace their steps, they continued following the railway line through the town. They were still wearing their flying suits and leather jackets and while most people stared and some waved, they were not stopped and no one spoke to them!

On the far side of the town they approached a man and asked him for help. The man was jittery and shouted '*Partez! Partez!*' (Leave, leave). Henderson and Heddleston immediately left the railway line and struck out across country through some woods. They came to a road and followed it but before long, a German lorry approached and the two men quickly jumped into a ditch by the side of the road. When the danger had passed, they realized that it was unsafe to follow an open road. They took to the hills again.

They came to a narrow stream and stopped to drink and wash. Shortly afterwards, they passed by a Frenchman working in his garden. They asked for help but he seemed reluctant to help them. The two Americans set off again and had barely gone a few yards when the Frenchman called them back. He had changed his mind and showed them a clump of bushes where they were to hide until he could get help. Heddleston and Henderson remained in the bushes, wondering if they had been duped. However, they were tired and hungry so they decided to chance their luck. After what seemed an age, the Frenchman returned. He carried a note, written in English, which read, 'Teacher of school will come at 5 o'clock. Courage, we are your friends.'

Impatiently, the two men waited for 5 o'clock to arrive. Punctually, on the hour, a man came to them, carrying a large suitcase. It was the school teacher, M. Benoit. The suitcase contained food, weapons, ammunition and whiskey. He led them from their hiding place to a farmer's house where they were given bread, cheese and wine. The teacher rode off on his bicycle and returned later with another man armed to the hilt. Stuck in his belt were pistols and knives, and grenades protruded from his pockets. The two Americans were given guns and escorted from the farmer's house through a town to the teacher's house. Shortly after their arrival, a car arrived and they were driven to another town, some distance away. There they were joined by Madame de Havrincourt, an English-speaking Frenchwoman, and taken to a farmhouse. There they met the leader of the local Resistance organization. That night they slept in beds with real sheets!

The next morning the Resistance leader came to the farmhouse accompanied by two women, an elderly man and a doctor. The doctor examined the Americans and treated their legs, which were badly swollen. Then he dressed Heddleston's head wound. That night, they were moved to an old abandoned house, where they were to remain hidden until arrangements could be made for their removal. For five days Heddleston and Henderson lived in total discomfort, waiting to be moved. Since there was no furniture in the house, they slept on a cement floor. Once a day, a Frenchwoman and a man came to the house, bringing a bowl of soup, a chunk of bread and a quart of water. Those were their provisions for each twenty-four hour period. They used the water for drinking, washing and even shaving. Behind the house was a good-sized lake but the men could not leave the house to get to it. At the end of five days the Resistance leader, accompanied by an English-speaking Frenchwoman, came for the men. The date was 5 May. Henderson and Heddleston were taken to the Frenchwoman's house where they were treated with every consideration. The Frenchwoman was eloquent in her condemnation of the plan which had kept them for five days on the cold cement floor of an abandoned house.

During their time at the Frenchwoman's house all necessary contacts and arrangements were made for their eventual journey out of France. However, their stay at the solicitous Frenchwoman's home came to an abrupt and premature end. On 14 May a woman visited the house and before evening the whole town knew that two American airmen were being harboured in their midst. As a result of the woman's talkativeness, Henderson and Heddleston were moved, early the following morning, to the Jean Crozet farmhouse, 6 kilometres away near St Germain Laval. There a rendezvous was made with the chief of another Resistance organization, which agreed to take over the two Americans.

They first stayed at the home of René Simone then for twelve days they remained at the home of M. Jean Boyer. During this time, the Gestapo made regular visits, since this was the farm which supplied them with fresh eggs. On 23 May Henderson and Heddleston were visited by the people who had sent the report to England of their aircraft crashing. These people had been hunting them for a month. They told how five members of the crew had been killed outright by the crash and how Jim Mooney, the dispatcher, had been helped away by a Frenchwoman but was betrayed to the Germans by a collaborationist and was now a PoW. The collaborationist's house, with him inside it, had been blown up by the French Resistance.

On 24 May the Resistance Chief brought a young English-speaking Frenchwoman to the house. Heddleston and Henderson were asked for their name, rank and serial number and for their escape photographs. It was explained that their photographs would be sent to England for corroboration. The next night they were moved from the farmhouse into a nearby town where they were to remain for more than two months, while verification of their identity could be received from London. At times, Henderson and Heddleston were taken on guided tours of the town. Their only activity in town, however, was occasionally to purchase cigarettes, which cost 150 francs ($3.00) for a pack of twenty. It was a far cry from the 3d pack of cigarettes at the Harrington PX! Despite the food shortage Madame Boyer made something extra for Jim Heddleston's 21st birthday on 19 June. She rounded up some Champagne and cake and Heddleston's birthday was celebrated in some style at the house of René Simone.

During their stay at the farmhouse the two Americans had one or two close calls. One day a German six-man patrol entered the town. It was reported that they were looking for 'two men'. While it was not clear exactly who these two men were, it was decided not to take any chances and Henderson and Heddleston were moved. They hid in an old barn until the Germans had left. Before they went, the patrol beat an old woman, demanding to know where her son was. She refused to talk, but eventually the son gave himself up in order to spare his mother further torture. Because of the language problem it was decided that the two American airmen would be 'deaf and dumb' mutes. However, this did not prevent them from taking part in several night-time raids with the French Resistance. On 18 July they joined a four-man party from the Resistance and, armed with British Sten guns, they mounted bicycles and rode 12 kilometres to their destination, a bridge used by German supply trains. The Frenchmen placed bombs at strategic points and set the fuses. Then they waited, hidden in nearby bushes as a train approached. Two German trains passed safely over the bridge but in the next moment, the bridge exploded! Future German supply trains at least would be delayed.

Five days later Henderson and Heddleston accompanied the same group on another operation. Their destination this time was the house of a collaborationist family. The purpose of the expedition this time was to frighten the collaborationists as well as gain some important information. The six men reached the house and surrounded it. The leader called out his orders but the frightened people inside the house refused to come out. They threw chairs and assorted bits of furniture out of the windows.

The leader's threat to set fire to the barn eventually forced the collaborationists out of the house. Henderson, armed with a machine-gun, took the wome in charge, while the men were questioned. The operation was completely successful. The necessary information was obtained and Henderson returned with the machine-gun in one hand and a gigantic ham in the other!

On 27 July the group who had sent the report of Lieutenant Ambrose's aircraft to England arrived to take Henderson and Heddleston on a reception operation. They drove their car, which contained a Eureka set on the back seat, to the reception ground and waited. There was intensive RAF activity in the vicinity and no aircraft arrived for the dropping operation at the ground, codenamed 'Astrologer'. Finally, the reception committee left. Next morning the BBC signal was received. 'Astrologer fell in the well', meaning that the previous night's operation had been cancelled, probably because it might have interfered with the RAF activities. Later in the day, another signal indicated that the same operation would take place that night.

Accordingly, the committee, accompanied by the two American sergeants, posted themselves again. After a period of waiting, the Eureka set indicated the presence of an aircraft. It was an RAF Stirling. The aircraft circled the reception and, from the unusually high altitude of 2,000 ft, made its drop of twenty containers. The wind conditions were favourable and none of the containers went astray. The reception committee worked feverishly until sunrise, gathering up the containers and hauling them, in a horse-drawn wagon, to a town 10 kilometres away, where the containers were hidden in an old barn. Just as the last of the load was being transported to the barn, the sun came up and people of the town were sticking their heads out of windows.

The following day, word was received that Henderson and Heddleston would be leaving in the next twenty-four hours to make connection with an aircraft which would fly them back to England. Accordingly, at 07.30 hours on the morning of 30 July, the two American sergeants were taken in a lorry to the rendezvous point, 110 kilometres away. The driver skirted around towns and villages, keeping to the back roads. He stopped only once, and that was to allow Henderson and Heddleston to see the five small crosses marking the graves of their fellow crew members, who had been killed. The graves were neatly trimmed and decorated with fresh flowers. Three kilometres further on, the truck passed by the scene of the crash and the men could see bits of wreckage around the burned crash site area.

Finally, the truck reached a town which was its destination. Henderson and Heddleston spent the next day waiting for the radio signal which would confirm the flight. In the course of waiting, they sat for a while in the terrace of a café. As they sat sipping drinks, a group of German soldiers rode by on bicycles. The Germans carried British Sten guns, which they had taken from the Maquis. As they rode by, they looked over in the direction of the two Americans but said nothing and did not stop.

At 13.30 hours and again at 19.30 hours the radio signal approved the flight but at 21.15 cancellation was signalled. Rather than spend another night in the town, Heddleston and Henderson were moved into a farmhouse on the outskirts. The farmer and his wife had a large brood of children and when everyone gathered for a meal, the table groaned beneath the combined weight of nineteen people. Ten quarts of wine were consumed at each sitting. In this domestic setting, the two airmen lived for three days.

Then a car arrived and they were driven to a hotel in the town, only for the flight to be cancelled again and they spent the night in the hotel. The following morning the flight was laid on but later in the day it was cancelled for the third time. Again they spent the night in the hotel. Henderson and Heddleston were beginning to get restless and nervous. The full moon period was waning and they looked with dread upon the prospect of remaining in France for another month.

Next day they were driven to a Maquis-liberated town where they remained for three days. They walked freely about town and everone seemed to know they were Americans. At last the great day arrived. The flight was approved all the way! From the Maquis-liberated town the two Americans were driven 10 kilometres to a rendezvous with a Maquis leader who, it turned out, had been recently to London and had spoken to Colonel Heflin.

Protected by carloads of Maquis soldiers, they were driven out to the landing field. The entire route was guarded by sentinels and all around the field, a total of 400 Maquis soldiers stood guard. It was known that quite nearby, a group of fifty-five armed Germans were stationed. However, the Germans, if they knew what was going on, showed an understandable reluctance to intervene. At the field, Heddleston and Henderson met the men who were to be their fellow passengers. These included, besides a group of agents, a Canadian Spitfire pilot and a Lancaster navigator.

Precisely at 01.30 hours, a Hudson of 161 Squadron from Tempsford arrived and began circling for a landing, lights turned on. It presented the most beautiful picture that the two American sergeants had seen for a long time. The Hudson landed and the two Americans, who had been given four and five priority numbers, boarded the aircraft. The flight to England was thankfully uneventful and in a few hours Heddleston and Henderson were safely back on English soil.

The RAF had first employed the Lockheed Hudson in the 'pick-up' role on 13 February 1943 when the CO of 161 Squadron, Group Captain Percy Pickard, delivered five agents to France with only moonlight and torches to guide the transport in for landing. A Hudson needed almost 1,000 yards to land and take off compared to only 250–300 yards required by the Lysander. Hudsons made thirty-six successful pick-ups, delivering 139 agents and bringing out 221 without loss.

6

FATEFUL MAY DAY

Special Operations OSS had for some time instructed its agents in France to seek out suitable landing sites where improvised strips could be laid out for the much larger and ubiquitous C–47 Dakotas to land valuable cargo and passengers and take out personnel. On the night of 1 May, after Harrington was ceremoniously handed over to the USAF by Squadron Leader E.D. King of the RAF, Colonel Heflin taxied a C–47 Dakota from dispersal while a handful of men, using torches, guided the transport aircraft onto a short stretch of runway. Heflin proved very adept at flying the Dakota at night and the practice take-off and landing was made without a hitch.

After this initial proving flight, a period of experimentation began to exploit the possibilities of C–47 landing operations in the occupied countries while normal Carpetbagger operations continued unabated. On the night of 5/6 May, when twenty-one B–24s were dispatched, Lieutenant Murray L. Simon's Liberator in the 406th Squadron was added to the loss list when it failed to return from a mission to France. Simon's crew were the victims of flak fired from guns mounted on a troop train, 20 kilometres north of Cheney le Chatel. The black bomber was blasted with 20 mm and 40 mm flak which knocked out the rudder control, interphone and electrical systems. The main fuel tank was hit and a flak shell exploded in the nose section between the navigator's and bombardier's stations, knocking out all the bomb levers. Flak punctured the port and starboard wing auxiliary tanks and fires began to engulf the entire wing. Simon smelled petrol fumes in the cockpit and ordered the crew to bale out.

Lieutenant John A. Reitmeier, the navigator, clambered from the burning aircraft and baled out. He pulled frantically on his ripcord but the parachute refused to open. Reitmeier struggled with the pack and by the time he finally managed to get the parachute open he was only 150 ft from the ground. Miraculously, although he was knocked unconscious by the force of the landing, Reitmeier suffered nothing more than cuts and bruises. Lieutenant John B. Mead, bombardier, who had been one of the original Carpetbaggers, followed hot on his heels and baled out at just 700 ft. Meanwhile, in the rear of the aircraft the enlisted men had also left the burning bomber. Technical Sergeant Phillip B. Latta, radio operator, Staff Sergeant Graham S. Hasty, gunner and Staff Sergeant Homer C. Collier, tail gunner, all baled out safely, although Hasty landed in a tree, injuring his foot, and was quickly captured by the Germans. Latta landed on the ground unhurt but Collier experienced the same terrifying feeling that Reitmeier had endured when his parachute also failed to open. Collier finally managed to get it open a few hundred feet from the ground and he landed unhurt.

Technical Sergeant Leo F. Dumesnil, flight engineer, also landed safely. He set out for a farmhouse after discarding his flying clothes. The American sergeant could speak perfect French but the inhabitants suspected that he was a German posing as an American and called the *Gendarmerie*. Four *gendarmes* were sent to arrest the mysterious stranger. Two of them were sympathetic and were in favour of letting Dumesnil go but the other two, who were pro-Nazi, overruled them and Dumesnil was arrested.

Simon and Lieutenant French M. Russell, co-pilot, remained in their seats until the rest of the crew had baled out and they then followed. As soon as he hit the slipstream, Simon, knowing their height to be around 5,500 ft, counted 1,000, 2,000, 3,000 and then jerked the 'D' ring on his parachute pack. Russell was right behind him. In the moonlight both men could see each other dangling on their 'chutes clearly. Russell shattered the peace of their descent by asking Simon if he was OK. The pilot replied that he was but not to make so much noise!

Simon's 'chute became snarled in a tree but he unbuckled his harness and dropped to the ground. He tugged at the parachute but it failed to budge so dropping his Mae West, Simon began to run through the woods in no apparent direction. Twenty minutes later he stopped, hid his flying suit trousers and checked his direction by the escape compass. Simon knew the wood was the obvious place the Germans would search so he turned due south to get out of the woods as quickly as he possibly could.

The American pilot traversed fields and hedgerows before falling wearily into a ditch. Simon slept intermittently until daybreak and was suddenly awakened by a passing farmer and his cart. Although he remained still the farmer noticed the American airman and glanced at him. Startled, Simon called out, 'Je suis Américain.' The farmer nodded but shook his head to indicate that he could not help. Simon put his finger to his lips to ask him not to give him away. The farmer nodded in agreement.

Some time later a woman cycled past and glanced in Simon's direction although he was still hidden in the ditch. Again he put his finger to his lips. She seemed to understand and rode on. Soon after, a man cycled past and looked in the ditch but pretended not to see the airman. He rode on and Simon decided it was time to find a way to leave the ditch, but without attracting the attention of some workers who were tending the fields in pairs nearby. Just as he was about to leave the ditch, the French cycle rider returned, bringing with him some clothes for the American airman.

Simon was fortunate to find help from members of the local Resistance who would ultimately help return him back to England via the escape and evasion lines. During his journey to freedom he was taken to the home of a Maquis chief who recalled many examples of Nazi cruelty, particularly when they captured and mercilessly tortured Maquisards to gain information. The Maquis chief also told Simon that Lieutenant John Mead, the bombardier, had evaded capture and had attached himself to a Maquis group. Mead had been picked up by a British agent called 'Victor' and the two of them had cycled to a secret Maquis HQ near Roanne, where, as an assistant to the British agents who controlled the Resistance forces in the area, he later joined in actions against the Germans. The first anyone at Harrington knew of his escapades occurred on the night of 29 May when an 858th Squadron Liberator, piloted by Lieutenant Jack H. Munn, was in the vicinity of Roanne, *en route* to its target deep in central France. Clarence H. Brown, Munn's radio operator, was taken aback to make S-phone contact with a voice in perfect English asking him if they were American or British. Perhaps because the voice from the ground had an unmistakable southern drawl, Brown replied, 'Neither. We're Yankees!'

'Who's your pilot?' the southerner asked. When Brown told him, Mead said, 'Well I'll be damned. Tell him hello. Tell everyone hello. This is Johnny Mead!'

Brown was almost speechless but managed to ask Mead what the state of the rest of the crew was. Mead replied that everyone was all right but he could not give details over the S-phone. By this time Munn was in a position to make his dropping run. Mead gave detailed instructions from the ground and the Liberator crew made a perfect drop. When it was completed Mead sent acknowledgement and instructed Brown to tell Colonel Heflin that 'the Colonel is doing a good job too'.

After a drop had been completed and packages and containers had been collected, Mead and his men would transport the load into Roanne, usually by ox-cart. Once, when a drop had been made quite late and dawn was approaching, Mead had driven the ox-cart, loaded with parachutes and containers, into Roanne, which was then garrisoned by 2,000 German soldiers. On his lap was resting a machine-gun. The Resistance used an abandoned warehouse of a textile factory in Roanne as a warehouse and assembly shop. Here they secretly stored the material they received by air, unpacked, cleaned and assembled it. At the time, Mead was living in the house of a prominent engineer. Every day, dressed in civilian clothes, he would walk to work at the warehouse. The route he chose to walk passed a German barracks, because it had been found that was the one place where no one was ever stopped for questioning. All of Mead's papers were in order, even to a bicycle tax receipt. He had French pin-up girls in his billfold and carried a lunch basket complete with a bottle of wine. (A Sten gun was secreted at the bottom of the basket.) If he had been stopped, his papers would have identified him as Jean Noel Dumbret, a deaf mute. Nothing more was heard from Johnny Mead until 4 July when a wireless telegraph message came over one of the circuits from the French underground, saying that Mead was now in command of a unit known as 'Maquis Violette', or the 'Groupe de Fragny' as the FFI called it. Mead operated from a mountain headquarters, sixteen kilometres from Roanne, instructing the French in American field equipment and in basic military tactics.

Meanwhile, John Reitmeier had regained consciousness after his heavy landing and had set off eastwards, walking until daybreak. Reitmeier found a vacant shed in a wood and, utterly exhausted, decided to sleep there for the rest of the day. That evening he awoke in great pain from a back injury. It began to rain heavily so he decided to build a fire to keep warm and at the same time camouflaged the shed with branches from the trees. He scooped some water from a stream nearby and sucked some malted milk tablets from his meagre emergency kit. Reitmeier remained hidden until mid-afternoon when he decided to set out again. Before long he reached the outskirts of Chenay le Chatol where he made a detour to avoid the town. On the road to Roanne Reitmeier met three French boys. They looked trustworthy and the American airman decided to chance an introduction. The boys immediately took him to a house nearby where he was fed and given a place to sleep. Three hours later he was moved to Marcigny where he spent the night and the next day. Members of a French family brought him food and drink.

Finally, in the early hours of the following morning a French Resistance worker came for Reitmeier. The two men cycled to Loddes, north-east of Lapalisse, where Reitmeier was put up at a French farmhouse. It was to be his home for thirty-five days. During that time attempts were made to obtain a forged passport for the American airmen but to no avail. Finally, Reitmeier, getting restless, decided he would continue on the evasion route without one. Working to a pre-arranged plan on instructions from his French friends, he walked to the train station at La Pacaudière and took a train to Roanne. At the first stop a French Resistance girl boarded the train carrying the magazine which was the pre-arranged signal for Reitmeier to follow her. Reitmeier and the girl were met outside the station by a man on a bicycle. In English the man said, 'How ya doin' Buddy?' Reitmeier almost fell over in amazement. The stranger went on to explain that he was a British agent and that his cover name was 'George'. George led Reitmeier to a house in Roanne owned by a man known as 'Babo', who was a French intelligence agent in charge of the district. At the house, to his complete surprise, Reitmeier was reunited with Johnny Mead. The two men had plenty to talk about during their week together before Mead left to operate with the Maquis in the district.

The *Maquis Violette* had been attacked in force by German troops and Vichy French *Milice* on 21 July and had been forced to withdraw and disband. The group later re-formed and began operating to the north-west of Roanne, interfering with German communications and blowing up telegraph lines and road and railway bridges. At Fragny, Mead's group of twenty-eight men found themselves on a hill surrounded by about 600 German troops. Mead skilfully led his men down the hill, through the advancing Germans and across a heavily defended road. They were fired on by an armoured car but most of the group made it to safety.

Pursued by six Milice men, Mead and three companions headed for the Loire. They split up into groups and Mead and his Alsatian companion were forced to swim the river under fire. They got safely across and later Mead had re-formed his group at Tarare. There he led a unit of sixty men, part of a force of 360, in an attack against some 1,200 enemy troops. Mead skilfully drove the Germans into the hands of Canadian paratroopers but the victory was not achieved without cost.

When Mead entered Tarare, he found the bodies of nine Frenchwomen and three Frenchmen who had been shot in cold blood by a retreating German officer. At St Yan he saw the bodies of thirty unarmed men who had been slaughtered at the entrance to the town's hotel. At St Gingolph there were 800 people, of all ages, massacred in a church. These casualties did not include the victims of individual torture, the mutilated, burned and broken bodies of Mead's own comrades who had fallen into German hands.

Reitmeier remained behind at Roanne for three weeks. One day three Gestapo men burst in and seized Babo. He had been betrayed by a French traitor. As they led him out of the back door, Reitmeier escaped unnoticed through the front. He walked hurriedly down the street and by chance, met George, who was cycling along in the direction of Babo's house. Reitmeier poured out his story and together the two men left for a house in another part of town. After a meal the American airman was escorted to the home of a French dentist. After two days Reitmeier was taken to a rendezvous point outside town where a lorry was waiting to take him into the mountains to join the Maquis and the reunion with Johnny Mead. Reitmeier could not take part in raids with his fellow American because his back was causing him much pain. Instead, he was put to valuable use instructing his hosts on the Winchester carbine rifle. During his stay Reitmeier learned that Babo had been liberated by the Maquisards one hour before he was due to be executed and that the traitor who had betrayed him had been summarily dealt with.

Reitmeier's back was troubling him badly in the mountainous terrain and it was decided to move him. Johnny Mead knew of a farmhouse near the village of Lac where he could stay. He was well received by the farmer's family and stayed with them for a week and a half before an incident occurred. One day German soldiers billeted in the village began shooting at random. Reitmeier was sitting talking to the daughter of the house in the living room when a couple of rounds entered through the window. Fortunately, no one was hurt but it was decided that the American would have to move on. Reitmeier was sent to the village of St Polgne. He had been there only a short time when he heard news of the family he had been staying with in Lac. About half a mile from the farmhouse a band of Maquis had attacked a platoon of German soldiers and had killed some of their number. Later, the survivors returned to the scene and as they were passing the farmhouse they caught sight of the nineteen-year-old son of the family, who was driving an ox-cart out of the farmyard, on his way to the village. Without provocation or warning the Germans attacked the young boy and slashed him twenty-seven times with their bayonets. After the Germans had left the boy's father came out of the house and picked up the body of his son, literally in pieces. Reitmeier recalled all the conversations he had had with the boy and how eager he had been to learn English.

For two weeks Reitmeier remained in St Polgne until the village was liberated by the FFI. There was little opposition from the Germans, who were at this stage of the war more willing to retreat than stand and fight. There was great celebration in St Polgne. Reitmeier ceremoniously raised a Tricolour in the village square. Everyone was told that the stranger was in fact an American and there would be more to come. He was made guest of honour at a large party and all the French girls vied with each other to kiss him and give him bouquets of flowers.

On 20 August, Roanne was liberated and Reitmeier was moved to the Central Hotel by Mead and an English captain in a Ford car. He remained there for eighty days and during his stay he visited a torture chamber used by the Vichy police. The blood-stained instruments he saw bore eloquent testimony to the barbarism and brutality of the French collaborationists. Reitmeier was also reunited with Babo again and heard from him many accounts of torture he had witnessed.

Meanwhile, on 23 August Mead had received the following wire from Colonel Heflin: 'Advise me present work not in line of duty. Suggest you return immediately if possible. Don't take any chances. Signed, Heflin.' The following day Mead joined up with Reitmeier and the two men waited for the roads to clear so that they could leave for Lyons. On 5 September Mead and Reitmeier presented themselves at the advanced headquarters of the 12th Air Force, 20 miles to the east of Lyons. From there they went to Amberieu where they caught a ride in a B–25 Mitchell bomber to Salon. A Carpetbagger Dakota piloted by Bestow Rudolph, flew them to Caserta in Italy where they were interviewed by General Cabel at MAAF Headquarters. As a result, Mead was sent back to France for a time to help in the work of the Air Force Recovery Unit. He returned

to England, at last, on 4 November, to find that he was now Captain
Mead and, moreover, had been recommended for a Silver Star 'for
gallantry in action against an armed and determined enemy, while
engaged in a special assignment with the FFI.'

Reitmeier, meanwhile, had been flown home via Algiers and
Casablanca. He finally got back to Harrington on 19 September. The
following day his fellow crew-members, Phillip Latta and Homer
Collier, also returned to base. Theirs had been an equally harrowing
series of close calls with Maquis groups always under threat from
German infiltration. Latta had walked for seven days after the crash
before he finally made contact with the French Resistance. He
was taken in by the Maquis and travelled with them, moving from
one hiding place to another. Finally, Latta reached a large Maquis
encampment in the mountains where he found Collier and seventeen
other Allied airmen living with the band of Frenchmen. For about a
week Latta and Collier lived unmolested in the Maquis camp.

On 10 June, two divisions of German troops attacked the Maquis
position. The Americans in the group decided it was time to leave
and slipped away at midnight. Next morning, the group split up,
with Latta and Collier teaming up with an 8th Air Force major. The
officer took them to a Frenchman he knew and he led them to the
secret hide-out of a Maquis group consisting of about thirty men.
Two days later the Germans launched an attack and the Maquis,
heavily outnumbered, were forced to retreat. They walked for three
days, sleeping in the woods during the day. Latta and Collier did
look-out duty while the Maquisards blew up bridges and picked
off the odd German soldier. On 10 July Latta and Collier joined a
third Maquis group and remained with them for just over a month.
On 12 August, wearing Maquis uniforms, they took part with the
group in the liberation of a French town. After a few false hopes,
Latta and Collier sought out the 8th Air Force major. Finally, on 6
September, they headed for the American lines, driven there in style
in a captured German staff car!

This now left only French M. Russell, the co-pilot, unaccounted for
at Harrington. After his brief reunion with Simon on the ground he
had run off in the opposite direction. Russell struck out across the
fields but he soon tired and his shoes were in no fit state for a protracted
hike. Russell decided to chance it and at a French café he revealed
his identity. Fortunately, he was taken in and soon passed along the
evasion lines after a close call with some Germans at another café

where he and his French guide were invited by the soldiers to play cards with them! Russell was thankful that the French people 'talked' so much with their hands, for his French was almost non-existent.

Russell was anxious to head for the Spanish border but he was continually passed from one group of helpers to another without seemingly making any headway in that direction. Finally, he decided to find the Maquis himself. With help he arrived at a town in Maquis territory where he met Lieutenant Jim Cater, an airman in the 8th Air Force. When the local people heard that Americans were in their midst the whole town turned out to welcome them, singing 'Tipperary' and other songs.

There was great excitement when news of the Allied landings in Normandy was announced. German attacks against the Maquis could be expected and after consultation with the Allied liaison officer in the group, the Americans were moved out of the area. Villages were burning as they left early in the morning of 11 June. Later, Russell, Cater and two RAF fliers formed their own unit and they struck out on their own. Later, the nationalities separated and the two Americans continued, aided by the French who provided false papers saying that they were deaf mutes! After a night in a hotel their French helpers packed them off on a train ride to who knows where. The slow train stopped at almost every station but their papers held up during checks by the feared French militia.

After changing trains they set off on foot and eventually reached the safety of a farmhouse in another area controlled by the local Maquis. Russell and Jim Cater felt they were in good company and decided to remain with the group. Besides, Russell reckoned to have walked some 200 miles in the past nine weeks.

Russell and Cater were well entertained during their stay with the Maquis group and ex-collaborators were anxious to ingratiate themselves now that the tide of war was turning. They opened up their cellars of wine and the two Americans spent much of their time drinking. They also made a couple of forays with the Maquis against German targets. It was a highly dangerous sideline because as Russell put it, 'The Maquis go looking for trouble.' They never considered stopping at road blocks placed by the Germans, a fact which worried the two Americans because they were stationed in the back of the car used on the forays, armed with sub-machine-guns to act as rear gunners. Fortunately and much to their relief, they did not encounter any trouble during the forays.

These armed incursions proved the only excitement during Russell's and Cater's enforced exile in France. Despite the good attentions of their French hosts, both men were anxious to return to their units. Russell remained confident, however, and told Jim Cater, 'Don't worry, my CO will be over to get us one of these days.' He could not know how true his words would prove.

7

NEW BLOOD

While the Norwegian and Swedish operations had continued from Scotland, the remaining Carpetbagger crews at Harrington continued to supply the Resistance Groups in France and the Low Countries. It was all part of the overall Allied plan to put more agents and sabotage teams behind the Atlantic Wall to harass directly and indirectly the very German units which would confront the Allied invasion forces when they landed on the shores of occupied Europe.

In May 1944 SOE–SO became Special Force Headquarters (SFHQ), responsible to General Dwight D. Eisenhower at Supreme Headquarters, Allied Expeditionary Force (SHAEF) for all Resistance operations within the Supreme Commander's sphere of responsibility.* After the landings all Resistance operations in France were to be brought under the authority of EMFFI (*Etat-Major FFI*), headed by General Joseph Koenig, who was ultimately responsible to General Eisenhower and not to SOE. General Koenig paid a visit to Harrington on 8 May, accompanied by Colonel Haskell and Major Gable of OSS. Speaking through an interpreter, the general showed a lively interest in the stories the crews had to tell at their interrogations, upon returning from their sorties over the continent.

The impending invasion of Fortress Europe meant that more agents and more Jedburgh teams had to be dropped into the occupied countries and France in particular. The Allies were gearing themselves for the onslaught, building up reserves, and in the case of the Carpetbaggers, increasing its strength. On 2 May an order marked 'Top Secret' was dispatched from SHAEF headquarters confirming that Eisenhower had 'approved the requirement for an additional twenty-five aircraft for SOE–SO.'

* *Helping The Resistance* Major-General R.H. Barry (Purnell, 1973)

Two additional Liberator squadrons officially joined the 801st Group on 11 May. The 850th Bomb Squadron, equipped with B–24H Liberators and commanded by Major Jack M. Dickerson, flew in directly from the States, although it had been earmarked to join the 490th Bomb Group in the Third Bomb Division.

The Second Bomb Division was also ordered to give up one of its squadrons, as Colonel Albert J. Shower, commanding officer of the 467th Bomb Group, recalls:*

> Shortly before 8 May General Peck, Commanding Officer of the 96th Combat Wing, invited me to Wing Headquarters at Horsham St Faith, along with Jim Isbell of the 458th and Art Pierce of the 466th. General Peck told each of us to get out a half-crown to toss. He explained that someone had to give up a squadron for a special mission. Coming up the 'odd' man, I decided to give up Bob Salzarulo's 788th Squadron, which he had commanded until he was shot down.

The loss of Major Robert L. Salzarulo had occurred on the mission to Berlin, on 29 April 1944, just nineteen days after the 467th had flown its first mission. Salzarulo was forced down in Holland and made a prisoner of war. On the same mission Lieutenant William B. Dillon, the pilot, had lost one of his waist gunners, Sergeant James W. Storey, when he fell out of the aircraft about five miles from the English coast. Although they had been in action for less than a month the 788th Squadron had lost several crews in combat. They had had a very bad experience on 22 April when Me–410s of the Luftwaffe had followed the Second Bomb Division home from a raid on the marshalling yards at Hamm and had strafed the 467th's base at Rackheath as dusk was falling.

Major Leonard M. 'Nate' McManus, who had served as 791st Squadron operations officer and assistant group operations officer at Rackheath, was named 788th Squadron commanding officer on 8 May. The previous day he had flown as command pilot on a PFF (Pathfinder) mission to Osnabrück. On 10 May eleven crews in the 788th were detached from the 467th Bomb Group and sent to Station 113 at Cheddington. The party of fifty-eight officers and 357 enlisted men arrived at the base by train during the early

---

* *Fields of Little America* Martin W. Bowman (PSL)

evening, anxious to learn more about their new role. Paul E. Gourd, the navigator on James E. Wilson's crew, recalls, 'We were one of only seven crews, with James A. Sevapco, the operations officer, that were sent to the 801st. Even so, each crew that went to Harrington left a gunner and an engineer behind at Rackheath.'

The ex–467th crews were fed and quartered for the night and the next day began their orientation and training under the 'faculty' of the 801st Group. Colonel Fish served as 'Dean' to acquaint the crews with their new duties and assignment. The crews were immediately schooled and sent on training missions. On 17 May the S–2 section, headed by Captain C. Malcolm Derry and Lieutenant James F. Stewart, left for Harrington to prepare for operations and arrival of the combat crews. Lieutenant Carl L. Black, the squadron armament officer, with twenty-five enlisted men, had to follow later because not enough barrack space was available.

The first shock to the system came when the crew were given billets two miles from the base. Lieutenant William B. Dillon remembers:

We lived in tent cities and the showers were cold. But the food was pretty good and later, the liberty runs into Northampton were enjoyable. None of us knew what we were getting into but everybody looked forward in anticipation to these night missions because some of our high altitude daylight missions had been pretty rough. Of course we found later that some of the night missions were pretty rough too.

My navigator, bombardier and myself all took separate flights for orientation over the continent. We started our missions as a crew in the latter part of May 1944. We flew mostly between 6,500 and 8,000 ft, trying to stay out of the range of light machine-gun fire, light ack-ack and the heavy stuff. This was just a little bit rough on the navigator but most of the time he compensated very well and got us to where we were supposed to go. In bad weather we had to rely on the navigator's dead reckoning. In good weather we could rely on navigation and pilotage. If I was flying then my co-pilot, Ralph Morrow, did the navigation and vice versa.

In all the flights we made over the continent with the 801st there was only one time we actually saw a Jerry night fighter. This was some place west of Paris. We had just levelled off and were heading over the coast to the Loire when we had a head-on closure. Evidently, he was on radar because he missed us by only about fifty ft. We saw his exhausts as he went over the top of us.

I think that one of the most exciting missions we flew was when we took a French agent from England to east of Bordeaux. Apparently, he had been over the continent about twelve times. On this particular mission he was the paymaster for the FFI and he had over a million dollars in francs. We got down there and everything went fine. We found the IP and the target but on our first run over the target we had a wrong identification signal. We tried again. But again the wrong signal was received. Our agent was very enthusiastic and really wanted to get out of the aeroplane and down on the ground again. I told the crew we would make a third pass. This time we got our third different identification signal.

Reception committees used three types of pre-arranged signals to guide the Carpetbagger aircraft to the pinpoints. The 'A' System, which consisted of a triangle of three white lights, with a fourth, red light at the apex, flashed the code recognition letter. The lights would be placed so that wind was blowing toward the flashing light and across the centre of the opposite side of the triangle.

The 'B' System was the same as 'A' except that a white light flashed and three red lights formed the triangle. The 'C' System was the most commonly used. It employed three torches, usually red, in a row with a white signal flashing light, set up at the down-wind light of the line. Aircraft always came in up-wind for their drop and sometimes bonfires were used instead of torches. On occasions, when there was a danger of discovery by the enemy, the aircraft would be asked to give an identification signal before the lights were turned on.

Dillon told the crew:

We've been here long enough. We'd better get out of here. Strap everybody down, we're leaving the area. We got to about 5,000 ft and were bracketed in searchlights. Evidently, the Germans were there. I was mighty scared at this time. We stood the B–24 on its wingtip and dived for *terra firma*. We headed for the Bay of Biscay just north of Bordeaux. I guess the good Lord was with us for we hadn't gone too far when we ran into a fog bank. We stayed pretty low and flew in cloud all the way around the Brest Peninsula and we hit Land's End before we broke out of this stuff. It was mostly instrument flying but we were very, very fortunate.

Our agent was disappointed. We never did hear what had happened, whether the Germans had infiltrated the group of if it was a case of mistaken identity. We got the agent safely back to Harrington and I suppose another crew took him out on a later mission.

Staff Sergeant Max B. Rufner was the dispatcher on Dillon's crew and recalls that the Joe drops were 'special nights':

I don't think it occurred more than three or four times that we had people to drop. I recall one night we had a woman radio operator. The poor girl was sick all the way over. We found the target and received the proper signal so out she went. She was a pretty brave girl I thought but I couldn't tell what she looked like because she was all bundled up in paratrooper's gear.

Dillon further recalls that 'over the dropping zones we could talk to the patriots on the improvised landing strips by using the S-phone. It would have helped if we could have spoken the language.'

The 'S'-phone and the 'homing S'-phone, first introduced on Carpetbagger aircraft in June 1944, proved especially valuable. The latter device, which had been developed by the US Navy, used a radio compass in the aircraft and permitted the navigator to direct the aircraft toward the ground operator, as on a radio beam.

Other night flying aids were also available to the Carpetbagger crews, as Bill Dillon recalls:

Sometimes we would take off in cloud cover and never see the ground again. We were on instruments most of the time. Around the British Isles the barrage balloons were fitted with 'bleepers'. We could fly in one direction and on our radio set the closer we came to one of the balloons the volume of these bleepers would increase. If we were lost we could go in circles. It seemed like every direction we went these bleepers got louder and louder. If we turned away they decreased for a moment and then they would pick up again.

'Gee' was very beneficial but by the time we hit the continental coast the Germans had the system jammed.

All Carpetbagger aircraft were fitted with a 'Gee' box, a British-developed radar navigational aid which picked up signals from ground stations in England. A 'master' station and two 'slave' stations sent out combinations of signals which were picked up and recorded on a grid which indicated the aircraft's position. The Germans had some success in jamming Gee signals in their own territory but by changing frequencies and other devices, the Allies were able to maintain effective use of the Gee set.

> One of the things about leaving the continent was that we had certain corridors into the British Isles. Some of these were pretty hectic. It was the same thing going out. If we were a little bit off-course and our Gee was not working properly or being jammed, we were fortunate we had good maintenance on our IFF (Identification Friend or Foe) equipment. I think this helped us more than once on our return from the continent.
>
> When returning, I noticed on several missions when we looked out in the darkness that British fighters were flying off our wings. They were always below our wings and a little to the left so we couldn't reach them with our top and tail turrets unless we tilted up 45°. We were thankful we were being watched over.

Meanwhile, the Carpetbagger Liberators at Harrington were also parachuting supplies and Joes into German-occupied Denmark. Resistance in this country was on different lines to that in France for example, where the Maquis had large bodies of organized troops, centred in mountain strongholds and had successfully liberated large areas of their country. In Denmark, however, there are not many mountains or large forests from which guerrilla fighters could operate. As a result, resistance was not fought on a large scale, but rather it was clandestine, consisting of individual acts of terrorism and sabotage, mainly of factories engaged in turning out material for the German war machine.

On the night of 6 May a Liberator, piloted by Lieutenant George Pipkin in the 496th Bomb Squadron, failed to return from a mission to Denmark. No further word was received until the night of 29 May when a returning crew brought news that an S-phone message from the field had confirmed a successful drop. General William Donovan, Commanding General of OSS, was present at the interrogation of the returning crews that night. He was no doubt pleased to learn that two men, Floyd N. Holmes, bombardier, and Jack C. Wengert, radio operator, had made it back to England. Colonel Heflin and Major Boone went to London immediately and brought back news that the two men were in the best of health and would soon be back to tell the rest their experiences.

On 3 June Lieutenant Holmes gave the Group historian a full account of his experiences. Holmes recalled that they had left the target area after successfully dropping their load. They headed back in the direction of the Danish coast at a height of 5,000 ft. About forty-five minutes after leaving the target, a single anti-aircraft gun had opened fire on their aircraft. From his vantage point in the nose Holmes looked down and saw clearly that only one gun was firing. He counted five shell bursts. Each shell struck home but none of the crew was hit. No. 3 engine caught fire and the flames spread rapidly to the fuel tanks. Pipkin told the crew over the interphone that he would attempt to put the fire out using some violent manoeuvres.

Pipkin's efforts failed and the situation worsened when No. 4 engine caught fire. Pipkin realized that it was useless and told Israel M. Barron, co-pilot, to sound the bale-out bell. When Holmes reached the bomb bay to jump, he found that the hydraulic system had burned out and the doors would not open. Wengert arrived on the scene and helped Holmes kick the doors open. The rest of the crew left the ship but Pipkin remained in his seat until the last possible minute, keeping the aircraft as level as possible to help his men make the jump. Lieutenant Clair van der Schaef, navigator, had trouble with his parachute harness and had to hit it with his sextant to get the troublesome clasp open. At the last blow the $400 sextant burst open and scattered over the deck.

Holmes baled out at 4,000 ft, delaying pulling the ripcord until he was 2,000 ft from the ground. He landed in a sandy area covered in pine needles, very near a small forest. Shortly after landing he heard a great explosion and saw the fiery evidence that the Liberator had crashed. Holmes buried his parachute and Mae West under the sand and headed south. He knew from the mission briefing that there were swamps located there and he wanted to foil any German tracker dogs that might be employed to look for him.

He walked a short distance when he heard his name being called by Wengert. The two men joined up and headed for the swamps together. As they waded through the water they heard dogs baying in the distance. They swam some canals and their scent was never picked up. Their plan was to make Sweden and they walked for several days, living off the land as they went, eating raw potatoes and drinking milk which they stole.

On the evening of the fifth day they came upon a farmhouse and a friendly Danish farmer asked that they join him and his farmhands for supper. It was here that the two Americans made the very first contact with the Danish underground. Someone mentioned that an English-speaking Danish minister in the village could help them. Holmes and Wengert left straightaway and walked all night to find the house. They stopped, tired and cold, towards morning and went to sleep in a haystack.

When they awoke they approached a nearby farmhouse. Here, also, they were told of the man who spoke English. While the two Americans were being fed by the farmer's wife, the farmer cycled off to get the minister. One of the Americans was seen by one of the farm-hands, who, it turned out, was of a talkative nature. When the minister arrived he insisted that to protect himself from suspicion he would have to hand the two Americans over to the police. However, he gave them five minutes start and agreed to rendezvous with them at his house after the police had finished their search.

Wengert and Holmes hid in a haystack for thirty-six hours while the Germans searched both the minister's house and the farmhouse where it was clear that the farm-hand had talked. The minister eventually arranged for Holmes and Wengert to pass through the Danish underground and after a drive north, the two Americans were smuggled into a boat bound for Sweden. In Sweden the two men stuck to their story that they were escaped prisoners of war. Before long they were England bound.

Crews who fell to the German guns were normally protected by the Geneva Convention. Agents who parachuted into occupied Europe were only too aware of the fate that awaited them if they fell into the clutches of the Gestapo. On 8 May the Carpetbaggers dropped a Frenchman, OSS agent M. Jean Remy, into his homeland, south of the city of Troyes. After several months of espionage activities he was captured, tortured unmercifully and dragged in front of a firing squad. At the last minute the German officer stopped the execution and threw Remy back into jail. The Frenchman tried suicide, unsuccessfully, very proud of the fact that he did not give his captors any information. Finally, this very brave French agent managed to escape in time to help welcome Patton on 1 September 1944 when he liberated Nancy.

On 17 May Carpetbagger crews heard at first hand the experiences of another French patriot, organizer of the Maquis Resistance group in the Haute-Savoie Department of south-central France.

Accompanying the organizer were an American captain from the London office of OSS, and a French officer. The American officer acted as interpreter when the going got tough for the organizer, who to some extent, managed to express himself in English.

Colonel Heflin introduced the speaker, who was a short, slightly built man, apparently in his middle thirties. He wore horn-rimmed glasses and resembled a bookish sort of school teacher. He was not physically impressive, but in the light of his work, of his direct contribution to the anti-Nazi struggle, he seemed a truly heroic figure. Heflin suggested that the meeting be conducted in the form of questions and answers.

The Carpetbagger crews responded with a series of questions. They were naturally anxious to learn how much material they dropped was actually reaching the French Resistance. The organizer told them that about 55 per cent reached them. He added that it was best to drop their loads from a height of 400 ft for accurate drops.

The Carpetbagger crews enquired how close the Germans were when they made their drops. The organizer grinned and related that sometimes the Germans were on the spot before the parachutes descended to the ground. At this point, the organizer told a story dealing with a large-scale pitched battle, fought by the Maquisards and a force of German soldiers, abetted by French militia. The French used weapons, ammunition and grenades that had been delivered to them, in large part, by the Carpetbaggers. The organizer told how 800 Maquisards were taken prisoner and summarily shot. For their service, some of the French militiamen received the *Croix de Guerre* from the Vichy Government. But, added the organizer, who was prone to much ironic humour in his answers, that was only their first cross – other crosses were due to them.

In the course of the meeting, the organizer related the stories of two of his face-to-face encounters with the Germans. The first story dealt with the time he was stopped by a German soldier who ordered him, in German, to produce his identification papers. The organizer brought out his papers with an agreeable, Germanic, *Ja, Ja*, which undoubtedly disarmed his questioner completely. He was stopped in this manner many times while travelling around in his car.

Once, he was driving along with 18 million francs in the car. It was in the dead of winter and the road was extremely icy. The car went into a skid, and turned completely about, so that, as the organizer put it, he found himself headed in the direction he had come from, instead of the direction he was going. The car continued skidding and when it finally came to rest, it was at the side of the road, with its back end in the ditch. The organizer got out and flagged down the next car that passed. He was startled to find that he had of his own accord, stopped a car carrying a German captain and two sergeants! However, having stopped them, he proceeded to enlist their aid in getting his car out of the ditch.

The captain immediately ordered his two sergeants to attach a rope to the rear of their car and to pull the Frenchman's car out of the ditch. They attached the rope but the organizer's car refused to budge. Thereupon, the captain commanded his men to put their shoulders to the wheel and get the car out of the ditch. The two sergeants carried out the order and eventually got the organizer's car on the road again. The German captain turned to the organizer and said, 'Well now, are you glad the Germans are in France?' The organizer replied, 'Oh yes!' Then, he got back in his car and drove off, with the 18 million francs intact!

Towards the end of the meeting Colonel Heflin announced that the organizer had brought word that one of their men was a PoW in a German hospital and that the Maquis would get him out when the opportunity presented itself. The organizer had also brought information about Lieutenant Ambrose's aircraft which had been lost on the mission to France on 27/28 April.

Starting on 18 May the base defences at Harrington were tightened up and all strategic sites on the base were guarded by armed soldiers. Paratroopers were much in the minds of the Allied planners during May 1944. They realized that the Allies' pre-invasion plans could be upset by German saboteurs being parachuted onto air bases in England, and Harrington would be one of the more obvious targets. Slit trenches were dug along the runways and men posted to guard the aircraft. A group of fifty men from all the squadrons were assigned the task of guarding the base.

A company from the 82nd American Airborne Division was also stationed close by and as Don Fairbanks recalls:

They were put in their own compound and weren't allowed to associate with anybody on the base. They had German shepherd dogs with them. One night in the barracks the PA system gave notice that an airborne parachute attack was imminent. A short time later the tannoy announced, 'Cease challenging. Shoot to kill!' I crawled down my bed and pulled the covers up. I wasn't getting out of that bed for anything. A little later they counter-manded the order. There was an audible sigh of relief across the runways.

Carpetbagger missions were flown in earnest throughout May. William G. McKee's crew, for instance, flew seven night missions that month, all of them to France.

On the night of 28/29 May, Lieutenant Henry W. Wolcott III and the seven members of his crew in 'Charlie' in the 858th Squadron, failed to return from a mission to 'Osric 53' in Belgium. An eighth man, Lieutenant Carmen J. Vozzella, the navigator from Sam Goldsmith's crew of the 859th Squadron, who was flying with Wolcott for navigational experience, was also lost. By 11 September 1944 all members of the crew, with the exception of Sergeant Richard G. Hawkins, the tail gunner, who was found dead on the ground at Aaigem, his parachute unopened, were back at Harrington. Wolcott and his crew confirmed that they had made three runs over the target but there was no evidence of a reception committee present. The Liberator had just swung around to begin its homeward journey, when it was suddenly attacked by a Messerschmitt Bf–110 night-fighter near Enghien. The Liberator received three damaging bursts but Wolcott managed to shake off the attentions of the night-fighter in some fierce avoiding action.

However, their troubles were not yet over. As Wolcott turned north, another sudden attack came from the side. Fifty calibre shells ripped through the right wing tanks, through the fuselage and through the navigator's compartment where William G. Ryckman was. Violent fires broke out and it only took a few moments for Wolcott to realize that the aircraft was doomed.

All the crew baled out and, apart from Hawkins, landed safely. The group split up and headed their separate ways. Wolcott, who had landed in a Belgian wheatfield, was taken in by a Flemish family and remained there for two days before being taken to the village of Ninove to meet a Belgian White Army official. The Belgian escorted Wolcott to the Catholic University in Enghien where the American remained for four days, hidden in a priest's room. At the end of this time Wolcott was taken to a farm, south of Enghien. There he discovered that there were eighteen Russians, who had escaped from forced service in the German Army, and also an American pilot. The next day Wolcott and the motley group left for other safe houses, having been warned that the Gestapo were only a mile away. Wolcott and the other American pilot were paired off with three Russians in a farmhouse further down the escape line. For three weeks they waited.

Then, one Sunday morning, 150 German troops surrounded the house. A traitor had talked. Warned in the nick of time, Wolcott hid in the attic in a secret hiding place under the floor boards. The Germans entered the house, searched it thoroughly and two of them even walked over the floor where Wolcott was hiding. The Germans finally left, taking the farmer, all the food and money they could find with them but without Wolcott and his comrades.

The farmer was released after two weeks but word of the American and Russian fugitives was becoming common knowledge. At another town on the escape route the Belgian mayor advised Wolcott to leave. The group split up at this point. Wolcott was escorted by a White Army official from one farmhouse to another. After a week of moving about, Wolcott finally came to a house on the outskirts of Brussels. Here he remained for five weeks. Then, a treacherous escape organization, unsuspected by Wolcott's helpers, came forward with a plan to get him to Switzerland. Wolcott was thereupon taken to an apartment in Brussels which later became known as the infamous 'Dog House', the place where Allied evaders were funnelled into German hands.

Wolcott remained in this apartment for three days. He was treated lavishly, then he was taken to a second house, where Gestapo interrogators, posing as members of an escape organization, asked him many questions. They brought out a questionnaire, which included questions about Wolcott's squadron, group and commanding officers. Wolcott filled in name, rank and serial number and handed the form back. The interrogators became angry and insisted that the form be filled in. Wolcott answered the question on religion and the question on names of the other crew members. The men asked for the name of his base. Wolcott replied, 'England'.

The next day, Wolcott was a prisoner in the infamous St Giles prison. There he met William G. Ryckman, his navigator, Robert F. Auda, co-pilot, and Wallis O. Cozzens, his bombardier. All of them had been betrayed in the same manner that Wolcott had been betrayed. The Americans were left to rot in St Giles prison for almost six weeks before their next interrogation. During this time they existed on a diet of ersatz coffee, carrots, potatoes and sour bread. Four times a week they were treated to watery, tasteless soup. Four to five men were crammed into one small cell and they slept on the floor, cushioned on straw sacks, crawling with lice. Once a week the men were allowed to bathe but they were strictly limited to five minutes in the bath. Once, when Cozzens was slow in leaving the bath, he was slapped across the face by one of the guards.

The Americans refused to give any further information about themselves or their Belgian helpers. Finally, on 25 August, the Gestapo's patience ran out and they were ordered confined to dark cells. Ryckman remembered the date well, because it was his father's birthday. Each dark cell was six feet long and four feet deep; the only ventilation came from three small holes in the floor. The Germans did not permit blankets in their dark cells, so the men slept uncovered on the cold, cement floor. In a corner of the cell was a bucket which served as sanitation. During confinement, which lasted five days, the Americans were not permitted any drinking water.

On the evening of 1 September the Americans were removed from their dark cell and again interrogated. There were only a few questions this time, asked mostly about the crew's duty positions in the aircraft. The next day, forty-two Allied airmen, including Wolcott, Ryckman, Cozzens and Auda, were taken from the prison and locked into the baggage car of a train. The men realized at once that they were being transported to a PoW camp. The talk was that British armour was approaching Brussels.

That night the train halted in a railway siding. At dawn the following day the train began steaming back towards Brussels. The German garrison troops on the train began to panic. They located a truckload of cognac and looted it. The train, with its drunken German guards and its carload of prisoners, made several more attempts to break through the ring of British tanks now encircling the city and each time it was forced back. White Army snipers began to concentrate their fire on the train.

The Germans attempted one last effort to break through the British lines. The train rolled slowly until it was 3 kilometres outside the city. Through a small window, the prisoners in the baggage car could see Very Light signals. Then the train stopped. The tracks had been blown up by White Army men. The train went into reverse, causing the baggage car to become derailed. Fortunately, none of the prisoners was injured. The guards, by now completely demoralized and frightened, abandoned the train. Sporadic shooting broke out in the wood beside the tracks and the prisoners had to dive for cover in the baggage car.

The prisoners decided to make a break for it. Using a pocket knife, they picked the locks and in groups of three and four, slipped unobtrusively out of the baggage car. Wolcott's crew headed for a canal where they were taken in by a patriotic Dutch barge owner. When he discovered the men he told them that open fighting had broken out in the streets of Brussels. Next morning the barge captain's son came running in, shouting 'Tommy, Tommy!' The British had completed the liberation of Brussels.

The four lieutenants were taken by Britsh Army supply lorry to France. At Amiens, an RAF officer told them there was a shuttle service to England from a local airstrip. They made their way there and before long, found themselves on a C–47 heading for England. Meanwhile, Lieutenant Carmen T. Vozzella, Technical Sergeant Dale S. Loucks, radio operator, Technical Sergeant Dervin D. Deihl, dispatcher, and Staff Sergeant Fred A. Tuttle, engineer, all from Wolcott's crew, were hidden in various places by patriotic Belgians until the liberation of Belgium by the Allies.

8

THE BELGIAN CONNECTION

By June 1944 it was estimated that in Belgium there existed forty Resistance networks dedicated to fighting the German occupation forces.* Belgium's small size and its absence of any suitable terrain, except in the forest of the Ardennes, prevented the establishment of a Maquis, so most Resistance activity was concerned with intelligence gathering. As happened in France, Belgium had produced a multitude of separate armed Resistance movements. This gave the Allies and the Belgian government-in-exile in London many headaches; not least of which was that a country the size of Belgium could not support twelve different movements without causing operational and political difficulties.

Resistance in Belgium had started towards the end of 1940 when some ex-officers of the Belgian Army, who were not incarcerated in PoW camps, formed groups called *Mouvements de résistance* which became known collectively as the *Légion Belge*. The existence of such groups was later admitted by the Belgian government-in-exile in London.* As it was the most important of all Belgian Resistance movements, the government-in-exile feared, wrongly, that the *Légion Belge* would oust the monarchy and take over the country after liberation.

Other groups,** like the *Front de l'indépendance* (FI), were very active but its members were predominantly communist. Their leader was Fernand Demany. Two other large groups, the *Milices Nationales Belges* (MNB) and the *Mouvement Nationaliste Royaliste* (MNR), also gave the German occupation forces many headaches. All these groups were known collectively as the *Armée Belge Secrète* (ABS). It was perhaps better known as the *Armée Secrète* (AS) or 'Secret Army'. Its leader was Lieutenant-General Pire and his orders for

---

* *Europe's Secret Armies* Dr Jean-Léon Charles (Purnell, 1973)
** *Home By Christmas?* Martin W. Bowman (PSL, 1987)

sabotage and resistance came from London via special radio contacts and coded BBC transmissions. His instructions were to raise an army 50,000 strong, to come under Allied direction when required.

The quantities of supplies dispatched from England were not always to the Belgians' liking. Often the situation created discontent among some groups which thought they were not receiving their share. This attitude persisted in other countries but few were aware of the difficulties the British and American clandestine squadrons had to solve to meet each group's needs.

Apart from carrying out acts of sabotage, the Resistance movement in Belgium had a very efficient escape line for downed Allied airmen.* By July 1941, stricken RAF crews were parachuting over the Low Countries in ever-increasing numbers. As a result, the 'Comete Line' came into existence. Patriots set up 'safe houses' along a route which led from Holland and Belgium through France to neutral Spain. Later, with the demise of the 'Comete Line' the 'Marathon Line' took over. Several Carpetbagger crews were among those who availed themselves of the escape lines in 1944.

On the night of 29/30 May, Lieutenant Ernest B. Fitzpatrick and crew in the 406th Squadron had failed to return from a mission, to 'Osric 14' in Belgium. Lieutenant Cornell 'Toby' Degrothy, the navigator in Bill Dillon's crew of the 859th Squadron, who was being checked out on night-flying procedures, was also lost. Dillon recalls:

> That evening, myself, my co-pilot, Ralph 'Angus' Morrow, and 'Toby' were all scheduled for orientation flights to the underground. This was group policy before a new crew went operational. Before take-off Toby approached me and said his intuition told him that something would occur that evening. Sure enough, it did. We heard nothing until late '44 or early 1945, when a PoW card came through the Red Cross stating at the time, 'all is well'.

'Osric 14' had been the subject of a successful visit by the Carpetbaggers the previous night. As a result of the activity, on the night of the 28th, the Germans had occupied the ground and all adjacent areas. Mobile flak units had been positioned in the vicinity and night-fighters alerted. Unfortunately for Fitzpatrick and

* *Home By Christmas?* Martin W. Bowman (PSL, 1987)

his crew, the Belgian underground were unable to transmit this information to London. Although he did not know it, Fitzpatrick was flying into a German ambush. An hour after midnight Lieutenant James S. Sherwood, navigator, identified the target below. There were no lights to indicate the presence of a reception committee. Then, as the Liberator circled, all hell let loose from a flak battery on the ground. The aircraft was hit. As it veered away, a Ju–88, waiting in the wings, came in for the kill, racking the bomber with 20 mm cannon fire. The Liberator was doomed.

Struggling with the controls, Fitzpatrick told Lieutenant Richard V. Theriot, co-pilot, to sound the bale-out bell. As the crew made ready to jump, Fitzpatrick first steadied the aircraft and then put it on auto-pilot before making his own exit from the burning bomber. Everyone cleared the aircraft before it crashed, 40 kilometres from Landen. Nothing further was known about the fate of Toby Degrothy and Staff Sergeant James E. Williams, gunner.

Fitzpatrick, Lieutenant Joe Lasicki, bombardier and Sergeants Walter W. Swartz, engineer, and William Schank, tail gunner, were reunited later when they passed into the hands of the Belgian White Army escape organization. Lasicki and Schack were captured later during a Gestapo raid on White Army safe houses and headquarters in Liège but Fitzpatrick and Swartz, who were warned in time, hid in fields until the danger had passed. They were taken to another house, where they remained in safety for seven weeks. From there, they were moved to a château on the outskirts of Liège. They lived in comparative luxury for four days, enjoying food and comfortable beds, hot water and pre-war whiskey. Then they moved again, travelling by train into Liège. The American advance had now reached the outskirts of Liège and the US Army had stopped to bombard the city. Street fighting began and snipers' bullets whined through the streets.

Fitzpatrick and Swartz remained in their safe house where they had been brought. Theriot and T/Sgt Paul P. Kazsa, radio operator, were in a house nearby. One day, a young Belgian, who had been their guide, was in the street and saw a man struck by a bullet. He was attempting to help the man when a German patrol passed, saw him and hit him on the chin with the butt of their rifles. They called him a terrorist and shot the young boy through the head.

Theriot and Kazsa were later moved to a farmhouse in Fallais, where they were reunited with James Sherwood. The three Americans remained there for eight weeks. Finally, contact was made with the escape organization centred in Brussels. In August arrangements were made for the airmen to pass along the evasion lines via Namur and Dinault. Theriot and Kazsa were joined later by eighteen other Americans and the group hid in a wood in the forest of the Ardennes until they were liberated.

Lieutenant William G. McKee's crew had flown a mission to Belgium on the night of 28 May when they dropped a consignment at Huy. On the night of 1 June the crew made another drop over Belgium, this time at Beaumont. Four days later McKee's crew made their last drop on Belgian soil at Givet. This was the crew's twenty-third mission of their tour with the Carpetbaggers. Don Fairbanks, McKee's tail gunner, knew they had only seven more missions to fly before they could go Stateside. Each mission had thrown up a variety of dangers and the ensuing missions would be no easier than the previous ones. Night flying brought its own dangers in the guise of night-fighters, flak and searchlights while problems could always arise with navigational errors and bad weather:

As tail gunner I used to ride backwards all the time. I recall one clear night with a full moon. We were just on top of a haze layer and the moon was reflecting off the layer. It gave a very definite horizon. All at once I saw an airplane coming from my right. An Me–110 was so close I could see both people in the greenhouse on top of the aircraft. He was maybe 100 ft above us. It seemed to me he was a sitting duck but we had orders not to shoot unless we were shot at so I didn't open fire. He floated right on by.

Another night we were just cruising along nice and quiet. The noise of the aircraft kind of blows itself out after a while and you can't hear it any more. Suddenly, it sounded as if someone was shaking a couple of buckets full of rocks. I turned around and looked back down the fuselage. (My tail turret doors had been removed because stories went that if they were hit by flak they could become jammed and the gunner couldn't get out.) Our flight engineer, Ed Cuplin, was lying on the floor in the waist. He had come back to use the relief tube. He hadn't brought his throat mike so he couldn't talk to anybody. For a moment I thought he'd been hit but 'Cup' had seen a Ju–88 flying on the left side of the aircraft about 500 ft out. (I hadn't seen the Ju–88 because the tail fin evidently blocked him out.) All of a sudden the Ju–88 had banked towards us and started shooting. It was machine-gun fire I'd heard. The escape hatch was clear and 'Cup' watched him go underneath. We didn't get hit. The Ju–88 made one pass and never came back. We didn't get one hole in the aircraft.

On another night I had trouble with the electrical system which ran the hydraulic pump for the tail turret. I manually hand-cranked the turret to one side, looked around and then let go of the crank. The wind blew the gun barrels and turned the gun turret back into position again. Then I would crank it the other way, hold it and let go. One time it blew back into the middle and there was a red light staring me straight in the eye. It scared the Dickens out of me. I hollered to McKee and Harwell, the co-pilot, 'Dive left!' Of course me being backwards McKee's left was one way and mine another so immediately I hollered 'Right!' The plane kept on turning and the fighter didn't come back.

On one trip when we had been fifteen minutes into France, we passed a small town. Five minutes later the flak opened up. I told McKee but it seemed too far back to be effective. Then all of a sudden there was a tremendous explosion right at our altitude and a great big ball of fire. An aircraft had been hit and had blown up. Big fingers of fire streamed to the ground. When we got back to base we learned that none of our planes were missing so it must have been an RAF aircraft.

On another occasion we were returning from drops in southern France. Norman Stoll, the navigator, made a 7° error. We crossed France and went over water and saw a couple of islands. Shortly after that we came over land which would normally be England. In fact we were right over the Bay of Biscay, having come up over the Brest Peninsula, one of the most heavily fortified areas in France! Stoll thought he was near Land's End. They started firing at us from the ground. I had a good view of it. Everything looked different at night. The tracer shells appeared to be moving slowly like balloons. It was coming up in all colours. I alerted the crew but it appeared they were firing over the top of the aircraft. I hollered to McKee to turn and we did, back over the Bay of Biscay. Stoll contacted England and we were told where we were. The navigator didn't believe his ears and challenged it. He received the right codes and we went west, heading for England. Low on fuel we landed at the first base we could find. It was a Spitfire base.

At night everything was black. When the moon was out and there was no external light our night vision would get very acute. Across the other side of the Channel there were times when somebody on the ground would open and close the door or up and down with a window shade and go 'dit, dit, dit, dah', which of course was 'V for Victory'.

We were coming back one night when we crossed a long east–west railway track. I could see a train on the track with a glow on the bottom of the smoke stack. He really put the power on to get to us. Then everything went black as he shut down the engine. I reported it at debriefing. The briefing officer said it sounded to him like a train with guns mounted on the cars. They would be moved around to try and get under the bomber streams.

We had a lot of respect for the Maquis. One night we were getting ready to board the aircraft. A car came out and we were told the mission was scrubbed. We turned in our parachutes and our equipment and went to bed. Next morning we were called in and told that the Germans had moved in some 88 mm guns to the drop zone. The Maquis had gotten the information back to England. We generally made our drops at 120 mph at 500 ft. If we had come floating through there nice and slow, with that type of gun, probably manned by some excellent gunners, we just wouldn't be here today.

Since we flew nights during the full moon we normally got our time off during the dark moonless period. Generally we had five days off. Then we went to London and stayed at the Red Cross Club. On one trip we were walking along Piccadilly Circus and we heard a buzz bomb coming over. It was about 400 ft up and sounded like a four-cylinder motor cycle. That morning the *Stars and Stripes* had published a three-view drawing of the V–1. I ducked in an open doorway and watched it. It looked just like the drawing. The engine quit right above us and spluttered and dived. It hit the ground about three blocks away. We ran over and it was the first time I had been near an immediate bomb blast. Everyone was covered with a light grey dust and had a stunned look on their faces. A tear ran down the dust on their faces and maybe a trickle of blood down their forehead. At the end of the street there was a horse-drawn cart. Evidently, the bomb had hit it and killed the horse. It had fallen over still attached to the cart. It was lying in a huge pool of blood. The buzz bomb was so impersonal.

The build-up to D-Day drew heavily on the resources of the Special Duty squadrons and the Carpetbaggers and all leave was cancelled. Replacement aircraft arrived to fill the empty dispersals caused by recent losses, and by the end of May 1944 approximately forty Liberators were available for missions to targets in occupied Europe.

On the night of 1/2 June the 801st dispatched twenty-two B–24s to the continent. The following night the group sent out eighteen Liberators and on the night of 3/4 June, twenty-three B–24s were dispatched. It resulted in seventeen successful sorties; the largest number of successes so far dispatched in one night. No losses were incurred during these three nights of operations.

On the night of 5/6 June British and American missions were mounted in support of the Allied landings in Normandy. SAS troops were dropped for the first time, in Operations 'Houndsworth' near Dijon, 'Bulbasket' south of Châteauroux and 'Samwest'.* 'Samwest', which involved 115 soldiers and thirty locally recruited French Resistance fighters, was less then successful but even so the group accounted for 155 German casualties. Operation 'Houndsworth' lasted until 6 September, during which time the party of eighteen officers and 126 soldiers from 1 SAS blew up the railway lines Lyons-Chalon sur Saône–Dijon–Paris and Le Creusot–Nevers twenty-two times. It also took 132 prisoners, killed or wounded 220 Germans and reported thirty bombing targets to the RAF.

The fifty-six soldiers from 1 SAS and 3 Patrol Phantom attached to 'Bulbasket' were to harass the 2nd SS Panzer Division on its move from Toulouse to Normandy. They attacked the railway lines Limoges–Vierzon–Poitiers–Tours, cut the railway twelve times and inflicted twenty enemy casualties besides sending vital information to the RAF, but had heavy losses themselves through treachery. On 3 July their main camp in the Fôret de Verrières was attacked by the 158th Security Regiment from Poitiers. Nine SAS members got away but thirty-one SAS and Lieutenant Tom Stevens, a USAAF evader who had joined them, were taken prisoner. One officer was wounded before capture and was tied to a tree and publicly beaten to death in Verrières. Three SAS prisoners were also wounded and taken to hospital in Poitiers where they were given lethal injections. The remainder, including the American and two other SAS captured previous to this engagement, were either shot in the Fôret de St Sauvant near the village of Rom or clubbed to death with rifle butts in the village square.

The SAS survivors signalled the UK with the information of their disaster and that the unit responsible was billeted in barracks at

---

* *The Special Air Service* Philip Warner (William Kimber, 1971)

Bonneuil Matours, near Poitiers. On 14 July, Bastille Day, eighteen Mosquitos of 2nd TAF destroyed the barracks. On 30 July the SAS learned that 2–3,000 Germans were massing for an anti-Maquis/ SAS sweep and the majority were billeted in the Caserne des Dunes barracks at Poitiers. This too was destroyed by Mosquitoes, on 1 August. When the SAS learned that the survivors of the 158th Regiment were now in the Château de Fou south of Châtellerault this was bombed on 2 August. It is estimated that 80 per cent of the regiment were killed, so that unit paid dearly for its actions. The surviving SAS troops were evacuated by air at the beginning of August by Hudsons and Dakotas.* (Altogether, the SAS carried out forty-three operations in the four months after D-Day.)**

Meanwhile, four Hudsons belonging to 161 Squadron at RAF Tempsford flew twenty-two sorties making radio contact with Resistance groups on D-Day.† The Carpetbaggers' contribution was no less effective. On 3/4 June twenty-three Liberators were dispatched to France and on 5/6 June, eleven Liberators were dispatched to drop zones in Belgium. Near Wavre, Lieutenant Kenneth Pratt's Liberator was hit by flak and three engines were put on fire in rapid succession. The fire quickly spread to the fuel tanks on both wings and the Liberator exploded. Three men are known to have been blown out of the aircraft by the force of the blast; the remaining five are thought to have perished in the Liberator, which crashed at La Hulpe.

Despite the shock they suffered as a result of being blown out of the aircraft, Pratt, Ralph Leindorf, co-pilot, and Sergeant Ollie Warren, dispatcher, recovered and managed to pull their ripcords. (Leindorf and Warren were later captured and made PoWs.) Pratt reached the safety of the Belgian underground and he remained with the White Army for three months until liberation. However, his stay was not without incident. Once, two German reconnaissance aircraft flew low over the White Army encampment in woods where Pratt was hiding. The Resistance, not wishing to take any unnecessary chances, moved that night to another part of the woods. Another time, the railway lines at Cincey were blown up at a point on the outskirts of

---

* *The Reich Intruders* Martin W. Bowman (PSL)
** *The Special Air Service* Philip Warner (William Kimber, 1971)
† *Flight Most Secret* Gibb McCall (William Kimber, 1981)

the woods. Although this was accomplished by another Resistance group, who had made good their escape to their own distant hideout, the Germans surrounded the woods with 2,500 troops. The Maquis sent diversionary columns in different directions, allowing Pratt and a P–47 pilot an opportunity to escape. Pratt was liberated by American tank crews on 7 September at the village of Sovet.

On 7/8 June, a further seventeen agents were dropped over France from five of the fourteen Liberators dispatched; the largest number of Joes dropped during a single night. One of these agents was 23-year-old Violette Szabo, the daughter of an English father and French mother and married to a French army officer. Violette had joined SOE in 1943 and was known to the Resistance as 'Corrinne'. She had already been landed by Lysander in April 1944 to spy out the closed zone of the Atlantic Wall. After her mission the brave heroine returned to Tempsford by Lysander and went on leave.* Shortly before D-Day she had returned to Hasell's Hall, the lovely Georgian house at Sandy concealed in woods, which was used as a clubhouse and dormitory by the Joes earmarked for SOE flights from Tempsford. Violette was the only woman agent among the large party of Jedburgh teams gathered at the house. (Altogether, just prior to and shortly after D-Day, 6 June, 100 three-men Jedburgh teams were dropped into France by the Carpetbaggers. British, French and American nationalities were all represented and they added greatly to the successful D-Day assaults.)

Violette's party consisted of four members. It was led by Major Charles Staunton, whose real name was Philippe Liewer and who was a Parisian by parentage and upbringing. The other two were Bob Mortier and an American radio operator, 2/Lieutenant Jean-Claude Guiet. All four would be dropped by a Carpetbagger crew into the Limoges area. Their mission had twice been cancelled. On the night of 4/5 June the B–24 was actually taxi-ing along the Tempsford runway when word was received that the weather up ahead was bad. It was the same weather which caused Eisenhower to put off the invasion for a further twenty-four hours. The following night, 5/6 June, the Liberator took off from Tempsford and passed over the invasion fleet heading for Normandy. All went well until the aircraft reached the drop area where failure on the part of the Maquis to flash their reception lights caused the mission to be aborted.

* *Carve Her Name With Pride* R.J. Minney (Collins, 1967)

The effect the two abortive missions had had on the four agents, already keyed up to a high nervous pitch, can only be imagined. But everything this time went according to plan and Violette and her three companions were dropped on the first pass. Four further containers, filled with machine guns, hand grenades, ammunition, explosives and the agents' suitcases, followed on the next run over the field. On 10 June, Violette and her companions were ambushed in Salon-la-Tour by advanced detachments of the SS *Das Reich* Panzer Division who were engaged in clearing the countryside of Maquis bands. Violette defiantly held off the advancing Germans with her tommy-gun before she was overpowered. Her brave actions allowed the others to escape. Violette did not survive the war. After torture by her Gestapo interrogators in Paris she was sent to Ravensbruck concentration camp where she was executed in January 1945. In December 1946 Violette Szabo was posthumously awarded the George Cross, the first British woman ever to receive it. Her daughter Tania received the medal from HRH King George VI at Buckingham Palace on behalf of her mother.

Experience was beginning to show and more crews continued to arrive at Harrington to replace men like Fitzpatrick and Pratt who had been lost on Carpetbagger operations. On 8 June Major Edgar F. Townsend, who had previously served as a navigator in the 453rd Bomb Group on Liberators, and lately with the 814th Squadron, 482nd Bomb Group at Alconbury, was assigned to Lieutenant Sam Goldsmith's crew in the 788th Squadron. Townsend discovered that the Carpetbagger routine was quite different to what he had been used to at Old Buckenham and Alconbury:

The crew of four officers and four airmen were alerted or awakened [the crew may have flown the night before] at 11.00–11.30 hours for the noon meal. At 13.00 hours the crews reported to the Operations room for briefing. Each crew was then assigned a target by the Squadron CO or the Squadron Operations officer. The crews that flew the previous night were normally assigned the short flights, and the long flights were given to flight chart to determine the general direction of the flight.

Intelligence briefing consisted of the latest information regarding the location of the battle line, possible night-fighter activity, new enemy tactics and the location and size of anti-aircraft guns. The details were plotted on a large map for the navigators and bombardiers to copy onto their flight charts. These charts were large scale and showed many more landmarks than normal charts including the shape of woods and forests. Charts were also available with 'Gee' lines so that all navigation could be done on one chart.

Radio briefing consisted of the correct IFF (Identification, Friend or Foe) setting, codes and frequencies to be used, depending on the time and area into which the flight was to be made. Normally, the IFF was used up to the battle line and then turned off. Radio was monitored but no transmissions were normally made until the craft were re-crossing the English Channel.

Weather briefing consisted of the detailed forecast for each general operational area. Crews were given wind directions and velocities at various altitudes up to 10,000 ft, also details of the type and amount of clouds and the position and movements of frontal systems.

After all the briefings were completed the crews then set up their own flight plans. First, a course was determined from the base to point of departure from England. After crossing the coastline, a zigzag course was used to the target to avoid known enemy anti-aircraft guns. By an unwritten law, the legs of the zig-zag course were limited to 30 nautical miles to prevent an enemy night fighter from lining up from behind to make an attack. Another zigzag course was set up for the return flight to the enemy coastline.

Operations over enemy-held territory had to be conducted in the period of total darkness, which during the summer was often as little as five or six hours in northern latitudes. Once the flight path was established, total flight time was worked out using the forecast wind speeds for the selected altitude. Each crew then turned in its forecast flight plan and Group set up the take-off times. At least ten minutes was allowed between planes entering the same area and those with the longest flights went in first.

When the target was given to the crew, they were also told the recognition signal they would receive from the ground. This could be three lights in a row with an extra light showing the wind direction. These lights could be torches or fires on the ground. [Few landing fields had radios to guide the Liberators in so most of the drops were made using hand-held lights. Sometimes, the Germans constructed dummy landing strips but the cargo seldom fell into enemy hands because they could not flash the correct signals.] When the target area was identified, the pilot lined up into the wind and approached at slow speed flying at 400 ft (600 ft if Joes were being dropped) using the radar altimeter. The bombardier controlled the time of drop. When the first light was immediately below he released the canisters from the bomb bay and signalled the drop man in the waist to kick out the large packages. A stop signal was given over the last light and if all the material had not been dropped, a second pass was necessary. This, of course, increased the danger to both the plane and the personnel on the ground.'

Throughout June Edgar Townsend and his fellow crew members continued night missions in support of the Maquisard groups in France as the Allies broke out of their Normandy bridgehead. Carpetbagger crews were heartened by the news that their missions had enabled Allied teams to be dropped into France to co-ordinate the Resistance groups and secret armies and thus prevent many German reinforcements reaching the Allied bridgehead at the crucial time of the invasion timetable. General Eisenhower was to record later: 'Thanks to the underground movement, the liberation of France was accelerated by some six months.'

9

NEW METHODS

It was essential that the Allies continued to prevent the Panzer units and German reinforcements reaching the Normandy bridgehead. One of the best ways of doing this was to hamper German lines of communication to the south of the region by blowing up railway lines. The German units would also be kept busy fighting off harassing attacks by the *Armée Secrète* and large bands of Resistance fighters led by experienced SOE organizers such as Major Richard Heslop.

Operating under his code name 'Xavier' since September 1943, Heslop had established the 'Marksman' Resistance network in Ain and Haute-Savoie. They fought a bitter, savage war with no quarter given. Villages were razed to the ground and rape, torture and execution of innocent villagers became a way of life, interspersed with attacks by the Wehrmacht and their allies, the Vichy-inspired GMR (*Groupes Mobiles de Réserve*) and the French *Milice*.

SHAEF estimated that about 16,000 Frenchmen were under arms and had received word that four French Departments were under French control but a further 34,000 Resistance fighters could enter the fight if an additional 340 supply-dropping sorties could be flown each month. The Carpetbaggers could, by operating at full stretch, extend their range of operations to Châteauroux and the Cantal area, south-east of Limoges, but more aircraft would be needed to supply the many thousands of potential Resistance forces in the south. In the mountainous region of Ain on the French–Swiss border a force of about 5,000 FFI (*Forces Françaises de l'Intérieur* or French Forces of the Interior) were more than holding their own but Heslop expected a major German push and radioed London for a large airborne drop of arms, ammunition and supplies to meet the threat.

The only way to do this was to temporarily divert Fortress groups of the Third Bomb Division, 8th Air Force in East Anglia from heavy bombing missions to large-scale daylight supply-dropping operations. On 14 June the Ain was almost taken by the FFI when lack of supplies and munitions forced them to break off. On 15 June SHAEF directed 8th Air Force Headquarters to be ready to begin supply-dropping missions. Special Forces Headquarters laid on supplies of containers to the five B–17 heavy bomb wing bases of the 8th Air Force Third Bomb Division in Suffolk, where approximately 180 aircraft were gathered for 'Operation Zebra', as the mission to supply the Maquisards was codenamed.

Originally, the drop was arranged for 22 June but bad weather prevented operations and the supply mission was re-scheduled for 25 June. Colonels Gable and Haskell of OSS flew in two B–17s in the leading 94th Bomb Group from Bury St Edmunds, led by Command pilots, Brigadier-General A.W. Kissner and the Group CO, Colonel Frederick W. Castle.

A large fighter escort protected the Fortresses and only two B–17s were shot down. Two other Fortresses turned back with mechanical problems but the remaining 176 aircraft managed to successfully drop 2,088 containers at five drop zones in the Haute-Savoie, although one Wing was forced to drop its containers south of Limoges after no recognition signals were received at the primary drop area around Cantal. Spurred on by their success, B–17s of the Third Bomb Division carried out further large-scale supply drops involving still more Fortresses during July, August and September.

Meanwhile, the Carpetbaggers continued to make a valuable contribution to the guerrilla war in France, parachuting more and more agents into the field. On the night of 12 June, Colonel Fish took off for a mission to 'Hugh 1' in France. In addition to the cargo of twelve containers and eight packages, he had aboard three Joes. The Joes were a Jedburgh team of two officers and a sergeant, all of them paratroopers, who were to be dropped near the Château Rouge for the purpose of organizing harassing units.

Fish brought the Liberator in quite low over the target and the containers, packages and Joes were dropped in that order. Unfortunately, the sergeant was killed when his parachute failed to open and one of the officers broke both his legs. Lieutenant Burton, OIC of the harassing unit, landed safely but discovered that he was 300 yards from where he should have landed.

Despite the inauspicious start to the mission, all went well and Lieutenant Burton was able to tell listeners in the 856th Squadron at Harrington all about it when he returned to the base on 3 November.

His opening remark was: 'The last time I was on this base, I was scared to death. Thankfully, the circumstances are a bit different this time!'

Burton looked none the worse for wear but his calm exterior concealed six months of hard fighting, blowing up bridges and railway tracks and generally disrupting enemy transportation and communications. Burton had been unhappy with one particular drop by the Carpetbaggers which was made from 1,000 ft. Several containers containing ammunition broke up in the air and he and his French colleagues spent many hours collecting every single precious round! Fortunately, incidents such as these were rare and he was able to recount several operations in which his unit took part, like the occasion they stole 10,000 lb of butter from a convoy, and the surrender of 12,000 German troops to the 83rd Division, which was due, in part, to the activities of Burton's army.

The problems of low flying occurred again on the night of 18/19 June, when Lieutenant John R. McNeil's Liberator in the 850th Squadron flew too low over its target at 'Historian 14' and hit a tree before dropping its containers. All eight crew were killed. It was the squadron's first operational loss. Unfortunately, the run of bad luck continued to dog the 850th Squadron. On the night of 27/28 June another Liberator, piloted by Lieutenant William E. Huenekens, which was on a training flight, was lost east of Bedford. One moment the B–24 was flying normally at about 2,000 ft, then suddenly the aircraft began shuddering violently. By the time the crew realized that they were under attack from a German night-fighter, the fuselage was ablaze. No one on board expected to encounter an enemy intruder in the sky over Bedfordshire. At the 'bale-out' signal, Robert L. Sanders, the bombardier, left his position in the nose and scrambled up to the flight deck to fetch his parachute, which was lodged near the bomb bay bulkhead. To his horror, he found that the area was a mass of flames and his parachute pack was burning! He quickly returned to the nose where Robert Callahan, the navigator, was about to jump through the hatch he had opened.

Sanders explained his fearful situation. Callahan knew there was only one thing he could do to save the bombardier's life. He sat down on the edge of the hatch and instructed Sanders to straddle his back and wrap his arms around him tightly. Then, locked together, both men dropped into the slipstream. The jolt when the parachute opened was a critical moment but the two men came down piggy-back fashion safely and landed in a wheatfield near Eaton Socon.

Their only injuries were a few cuts and bruises and a broken ankle sustained by Callahan. The only other crew member to escape from the burning aircraft was the badly burned radio operator, Randall G. Sadler. Callahan was later awarded the Silver Star for his bravery.

The month of June 1944 saw the 801st breaking all records, flying 424 sorties of which 347 were successful. Seven of these were to Belgium but the remainder were all flown to France. It was a far cry from January when during the Carpetbaggers' first month of operations, only eighteen sorties were flown. The run of success had continued, for one crew at least, when on the night of 3/4 July, Lieutenant Jackson's crew of the 36th Squadron chalked up their thirteenth consecutive successful mission. However, Independence Day, 4 July 1944, marked a black day in Carpetbagger operations. On the night of 4/5 July the 801st dispatched thirty-six Liberators to France. Three Liberators failed to return while a fourth ship crashed on landing; the highest losses sustained by the Group in a single night. One ship, piloted by Lieutenant John C. Broten, belonged to the 36th Squadron, while the other two, piloted by Lieutenants John J. Meade and Charles R. Kline, came from the 850th Squadron.

Meade's Liberator was attacked by a Messerschmitt 110 night-fighter about 40 miles south of Paris. The German crew approached from seven o'clock low and raked the tail and fuselage, killing S/Sgt Ellis H. Syra, tail gunner, instantly. Lieutenant John D. Bonnin, bombardier, recalls, 'We tried to lose the Me–110 in the clouds. We didn't have a chance. We had a runaway gun in the tail and we were only able to fire a few bursts. The bomb bay caught fire and two engines were out.'

Meade ordered the crew to bale out. Lieutenant James L. Lovelace, co-pilot, apparently collapsed his parachute when it opened under him. His body was found wrapped in his parachute by Frenchmen. Meade was later shown Lovelace's grave by the French, who told how the Liberator had headed directly towards their village, burning and diving, and how by some miracle it had pulled up and cleared the houses before crashing. The rest of the crew landed safely and were sent along the escape lines before eventually being repatriated to Harrington in August.

Broten's Liberator, meanwhile, was brought down near Orléans after a successful drop in the area. The aircraft was still climbing for altitude when the attack came. A German night-fighter suddenly appeared behind and below the Liberator. It came in fast, spitting flame and firing with deadly accuracy. Edward Tappan, the co-pilot, reported that only the first three rounds missed the aircraft. In the next split second the big bomber had been raked from nose to tail. Shells whistled into the cockpit, ripped through the bomb bay and up through the ship, so that they clipped Tappan's sleeve off and nicked his wrist. In another second the left hydraulic accumulator had caught fire, filling the cockpit with flames and black smoke. Broten told Tappan to ring the bale-out bell and get out of the aircraft. As Tappan made his way to the top escape hatch there was a tremendous explosion. By some miracle, the blast's combustion propelled Tappan out of the escape hatch. The rest of the crew were doomed. They died in their ship.

When he was blasted out of the escape hatch, Tappan's head struck the stabilizer and he blacked out. He had no memory of pulling the ripcord on his parachute. His first recollection was of being almost to the ground when he regained consciousness, and found his fist still clutching the ripcord. Tappan later made contact with the French Resistance and by early August he had been returned to England.

No word was received regarding Kline's crew. A fourth Liberator, piloted by Lieutenant Oliver C. Carscaddon, also from the 850th Squadron, was attacked by three Junkers Ju–88s, 15 miles inside the French coast while flying at 8,000 ft. The German fighters knocked out the Liberator's No. 2 engine and it caught fire. Technical Sergeant Franklin J. Hasty, the engineer-gunner, claimed one Ju–88 probably destroyed. The Liberator crew had to fend off constant fighter attacks all the way from the River Seine to Elbouf, where a brief respite ensued when flak guns opened up on them.

After passing the town the German fighters resumed their attacks. Staff Sergeant Laurie Salo, the tail gunner, was wounded by a burst of 20 mm cannon fire. One of the waist gunners was also hit and a fire broke out in the bomb bay. During a lull in the attacks Carscaddon ordered the crew to bale out. Six of the crew left the aircraft but Hasty discovered that his parachute had been holed by flak and he remained on board with Carscaddon. The fire, which had been raging in the bomb bay, had died down so he decided that they would try to get the aircraft back to England.

Carscaddon took the Liberator down to treetop height and headed for the French coast amid machine-gun fire and the occasional burst of flak. Hasty beat out most of the fires on board while Carscaddon took evasive action to wrest the aircraft from a searchlight beam and machine-gun fire at the coast. Carscaddon limped across the

Channel and crossed the coast at Shoreham. He was directed to an airfield at Ford by RAF aircraft where he landed without brakes and the bomb doors open. The Liberator hurtled down the runway, hit a ditch and finally came to rest in a field with a smashed nose and damaged right undercarriage.

Carscaddon and Hasty returned to Harrington and were joined a month later by their co-pilot, Otis W. Murphy, who had evaded capture. Murphy had been fired on by one of the Ju–88s after baling out. The German pilot dropped flares and had continued strafing him on the ground. Despite a hit in his leg from a 20 mm shell, Murphy managed to drag himself to safety, as the Ju–88 continued to fire at his disregarded parachute harness. He was picked up by the French underground and waited in hiding until liberation.

During his sojourn in France Murphy saw the Germans at close hand:

> The Jerries lived like kings and those that went through our village said they were going back to defend the fatherland. I saw five SS officers one day retreating in an ox-cart. The roads were lined with wreckage and burned vehicles. They were scared of the strafing done by the P–47s and P–38s. They really took to the ditches and cover when the fighters appeared.

Unfortunately, the strafing produced civilian casualties as well as German ones. Later, Murphy wrote poignantly:

> While I was staying with the French I was taken on walks and one day they took me to the cemetery. I was kissed by a woman who had lost three children that were killed when a P–47 strafed the truck in which they were riding. The children had only been buried there the day before and this woman with no hatred and only grief in her heart kissed me because I was an American. They are wonderful people and every Sunday they put red, white and blue flowers on every American and British grave in the cemetery.

Eventually, Murphy was flown to the American lines in an L–4 Advance Artillery spotter plane.

Edward Tappan, co-pilot on the Broten crew, also evaded capture after their Liberator was shot down by a night-fighter near Orléans after their drop had been completed. Tappan, who was the only survivor in the seven-man crew, was taken in by the French underground and holed up in a French village until the American 3rd Army overran the village on 13 August. He was driven to 9th Air Force Headquarters on the Cherbourg Peninsula and flown back to Harrington by Ferry Command.

During July 1944 the Carpetbaggers flew a total of 397 sorties, dropping thousands of containers, packages and bundles of leaflets and sixty-two Joes. The increase in sorties was bound to lead to a relatively high incidence of accidents and losses to both the American Carpetbagger Group and the RAF special duties squadrons, which also increased its operational ability in the summer of 1944.

However, night flying at low level brought with it its own particular problems and restraints and not all losses could be attributed to enemy flak or fighters. One such tragedy occurred on the night of 18/19 July. A Liberator piloted by Lieutenant David A. Michelson failed to return from a sortie to target 'Dick 89' in France. Two weeks later news of what had happened filtered through during another sortie, flown by Bill Dillon. While using the S-phone, his radio operator received a message from the field which indicated that Michelson had collided with another aircraft from RAF Tempsford.

Apparently, the French said, both aircraft had flown over the drop area without replying to the signals from their Eureka set. The first aircraft turned over a local village, probably to drop its load on 'Dick 89a'. The other aircraft had also turned, onto a collision course, and both aircraft collided over the village. Eight bodies had been recovered from the wreckage.

Among the crews who took part in missions during the month was Major Edgar Townsend, the navigator on Lieutenant Sam Goldsmith's crew. He recalls two distinct problems the Carpetbagger crews had to contend with.

One night in July 1944 we were crossing the English coast in the vicinity of Brighton on a south-easterly course. At the same time an RAF Halifax flying on an easterly course and about twenty feet below, crossed right under our nose. Even in the black of night with just a little moon, we could see the markings on the fuselage and tail. Mid-air collision was probably one of the greatest fears of night-flying personnel. I never looked out again except during the drops over the target.

One of the long missions was made south-east of Bordeaux about 100 miles from the Franco-Spanish border. On the way home we crossed the French coast at 5,000 ft just south of Bordeaux. The enemy started hunting our plane with three searchlights criss-crossing the sky several times. Finally, one caught us for a few seconds and moved on still searching. I feel sure they were unable to see the plane even in the light. My bombardier later stated the light was so bright he could have read a newspaper.

Don Fairbanks, now nearing the end of his tour, also had problems with a searchlight: 'I put my hand over my eyes. It was so bright even then I could see the bones in my fingers. On another night we dropped a five-man American team. They only swung two or three times before they landed so they must have been low.'

McKee's crew were biting their fingernails. Fairbanks recalls: 'One night near the end of our tour we made a drop near the Alps. There was a bunch of us including, I believe, British aircraft and we went over in trail. It was a huge area and we could see trucks waiting to take our canisters.' (The crew finished their tour on 1 July 1944.)

It was not unusual for Carpetbagger crews to undertake long-range missions as far afield as Bordeaux and near the Alps because the Liberator had the necessary tankage. In addition, the B–24's large, cavernous fuselage could accommodate a large combined cargo of passengers and supplies. Unfortunately, the Liberator's wide high-aspect Davis wing, its relatively high landing speed and weight made it impossible to put down behind enemy lines. During July SHAEF received a request from 'Xavier' in the Haute Savoie for heavy machine-guns and mortars but these could not possibly be dropped by parachute or transported by a Liberator. Providing Heslop could lay out an improvised landing strip, a C–47 Dakota was another matter.

10

FRENCH ESCAPADE

Since 1 May, when Colonel Heflin had made the first night take-off and landing in a Dakota, Captain Wilmer Stapel of the 406th Bomb Squadron had started flying the C–47 in preparation for missions to come. He recalls: 'On nights that our crew wasn't flying combat missions, I was making landings on an improvised field near Harrington. Captain John Kelly was my assigned co-pilot for these flights. We helped train OSS and SOE personnel in the setting up of the night landing flare path for future missions. On 14 June my crew completed their thirtieth mission and rotated back to the USA. I stayed on for future operations.' Stapel performed as many as twenty C–47 landings in a day to demonstrate the possibilities of this type of operation.

During the late afternoon of 6/7 July cars motored along the narrow winding lanes around Harrington and alighted at the base flight office to disgorge six French politicians and three SOE operatives. Three thousand pounds of baggage, ammunition, medical supplies and even several up-to-date, British-produced propaganda films such as *Desert Victory* and *The Blue Angel*, with Marlene Dietrich,* were loaded aboard the cavernous C–47.

Meanwhile, Colonel Heflin and his crew were briefed behind closed doors by the S–2, Captain Robert D. Sullivan and by Group weather officers. In addition to regular navigation maps, a map and an aerial reconnaissance photo of the landing field were used at the briefing. Wilmer Stapel was flying as co-pilot for Heflin on the inaugural C–47 mission, while Major Edward C. Tresemer and Major Charles R. Teer would by flying navigator and bombardier respectively. Technical Sergeant Albert Krasevac would complete the crew as radio operator. This constituted a normal Carpetbagger team, since Major Teer would perform the bombardier's duties of map-reading and pinpointing.

---

* *Xavier* Richard Heslop (Rupert-Hart Davis, 1970)

Their destination was an improvised Resistance airstrip at Izernore a few miles from Nantua near Lyons, codenamed 'Mixer 1'. Stapel recalls: 'We were well aware of the fact that we would have to remain overnight as there was not enough darkness at this time of the year to complete the mission in one night. Planning was done accordingly by both our crew and the reception party.'

There could be no refuelling during the flight, a round trip of 1,000 miles, or at Mixer 1, so throughout 6 July a tank holding 100 gallons of fuel was installed in the Dakota's fuselage. This brought the twin-engined transport's capacity up to 906 gallons, enough for the nine hours' flying time involved.

At 20.00 hours all was ready. A half-hour later Heflin was airborne and Tresemer set course for Bolt Head near Plymouth. To save on fuel for the actual flight from England it had been decided that the C–47 would be refuelled there for the flight across to France. The flight south-west was made without mishap and the C–47 touched down at the Devon base at 23.00 hours. Arrangements went smoothly. The transport aircraft was refuelled and was soon in the air again, heading for France.

Less than an hour later the C–47 crossed the French coast at Penenan. The main fear now was the possibility of enemy night-fighters for the C–47 was unarmed, had no armour and no self-sealing petrol tanks. In addition, the aircraft could not carry an observer in the tail who could keep an eye open for night-fighters and so there was a strong risk of an unexpected fighter attack from the rear. Captain Stapel moved to the astrodome in the nose to maintain a 360° lookout from the top of the aircraft. Luckily, a solid undercast reaching to 7,000 ft between Penenan and the Loire provided excellent cover. The cloud began to break up to the south of the Loire and Teer was able to pick up checkpoints on the ground.

Fifty miles from the river there was no cloud at all. Heflin dropped to 4,000 ft. His passengers, although outwardly composed, must have begun to feel naked and uncomfortable knowing that they were an easy target for any prowling night-fighter in the vicinity. At least navigation was relatively simple from this point on. Heflin's passengers became a little restless, when at 01.20 hours the engine began spitting. Krasevac, who was in the passengers' compartment, told the Joes to fasten their safety belts. He and the two pilots knew that it was simply a matter of transferring petrol. Stapel explains: 'We waited until the fuel tanks ran dry before switching to the alternate fuel tanks so the engines ran out of fuel and stopped. I frantically worked the wobble pump while Colonel Heflin changed the fuel tank selector valve. For a minute or two we made like a glider until the engines re-ignited.' Soon the two engines were humming reassuringly again.

Heflin maintained a height of 1,000 ft while in the clear moonlight below the crew could see that the terrain was becoming more mountainous. The obstructions prevented Tresemer from picking up a Rebecca signal at any great distance. However, 4 miles from the target his Rebecca scope registered a clear signal. The time was now 02.57 hours. A moment later, the row of four reception lights, set at intervals of 150 yards, came into view. The code letter 'N' was flashed from the ground and the aircraft's downward recognition lights replied with 'R'. The Rebecca signal had brought the Dakota on the downwind leg into the lights, so that, after the code letters had been exchanged, Heflin only had to swing his aircraft around and land. Altogether, the reception lights had been on for no more than sixty seconds.

Heflin made a perfect three-point landing on the improvised landing strip, which only a few days before had been a wheatfield and which, even now was only 50 per cent harvested! The powerful beams of his landing lights split the darkness and the C–47 came straight in. A Maquisard guided the transport to the edge of the field. When it came to a halt, Major Tresemer got out to direct the taxi-ing procedure. Out of the dark the first words Tresemer heard when he stepped onto French soil were, 'Jesus Christ, Yanks. Am I glad to see you!' Somewhat taken aback, the Major at first thought they had got back to England by mistake. However, the words were spoken by a Canadian gunner who would be returning to England in the C–47. The French had never seen such a large aircraft before and curiosity got the better of them. Some attempted to climb all over it, investigating its equipment and exclaiming at its size.

The first person to greet the aircraft officially was an American lieutenant, who was simply known as 'Paul', actually Paul Johnson, a highly trained radio operator who had worked in North Africa with OSS and had been seconded to the SOE in France. Paul took charge and helped Tresemer direct the Dakota to a suitable parking space a few hundred yards distant at the foot of a mountain where there was a small copse of pine trees for camouflage. Immediately, two large groups of Maquisards marched towards the aircraft and stood to attention while the American officers climbed out of the C–47. They were told to fall out and immediately they began concealing the aircraft by 'planting' more pine trees around the Dakota.

Meanwhile, all nine passengers had alighted from the aircraft and were being greeted by the Maquis. Richard Heslop noted with disdain that the first six were in plain clothes – 'bloody politicians'. Xavier had been asking London for some months for a surgeon and he was pleased to see Major Parker, known as 'Parsifal', emerge. He would later organize the Maquis field hospital and save many lives with his skill. Next came 'Bayard', or Captain George Nornable, a small arms expert and instructor. The ninth man was Yvello-Veilleaux, a French Canadian radio operator, needed as an assistant to Paul.*

The French greeted the arrivals with a good deal of kissing and hugging. Colonel Heflin, meanwhile, ceremoniously pinned a pair of captain's bars on the shoulders of the agent Paul. Stapel recalls: 'We all got into vehicles and took off. We looked back toward the aircraft and it was almost impossible to see where it was parked. The camouflage was good.'

The crew were taken in two large French cars to the Maquis headquarters at Château Wattern, which lay on a steep hillside overlooking the landing area. It was a large 'U'-shaped building with administrative offices, mess, club rooms and a barracks and was known as the 'castle'. On entering the building the crew were taken aback to see a large red and silver Nazi eagle and swastika emblem which had been captured during a raid on a German headquarters two days before. Heflin and his fellow officers were shown into a dining room and seated at a long table expertly set with tablecloth and napkins. The officers noticed too the array of roses and the dozen bottles of wine. Before they tucked into barbecued beef and potatoes Paul introduced Colonel Heflin and his men to the twenty guests who were to dine with them. The enthusiastic French clasped their hands and talked excitedly.

Conversation at the table flowed freely and mainly concerned details of the C–47 flight. None of the crew could speak French but this proved no limitation to their French hosts, some of whom could speak English. Paul filled in the gaps with some interpretations. One crew member asked how long the reception committee would have been prepared to wait for the Dakota if it

---

* *Xavier* Richard Heslop (Rupert-Hart Davis, 1970)

had been late. A Maquisard replied that they would have waited until morning if necessary!

The French were unanimous in their praise for the way Heflin had landed the large Dakota at the strip. Their only regret was that the C–47 had not brought a cargo of ammunition and heavy weapons. Heflin explained that future C–47 flights would indeed bring them the necessary supplies. With this their hosts were eager to know when the next mission would be and they repeated the need for arms, mortars, ammunition, clothing and shoes. The Maquis chiefs must have been pleased with the assurances for the meal finished around five in the morning with many toasts to 'les Américains' and at one point, Colonel Heflin stood and proposed a toast: 'Vive le Maquis!'

The crew were escorted to properly prepared bedrooms to sleep, safe in the knowledge that they were in a securely held area of France. Space, however, was limited so some of the crew doubled up and shared rooms with members of the Maquis. Major Tresemer bunked in a room with a Maquisard who had composed the Maquis song, Captain Stapel with a Frenchman who was the bodyguard to a Maquis chief. The bodyguard's brother had been captured and knifed to death by the Gestapo and the man had taken up the fine art of handling a knife. He demonstrated this art the following day by making a few mock thrusts in the general direction of Major Tresemer's innards!

At 09.30 hours the crew arose to find Paul waiting for them with a car. They drove to the area where the Dakota was hidden but the job of camouflage had been so well handled that no one could see it! Paul showed them where the aircraft was hidden and after all had assured themselves that everything was in order they were driven to Nantua. The town lies on a smooth plateau 3,000 feet high, eight miles from the level ground at Izernore on the side of the beautiful Lac du Nantua. On 25 June its residents had watched the Fortresses, flying as low as 500 ft, unleash 400 tons of supplies over two dropping zones at Izernore and Port. The sight of the bombers had been a massive boost for French morale in the town, now liberated from the Germans.

Heflin and his officers were vividly impressed by the free and easy atmosphere of Nantua. Shops were open for business and people were calmly walking about in the streets. It was hard to believe that this was happening in a country occupied by the German Wehrmacht.

On their way through the town the men saw a gang of German prisoners working. The sight of these members of the 'master race' reassured the Americans that the town was secure. The prisoners were wearing sabots, or were barefooted and it was explained that this was to stop them running away.

Paul told his passengers of a Maquis exploit which had taken place the day before. The exploit involved the capture of a German train containing a store of cigarettes which was being moved up to the front. The Maquis brought the carload of cigarettes to their headquarters and then had teamed up the emptied car, sending it crashing down into the train parked at Bellegarde junction. This was why there was an abundance of cigarettes around Nantua.

By this time the car had arrived at the house occupied by the Governor of Nantua. Paul escorted them men in and introduced them to the Governor, who was a solidly built man, popularly known as 'Big Jewel'. The Governor was very proud of his town. One of his strictest edicts was that cars must not be parked in the open street but under the trees, in order to prevent the Germans from observing activity in the town by aerial reconnaissance.

When the Governor told them this they all had the same thought – that their own car was parked out in front and not under a tree. Paul had assured them that this would be all right. Accordingly, they spent time with the Governor, drank wine at his invitation and finally took leave of him. When they went outside they found that their car was missing – it had been driven off in accordance with the Governor's standing orders! However, under the circumstances, it was quickly returned and the men continued on their way.

Paul then drove Colonel Heflin and his men to a field at nearby Port, to show them evidence of a bombing attack by Stukas, which had taken place the day before. The field was under cultivation but had a very good landing strip. Bombs had been dropped in train, directly on the strip, leaving craters six feet deep and twelve feet across. The American officers wondered, naturally, if the Germans had somehow known of the next day's Dakota landing but it was more logical to assume that the field had been bombed because it had been one of the drop zones for the large-scale daylight dropping mission two weeks before. The French were very enthusiastic about the part played by the 'big bombers' in making the perfect drops.

When the Americans had finished inspecting the bomb damage, they returned to the car and Paul drove them on a tour of the area.

The roads were wide and invariably good although every quarter of a mile they were barricaded and manned by armed members of the Maquis who checked their passes. Paul was heading for Izernore where Colonel Heflin had been told that two lieutenants, both pilots, were waiting to be picked up for the return flight to England.

Heflin and his men met the two men at the local hotel. One of them, whom they knew as 'Jim' (Cater) was seated at a table when they entered. They were at the table, talking to Jim, when they heard the exclamation behind them 'You too!' They turned around and found French M. Russell, who had gone missing in action with Murray Simon's crew on 5 May. Russell's reactions at seeing the Colonel were mixed. He had been in France for some nine weeks and was glad to see his group commander but his first thought was that the Colonel had been shot down and that was the reason he was there.

When the excitement of the reunion had died down a little, Colonel Heflin related the story of the Dakota mission and said that the two lieutenants would be returning to England with them. Russell and Cater went wild with emotion. Recalling Russell's prophecy that his CO would eventually pick them up, Jim Cater for a long time could not get over the idea that this was the primary purpose of the Colonel's flight. A celebration in the presence of several attractive French women followed and wine flowed freely. Then Cater and Russell went to their rooms to get their gear together. Shortly afterwards all the Americans left in Paul's car. It was 13.00 hours when they returned to the castle and dinner was ready for them. The meal, consisting of five courses, including medium rare steaks, surpassed even the meal they had the night before. Each course was liberally washed down with wine or champagne.

After dinner the Americans, accompanied by various Maquis chiefs and organizers, went in three cars to the nearby village. They had not been told anything of what was in the wind. The cars stopped at the outskirts of the village and looking down the mainstreet, the Americans could see Maquis troops lining both sides of the street and civilians behind the troops. In a body, the Americans and their hosts began walking down the street. Immediately, a great cheer of 'Vivent les Américains!' went up. The first person to gree them was a small French girl, who offered bouquets of flowers to Colonel Heflin and the French Commandant.

At the end of the street there was a monument which had been erected to honour the memory of the Free French who had died in the war to liberate their country. Behind the monument, a platoon of German prisoners had been brought up. The prisoners included a woman who had been the mistress of a German adjutant. French flags were waved everywhere, in the street and from every window. The French Commandant told Heflin how sorry the people were that they had no 'Stars and Stripes' to wave and he asked that a quantity of them be included in a future delivery.

With simple but impressive ceremony, Colonel Heflin and the French Commandant placed the flowers at the foot of the monument. Then the platoon of prisoners was marched off and the Commandant made a five-minute speech. He told the people that the American crew had come to see the Maquis and to help them in clearing the hated Boche out of France. There were enthusiastic cheers and a great waving of flags. Then, standing before the monument, Colonel Heflin reviewed the march past. In perfect formation, the Maquis troops marched smartly up and down the street before finally resuming their positions on both sides of the street. Colonel Heflin and the Maquis chiefs returned to their cars and drove back to the castle. The Americans were very moved by the whole experience.

After a stop *en route* at an inn where more wine was served, the Americans returned to the castle. They slept until 20.30 hours when they awoke to listen to their codewords on the BBC news broadcast for final verification that they would fly home that night. The flight had been approved on the 13.00, 15.00 and 19.00 hour broadcasts but now, as they listened to the 21.00 hour broadcast, they found that the flight was cancelled because of adverse weather. The French, undismayed, arranged another champagne party in honour of the Americans! Innumerable toasts were proposed and the singing never stopped. At midnight the celebration was over and the Americans returned to their beds.

Next morning Paul drove Colonel Heflin and his men to the printing shop where the Maquis newspaper, *La Voix du Maquis*, was prepared. The Americans picked up bundles of the newspaper and drove to within 5 kilometres of the Maquis front lines to distribute them. On the way back Paul took the officers to the headquarters of the Maquis Secret Intelligence where they received a summary of a daring raid on a German train containing an armoured car the preceding night.

On the return journey to Château Wattern Paul pointed out places where houses had been burned to the ground in reprisal for Maquis activities, where executions of Maquis soldiers had taken place and where skirmishes had been fought with German troops. He also pointed out a spot where at one time, patriot sentries had been posted equipped with 'walkie talkie' sets to warn the Maquis of approaching Germans.

Paul told the story of Lieutenant Naucourt, a Maquisard who had been captured and tortured by the Gestapo. To illustrate the point, he showed the American officers a photo of the tortured man. His arms had been broken, both his eyes had been gouged out, his testicles cut off and his naked body brutally burned, but he had died without giving his captors the satisfaction of a single word. Colonel Heflin recalled later that 'nearly every family I talked to has had one or more of its members tortured or killed by the Germans'.

Heflin and his officers were shown the political prison where prisoners were guilty of black market activities or collaborationist crimes. From there they proceeded to the German prisoner of war camp, which was considerably worse than the first prison. The prisoners seemed old and shabby and presented a picture of utter dejection. This was quite understandable because of the new Maquis policy of executing three Germans for every Maquis who was killed or tortured by the Germans. The day previously, fifty-seven Germans had been shot, in line with this policy. Some of the prisoners the Americans inspected were shot later that same day.

The Maquis were anxious to give the Americans souvenirs of their visit to France. Colonel Heflin was given a P–38 pistol by one of the Maquis men which had been taken from a Gestapo officer. German caps were declined however, because Heflin and his officers were not certain that the wearers of the caps had been deloused. Uniform insignia, which the Maquis ripped off at random from the prisoners, however, made interesting souvenirs which several crew members brought back with them.

On 10 July the Americans made one last visit to see 'Big Jewel' and were entertained at an inn beside Lake Nantua before making preparations for the flight home to England. Take-off was planned for 23.00 hours and the 21.00 hour BBC broadcast confirmed that all was well. An hour later the Maquis began removing the skilful camouflage of the C–47 and amid scenes reminiscent of the landing three days earlier the officers began clambering aboard.

With them on the return flight were nine passengers including Heslop, who decided to hop aboard at the very last moment to attend a de-briefing in London before returning to the Ain. The rest of the passengers included Loulette Miguet, one of the Heslop's couriers and sister of his transport officer, Jim Russell, the Canadian gunner who had greeted Major Tresemer when the C–47 landed, a British gunner, an RAF navigator in Bomber Command and a young French girl and a Frenchman, who were to attend a school for saboteurs in England. Two Hindus, who had been in a group of Hindus rescued from the Germans by the Maquis, completed the party. Originally, it had been decided to send a captured German sergeant to England in the C–47 but the Maquis had already disposed of him in quite another way.

By 22.45 hours the weather had closed in badly and it began to rain. Heflin finally took off on instruments at 23.15 hours with visibility down to only 200 ft. For two hours the C–47 flew through solid overcast and with no winds from which to gain navigational information. Finally, at Poitiers, below the Loire, the Dakota broke through the clouds and winged its way to the French coast and on home. Heflin re-crossed the coast at Penvenan and decided that as the fuel supply was plentiful he would head for Harrington rather than the planned landing at Exeter.

Heflin touched down at 04.30 hours. With him he carried the red and silver emblem that had been on display that first night at Château Wattern. The emblem was now inscribed, in black crayon, 'A mes amis Américains, ce trophée du Maquis de l'Ain – 7 Juillet 1944. Prix aux Allemands dans la nuit du 5 et 6 Juillet au Pillay par l'Ain.' (To my American friends, this trophy of the Maquis of Ain. Taken from the Germans in the night of 5/6 July at Pillay, by the Maquis of Ain.)

Colonel Heflin was later moved to say, 'I recommend that every assistance be given to the Maquis troops, as I have never before seen such spirit as was displayed by these people. By giving them much-needed supplies, I think it will shorten the war and save thousands of Allied lives.'

11

FRESH FIELDS

The first Dakota mission to France had been a great success and had come just before a major push by the enemy forces in the Ain. For seventeen days, beginning on 14 July, the area came under savage attack by up to four German divisions. While he champed at the bit to return to the Ain, Heslop managed to persuade SOE to make several drops of heavy machine-guns, ammunition and mortar equipment to the beleaguered French forces. Colonel Buckmaster, head of the French Section at SOE, arranged for 'Xavier' to be flown back to Izernore in the same Dakota.

On 24 July Heslop, now promoted to Lieutenant-Colonel, gave a talk on the Maquis to the combat personnel at Harrington. He began with a word of congratulations to the Carpetbagger crews for the manner in which they had been delivering supplies and arms to the Resistance. He added that the Maquisards welcomed all the weapons they could get and were hungry for more. Heslop went on to explain that this group, operating under the codename 'Marksman', held a section 60 miles long and 40 miles wide north-west of Lyons. Their strength was between 4,000 and 5,000 and in the past ten months they had killed over a thousand Germans.

Since D-Day, he said, the ranks of the Maquis had swelled considerably. Now, the only limitation on the numbers of personnel was imposed by the quantity of arms available. Xavier explained that attacks were continually being pressed by the German forces against the Maquis and at the present time some 40,000 Germans were attacking the Resistance forces. Arms and ammunition were badly needed, especially light weapons, mortars and heavy machine-guns.

It was pointed out to the crews that an established practice of the Germans was to make reprisals against the civilian population. The attacks were being made most of the time by the Germans and abetted by Vichy-led French forces, such as the *Groupe Mobile*, most of whom wore distinctive black military uniforms and the plain-clothed Milice who were the most ruthless. Heslop told them that the Milice were as dangerous as the Germans, since they formed a French Gestapo.

Heslop told a hushed audience of how a German reprisal took place. During the large-scale attacks of February and April, the Germans occupied some villages which had previously been liberated by Maquis forces. When the Germans moved in, they executed seventy non-Maquis civilians and wantonly burned down 300 farmhouses. Recently, Xavier added, the degree of German barbarity had been intensified.

The crews asked Heslop many questions concerning their drops and were anxious to know if the Maquis were short of food. Xavier told them that in general the food situation was satisfactory, although in times of major battles, serious shortages did develop. He added that the Maquis were very appreciative of the American 'K' rations, as dropped to them by the Carpetbaggers. The question was asked that if a target is laid on for a number of aircraft, did the Maquis know how many. Heslop replied that they did and he cited a case where two grounds, one fairly close to the other, were prepared to receive three planes each. But, at the last minute, one of the grounds was rendered unusable by the Germans. By S-phone contact, all six aircraft were directed to drop at the safe ground. The six drops were successfully accomplished.

Heslop told the men that a good drop was material which landed within 400 yards of the reception lights. The danger of dropping material outside that 400-yard radius, was that the ground might be given away. He recalled that during one dropping operation, some of the material was found 4 miles away from the reception lights. Crews were relieved to hear that lorries taking the supplies from the dropping grounds rarely ran into German road patrols because patrol schedules were checked beforehand. Heslop paid tribute to the Maquis drivers. Since January, he pointed out, they had worked tirelessly, transporting supplies both day and night. To date, they had lost six drivers killed by the Germans.

Some crews asked Xavier why Eureka was used on some missions and not on others. Heslop put this down to the simple fact that there were simply not enough Eureka sets. The Maquis of Ain, he explained, at present only had three sets and these were used at grounds where the most difficulties would confront a dropping operation or where a multiple operation would take place. Many more sets were needed, he added.

Milton Ernest Hall pictured in the winter of 1942–43 before American occupation. *(Connie Richards)*

The impressive Carpetbagger memorial at Harrington, designed by the late Douglas and Jacqueline Walker and based on a concept by R. Wallace Clarke, was dedicated in 1987. *(Author)*

Colonel Clifford Heflin, CO of the Carpetbaggers with Lieutenant Colonel Robert Fish, deputy CO, at Harrington. *(Seb Corriere)*

Lysander III (Special Duty) fitted with a 150 gallon long-range tank for SOE operations. These special 'Lizzies' flew over 400 operations with four squadrons (and also 1419 Flight in Europe and the Far East between August 1941 and 1944). *(Westland Aircraft)*

Queen Elizabeth is introduced to American crews at RAF Tempsford by Major (later Lieutenant Colonel) Robert Fish (centre) while King George VI talks to Colonel Cliff Heflin (back to camera). *(John Reitmeier)*

Finedon Hall, Wellingborough today. *(Author)*

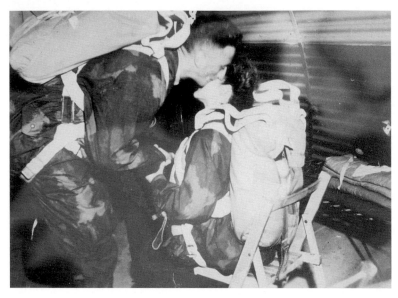

An OG Group commando and a female agent steal a final kiss before boarding a Liberator at Harrington. *(via Ron Clarke)*

Brock Hall today. *(Carl Bartram)*

Stirling IV 'Y' *Yorkshire Rose II* LJ566 at Fairford being readied for D-Day. Flt Lt Derek De Rome flew this aircraft on the Operation *Donald* mission to Brittany on 5 August 1944 carrying NORSO personnel whose task was to prevent the Morlaix railway viaduct being destroyed by retreating German forces. *(Noel Chaffey)*

Milton Hall near Peterborough pictured in 1987. Agents were billeted in the stable complex at the rear of the hall. *(Author)*

Holmewood Hall and its grounds (below). Holmewood was code-named 'Area H', a holding area for agents and OG Groups from Brock Hall, who were accommodated in the grounds under canvas. If their mission was unsuccessful they would be flown back to Holmewood and not Brock Hall, but would return to Brock Hall once the mission was successful. 'Officer X' and Major Colby later alleged that Glenn Miller was taken and executed here by the OSS.

American singer Irene Manning joins Major Glenn Miller for 'Music for the Wehrmacht' broadcast by ABSIE from London in November 1944. *(US Army)*

Agents leave for the flight into Occupied Europe. *(Dept of the Army via Carl Bartram)*

Above: Black B–24 on the line at Harrington (note the Rebecca aerials and flame dampers on the guns). *(Joseph Staelens)*

EN SOUVENIR
DE CINQ
AVIATEURS AMERICAINS
TROUVES MORTS SOUS LES
DEBRIS DE LEUR AVION
ECRASE EN FLAMMES EN CE
28 AVRIL DE L'AN 1944

Left: Memorial stone at St Cyr de Valorges to Lieutenant George W. Ambrose and four of his crew of B–24D 42–40997 *The Worry Bird,* which crashed near the village during a drop on the night of 27/28 April 1944. *(André Pecquet)*

Above: Johnny Mead proudly displays the French Tricolore at Lake Annecy following liberation of the town by American troops. *(Bestow Rudolph)*

Right: An S-phone operator demonstrates how contact was made with aircraft. *(Ron Clarke)*

Above: Carpetbagger crews are de-briefed at Harrington. *(via Ron Clarke)*

Left: Violette Szabo, who was parachuted into France on an ill-fated mission on the eve of D-Day June 1944.

Above: Hasells Hall near Tempsford where Violette Szabo waited for her flight in a USAAF Liberator to France in June 1944. *(Author)*

Right: Commemorative plaque at Troucrainville, in Eiuve-et-Loire in memory of Lieutenant John O. Broten's crew who were lost on the night of 4/5 July 1944. Edward Tappan, co-pilot, the only survivor from the mission, was present at the 50th anniversary ceremony on 14 August 1994. *(André Pecquet)*

Colonel Cliff Heflin studies the operations map of France. Heflin made the first of the C–47 Carpetbagger flights to France on the night of 6/7 July 1944. *(Seb Corriere)*

Rare photo of a Carpetbagger C–47 pictured in a French field just after touching down behind enemy lines during a delivery and pick-up operation. *(Seb Corriere)*

Classic shot of a Carpetbagger Liberator piloted by Lieutenant Paul Karr taking off from the east-west runway at Harrington with Foxhall cottages in the background. This photo forms part of the inscription on the Carpetbagger memorial at Harrington where the cottages still stand. *(USAF)*

Paul Karr's crew who flew the Liberator in the previous photo. Standing, L-R: James Watson, co-pilot; Paul Karr, pilot; George Miller, navigator; Douglas Granzow, bombardier. Front row L-R: Robert Sanchez, flight engineer; Leyland Garlock, tail gunner; Floyd Jensen, dispatcher; Talmadge Fletcher, radio operator. *(Douglas Walker)*

Rare photo of Carpetbagger Mosquito at Harrington, 9 May 1945. *(Art Carnot)*

An A–26 Invader, pictured at Harrington, the type used in the Hammer mission to Berlin on 1 March 1945. *(André Pecquet)*

SUPREME HEADQUARTERS
ALLIED EXPEDITIONARY FORCE
REAR HEADQUARTERS
APO 413

AG-201-AGF + Miller,Alton G. (Off)   12 December 1944

SUBJECT : Orders.

TO : Major ALTON G. MILLER, 0606271 G-1 Division, Supreme HQ

 1. You will proceed by military aircraft (ATC) on or about
16 December 1944 from present station to SUPREME HQ,ARMY AG-TM
on the Continent to carry out the instructions of the A.C. of S
G1,SUPREME HQ AEF,and on completion thereof return to present
station.

 2. Travel by military aircraft is directed. Baggage allowance
limited to sixty-five (65) pounds.

By command of General Eisenhower

Above: Confidential orders given to Glenn Miller by General Eisenhower to proceed to Paris 'on or about 16 December'. Note the incorrect serial number. It should have been 0505273.

Right: Colonel Norman Baessell – chief protagonist or fall guy in the disappearance of Glenn Miller? *(via Connie Richards)*

More than one UC–64 Norseman aircraft figure in the mystery surrounding the disappearance of Glenn Miller. This Norseman, which belonged to the Carpetbaggers, crash landed in a field on 20 June 1944. *(Seb Corriere)*

The plane that could actually have been used in Glenn Miller's final flight, rather than the Norseman that has often been suggested.

The question and answer session continued for some time and when the meeting was finally over, the muscular, soft-spoken Heslop left the briefing hut. His was one of the most hazardous jobs of the war but he left the vivid impression that he was eminently capable of carrying out that job.

During the last week of July Xavier prepared to return to France. Captain Wilmer Stapel and a four-man crew were selected for the return flight to the airstrip at Izernore, on the night of 2/3 August. Acompanying Heslop were three other passengers, including a cameraman from MGM, who was to make a full documentary of life in the Maquis. Stapel recalls:

We flew wide of the battle area going in and headed for Lyons. It clouded up before we reached the landing area and we became lost and confused. After wandering around for a while, I made the decision to fly south and get out of France before daylight. Neither the navigator or I had brought any maps for any point south of our proposed landing area so we were flying without any navigational aids. I knew Africa lay somewhere across the Mediterranean, so we kept going.

We crossed the coast of France outbound somewhere near Marseilles. When the fuel tanks got low I instructed Krasevac, the radio operator, to start sending out SOS signals on 500 kilocycles. We proceeded further in a southerly direction and it was then that we saw some fighter aircraft coming toward us from the east. I turned on my landing lights and dropped the undercarriage in case they were German fighter 'planes. Another thirty seconds went by and then we could see that the fighters were P–38 Lightnings. I pulled up the landing gear and proceeded to follow them. We landed at the 63rd Fighter Wing base near Bastia on Corsica.

We got a message off to London, refuelled the airplane and got us something to eat in the mess hall. A decision had to be made as to what we were going to do next. No one on the crew spoke any French but between all of us we finally made out what the Joes were trying to get across to us. They wanted to be taken across the island to the town of Borgo near Calvi. We took off from the fighter base without informing anyone where we were going, since our mission was secret, and flew over to an RAF fighter base near Borgo and landed.

We were met by the commander who politely informed me that I could stay there if I so desired but there were no rations or quarters available to us so we would have to remain by the airplane. The Frenchmen took off on foot for Calvi. The crew was tired so we propped ourselves under the wing of the C–47 and dozed off. We were aroused by a couple of the Frenchmen, who had returned from Calvi. They brought us some goats-milk cheese, some hardtack, orange marmalade and a can of vino. They said they would go back to their underground headquarters and keep in contact with the BBC. They would let us know when we should go back into France and complete the mission.

Stapel's enforced flight out of France to Corsica prompted a flurry of telegrams from London and Caserta, Headquarters of MAAF Command. Caserta sent Borgo a coded telegram to the effect that Captain Stapel and 'Charlie Four Seven [C–47] 42–92840, call sign 'Garbage Queen' is believed to have landed at Borgo.' Stapel was instructed to 'Try target tonight. Weather is favourable. PD for instructions Colonel Heslop. Listen to Baker Baker Charlie [BBC] for confirmation.' Stapel recalls:

On the afternoon of 7 August word was passed to me by the RAF commander in a radio message that we were to try the target that night. No fuel was available from the RAF for the aircraft so we all climbed aboard and flew back to the 63rd Fighter Wing base, refuelled and that night flew to Izerdore. [Heslop was dropped off but the MGM cameramen had had enough excitement for one flight and decided to accompany Stapel to England.] Again we gave the battle zone a wide berth but this reduced our fuel supplies. By the time we reached the coast of England the aircraft was about out of fuel. I landed at a base near Eastbourne, refuelled and flew on to Harrington.

After crew de-briefing I went to my quarters and found that the troops had removed my belonging to supply. Since no word had been passed on to the officers in my quarters and we had not returned as originally planned, they assumed we had been shot down. I moved back into the quarters in short order.

Meanwhile, Xavier and his brave band of Maquisards fought on until the day of liberation by American forces.

During Stapel's absence the Carpetbaggers at last lost their provisional label. On 5 August the 801st Bomb Group were afforded the dubious honour of being re-designated the 492nd Bomb Group. The previous holders of this label in the Second Bomb Division had been withdrawn from combat after losing a staggering fifty-one B–24s missing in action in just sixty-four missions in less than four months. No Liberators and personnel were forthcoming from their base at North Pickenham but the Carpetbagger squadrons also took the old 492nd squadron numbers. The 36th became the 856th, the 850th became the 857th, the 406th was now the 858th and the 788th became the 859th.

On 2 August 1944 the Carpetbagger crews gathered in the briefing hut at Harrington to listen to an organizer in the Danish Resistance movement from 'Area O'. Colonel Heflin and an RAF officer entered the room with a tall greying Dane with a weather-beaten face and dressed in a civilian suit. Crews came to attention as the three men walked towards the rostrum where a huge briefing map was displayed on the far wall.

After the introductions the Danish organizer began outlining his country's Resistance efforts. He explained in clear modulated tones in very passable English that in the last couple of months, opportunities for sabotage in his country had increased. Since the D-Day invasion, he said, the Germans had attempted to rush reinforcements from Norway and Denmark to northern France. The movement of these troops had to be via boat or train, a situation ripe for exploitation by trained saboteurs. In Denmark there were only two main railway lines, making it relatively easy to plan and perform acts of sabotage. By effective sabotage of dock and railway installations, the Danish Resistance had delayed troop movements by up to twenty-four hours in some cases.

The Danish organizer explained that to accomplish their brand of resistance, the Danish underground needed quantities of high exposive and pistols. They did not need machine-guns at the present time, since they did not fight the kind of pitched battle with German forces that the Maquis did so frequently. Substantial quantities of explosive were delivered to the Danes during 1943 but the organizer told the hushed crews that all stocks had now been used up and he appealed for more to be delivered as soon as possible.

The organizer elaborated on the difficulties of dropping missions in Denmark while outside, the normal air traffic at Harrington went on in the summer sunshine. 'Since Denmark is small,' he said, 'and flat and densely populated, a committee is hard-pressed to meet secretly at an isolated dropping ground.'

'A square mile without houses is rare,' he explained. Moreover, it was difficult for a Carpetbagger aircraft to fly over Denmark at the low altitude required for its particular kind of mission. There were no mountains to screen the flight of the aircraft and the land was studded with German fighter airfields. The only solution, he told them, was to reduce to a minimum the time spent in flight over the country. For this reason the northern tip of Denmark was best for Carpetbagger operations and the distinctive northern coastline was most suitable for navigation purposes.

The Dane emphasized the necessity for accuracy in making drops. The least deviation would undoubtedly lead to the loss of the material. At most, a committee had only half an hour after the drop in which to gather the containers and packages and leave the drop area. The Germans had many direction finder stations and detector services and they could be expected on the spot an hour after the aircraft reached its target. Therefore, there could not be very much circling around over the target, he warned, and the target must be hit accurately and without delay.

Sometimes, the organizer went on, a Carpetbagger aircraft had circled over its target after completing a drop in order to check results and make sure that the material was being picked up. The Danes appreciated such solicitude but would prefer that the aircraft make for home immediately after dropping, since its presence over the ground became a beacon for German observers.

The organizer also told the story of an aircraft whch was approaching a target when three lights were laid out in a triangle as the reception signal. The committee heard the engines of the Liberator when it was three miles north of the target. However, at that point, the crew noticed a similar pattern of lights created through sheer chance, by signal lights at a railway station. The Liberator went down to make a drop, discovered the error in time, and, while it fortunately did not drop in the railway station lights, was then unable to find the real reception, and headed home without dropping.

To prevent this sort of mischance, it would be very desirable for the Danish patriots to have more special equipment. They had a few Eureka sets but needed more. As for the S-phone (a two-way instrument for air to ground communication with a range of up to 10 miles), the organizer seemed to have little faith in them. He recounted the story of the drop which was bungled because the S-phone operator in the RAF aircraft spoke only Polish and so was unable to communicate intelligibly with the Danish operator on the ground.

The organizer also belittled the importance of code letters flashed by the reception lights. An incorrect letter, he said, should not deter a pilot from making a drop. He told of a reception committee leader who was, to say the least, unfamiliar with the ins and outs of code. He never did manage to flash the correct letter but nevertheless took part in eight consecutive successful dropping operations.

The most desirable condition, he said, was one created by multiple operations in one night. It was better to have six aircraft in one night, than one aircraft on six consecutive nights, because multiple operations helped to confuse the German observers and made it difficult for them to plot the course of any individual aircraft. The Carpetbagger crews noted this warning that they could expect many German night-fighters in Denmark.

The organizer stated that people in the underground movement in Denmark were always impressed by the excellence of weather-forecasting from England. Often, it happened that the weather appeared perfectly clear but the BBC signals cancelled the night's mission. The underground could not understand the cancellation, until, sure enough, the fog moved in during the night.

The organizer finished with several tips and points to consider if any of those seated were unfortunate enough to have to bale out over German-held Denmark. Meat and dairy products were in quite plentiful supply if the airmen had to live off the land. Once they had made contact with the underground he warned them that they could expect a heavy and detailed interrogation to safeguard against possible Nazi plants. Once passed as bona fide airmen, the Carpetbagger crews could expect to be dispatched by boat to neutral Sweden.

All the crews assembled in the briefing room must have been cheered by the knowledge that if they were brought down in Denmark many Danes would give them help and sustenance. As the official historian recorded: 'In the minds of the Carpetbagger crews, the tall Dane had become a symbol of Danish Resistance; strong, assured and unconquerable.'

Meanwhile, Carpetbagger missions to France and Belgium continued. On the night of 6/7 August, 36 Liberators were dispatched from Harrington. Lieutenant Robert C. McLaughlin and his crew, who were flying their 33rd mission, failed to return from a sortie to Belgium. McLaughlin made a run over the target but although his dispatcher, Fred Heath, managed to get the packages away safely, the containers hung up in the bomb bay. After their partial drop McLaughlin began climbing. At about 2,500 ft and some 10 miles from the target the Liberator suddenly came under fire from anti-aircraft guns. At least two of the fuel lines to No. 1 and No. 2 engines were ruptured and then burst into flames. McLaughlin immediately told Daniel Olenych, co-pilot, to hit the fire extinguishers while Bert Knapp, bombardier, salvoed the stubborn containers.

McLaughlin tried to control the torque of the ship, which was fast becoming too much to allow control, either by trim or manually. He quickly realized that his efforts were in vain and the pilot punched the alarm signal. At this time the whole aircraft seemed to be on fire. Sergeant Warren Lee, tail gunner, was in the bomb bay fighting the flames. When he heard the alarm he put on his parachute, which was just forward of the bomb bay, and jumped. Leo Arlin, navigator, baled out and was quickly followed by Bert Knapp. Knapp landed in the underbrush of a wooded area, wrenching his knee and spraining an ankle. John Y. Bear, engineer, went forward and baled out of the front bomb bay with Donald Adamson, radio operator. Heath, Olenych and Lieutenant William F. Reagan, who was flying as a passenger, also tumbled from the ship. McLaughlin was the last to leave. He left with a great deal of regret because everything that mattered seemed to be attached to the aircraft; getting back to base safely and going home after two more missions. He was in a low mood, for there seemed little prospect of anything good coming out of this.

McLaughlin landed beside a wooded area and immediately hid his parachute and Mae West. That night he slept in a shed filled with straw in a farmyard. Next morning McLaughlin asked an old maid who lived at the farm for help. She responded to the American airman's request and soon he was on his way through the French underground. On 2 September the Allies arrived and McLaughlin went north with the 3rd Armoured spearhead to Mons. While with them, McLaughlin saw some action and a lot of dead Germans. He decided that 'there weren't half enough of them.'

Leo Arlin had landed in a high tree after baling out. Having trouble with his harness he was forced to spend the rest of the night up the tree cursing his luck. He did manage to climb down from the tree next day and be began walking south-west. Arlin later met Knapp and the two men shared some adventures with their French hosts until they were finally liberated by units of the FFI and White Army. Adamson, Bear, Lee and Heath also hid out in the French and Belgian countryside with patriotic families until liberation. Adamson had a narrow escape when the Gestapo searched the house he was staying in but they had been forewarned and escaped by hiding in a secret cellar. Olenych and Reagan were not so lucky. They were helped across the Belgian border into France, where they stayed in a farmhouse one night. The next day they were arrested by the Germans.

The night after McLaughlin's crew went down, on 8 August, a B-24 flown by Captain William L. Bales, returned to Harrington after a sortie to Belgium with over 1,000 flak holes in the fuselage. Tail gunner, Staff Sergeant Silas S. Stamper, and the radio operator, Technical Sergeant Leo J. Ensminger, were both wounded after the aircraft came under fire while flying at 7,500 ft from anti-aircraft guns and by several Ju-88 night-fighters.

A few nights before, Carpetbagger Liberators in codename 'Salesman 21' were despatched from Harrington as part of OSS Operation 'Percy Red', to drop eighteen men in the Haute-Vienne area of France. Their mission was to block a major French highway and a railway line and to destroy a Wolfram mine near St-Léonard-de-Noblat then harass the Germans in every possible way and with the help of the Maquis carry out demolitions wherever it would hinder the enemy's advance. At about this time it was estimated that the Maquis in the Haute-Vienne had under its control approximately 5,000 Frenchmen engaged in operations against the German occupiers. The group had been largely armed and organized by Special Forces Headquarters and the chief organizer, Major Charles Staunton, known as 'Hamlet'. His real name was Philippe Liewer and he was a Parisian by parentage and upbringing. He had flown out from Tempsford with Violette Szabo as leader on both her missions.

A heavily armed five-man OG, led by Captain R.J. Grunseth of 'Area E', with containers filled with mortar rounds, ammunition and grenades, was dropped in the Haute-Vienne at 01.30 hours on 1 August but the three other B-24s failed to find the dropping zone and the 13 men had to be dropped on following nights. A B-24 carrying five men again returned on 2/3 August when no signal was observed from the reception committee. Finally, the last Liberator dropped on 5/6 August. Some of the drops were far from the drop zones and on at least one occasion it took four hours for the unit to assemble. Fortunately, their reception committee, organized by Hamlet, was very efficient and soon the group was assembled. They were taken to a farm which the Maquis had arranged for them.

When the full complement of sixteen men and two radio operators had arrived they moved to a location between Sussac, where they set up their HQ, and La Croisille, about four miles away. Word was received that a German armoured train was going to attempt to open the railway south of Limoges. Up to now the Maquis had succeeded in keeping the line out of action for most of the time. On the morning of 11 August the group located the train and followed it, trying to find a good spot to attack it. When the train, with fifty Germans aboard, stopped at St Germaine, they planted demolitions ahead along the track at a spot between Salon-la-Tour (where Violette Szabo had been captured while bravely holding off the SS Das Reich Panzer Division which allowed a comrade to escape) and Uzerche. The train was travelling at only about 4–5 mph with a soldier stationed in front on lookout for sabotage. When it approached the spot where the demolitions had been set up, the train stopped dead. Unnoticed by the group there were some electric wires across the track which the Germans got out and cut.

A few SAS troops had set themselves up at one end of the trap with the OGs further down the road. The SAS had joined the group a few days previously. (On the night of 4/5 August the RAF dispatched forty-two aircraft from five airfields to twenty-two drop zones with a total cargo of 150 SAS troops, four jeeps and 700 containers of miscellaneous stores (see Chapter Two). Meanwhile, 11 gliders, 45 troops and 11 jeeps were landed behind the enemy positions in Brittany.)* While the train was stopped German sentries were posted about the area. One sentry came face to face with one of the SAS. He raised his weapon to kill the sentry but was stopped by a Maquisard as it had been agreed to have no gunfire until the demolitions had exploded. About forty men took part in the ambush, including Maquis. They used Bren guns, Thompson sub-machine-guns and rifles. Naturally, the German gave the alarm immediately, so when the group did start firing they were faced with German machine-gun fire but it was inaccurate because they could not locate the OG's exact position. At this point four of the group, T/5 Stiansen, Corporal Alf Paulson, T/5 Olaf Eide, and T/5 Twingley, stood up and while exposed, fired at the enemy with Bren guns. This threw the Germans completely off guard and probably saved the lives of the whole group.

---

* *The Special Air Service* Philip Warner (William Kimber, 1971)

Two SAS were captured, so the remaining few withdrew. This left one flank entirely open, so the OGs had to withdraw too, blowing up the whole track as they did. It was now about 0930 hrs. The ambush had not proved entirely successful, but the railway was not opened. The train stopped about ten yards short of the last charge so it was not damaged, but flying steel fragments and debris probably killed some of the Germans. After this ambush the Germans returned to Limoges and never again attempted to open the railway line.

When the group was reassembled 'Leander' (Captain William F. Larsen, the OGs section leader) and a sergeant were missing. The sergeant turned up later but Larsen had been killed in a grenade explosion. He was given a full military funeral by the Maquis and was buried in the grounds of Château de La Vialle near La Croisille. The French brought masses of flowers and laid them on his grave. Later, in Limoges, the SAS men who had been captured were found. When the Germans had questioned them, they had reported that there were American and French troops in the area. This probably accounted for the German retreat in large numbers immediately after the encounter.

After the ambush the group continued to follow the train as it returned to Limoges. About a day later they received word that 2,000 Germans were moving north out of Limoges. The Maquis were not equipped to try to stop them here, so the OGs set out for St Léonard, where there was a bridge the Germans would have to cross. Outside of St Léonard they located 200 Germans guarding a Wolfram mine. The bridge, however, was inside the city. They had received varying reports that it was guarded by Germans, then by French, so they sent a reconnaissance group to look over the set-up. With the group now was Jedburgh team 'Lee', of which Captain Charles Brown ('Gerbert') was a member. They had joined up with the group the day after the ambush. On 14 August 'Gerbert' radioed Colonel Obolensky requesting four bazookas, 160 mortar shells, two Bren guns and fifty cartons of cigarettes. 'Lee' added that they needed petrol urgently. (On the night of 14/15 August thirty-seven Carpetbagger Liberators took off from Harrington for deliveries to France. Lieutenant Richard R. Norton and his crew in the 856th Squadron failed to return. Sgt John W. Gillikin, the dispatcher, was the only survivor. Earlier that day another B–24, 'Slick Chick', had taken off at 12.45 hours to drop a Jedburgh team codenamed 'Bruce', consisting of Lieutenants Jacques P. Favel, Louis Giry and Major William E. Colby near Montargis in France. (Colby was appointed director of the CIA long after the war.)

Meanwhile, Captain Brown, a few Maquis, and a few OGs went into St Léonard and found four French civilians guarding the bridge. They arranged for them to leave the town with their families, and the whole group moved in. There were no Germans there at all. They started placing demolitions around the bridge immediately upon their arrival, but it was extremely difficult because two men were compelled to climb down into the river bed. In case of an attack, it would have meant certain capture or death for these two men. Corporals Sverre Aanonson and Arne Herstad volunteered for this hazardous task.

The bridge was constructed of railway ties in such a manner as to make it difficult to place demolitions. It took about an hour and a half to complete the job, but a German garrison a mile away evidently did not get word of it as they were not attacked. The whole town was warned of the placing of the charges by the group. An explosion occurred at about 06.15 and the windows of many houses in the city were broken. Nevertheless, the French civilians all came out and cheered the OGs wildly.

On 14 August, having completed the destruction of the bridge at St Léonard, the group moved out. They later learned that 2,000 Germans were just moving out of Limoges when the bridge was blown. This naturally delayed their advance. In addition, the Maquis blocked the roads they were using and held them in Limoges. After the group had left St Léonard, 200 Germans moved into the city and warned the Maquis that if the bridge were blown again, the whole town would be burned.

At this point the OGs began to lay plans to take the German garrison at Limoges. They requested air support from London and received confirmation. However, twenty-four hours before the attack was to begin, Staunton received a message from the commanding general of the German forces at Limoges saying he would like to arrange surrender terms. Consequently, Staunton, Captain Brown and Captain Vigny of the Jedburgh team held a conference with him and complete surrender terms were arranged. While arrangements were being made, however, the Germans received orders to move at any cost. The general returned to the garrison after the meeting and was never heard from again.

The Germans retreated by a road that had been left unguarded. However, the Maquis attacked the group and captured 300 Germans. It was feared that another attack might be forthcoming at Limoges, so the group blasted the national highway about 35 kilometres south of

Limoges. The local population assisted them in making a tank ditch across the road. They still had a supply of mines so the surrounding terrain was mined and trees were cut down and booby-trapped. All the side roads were booby-trapped too. A railway bridge was blown to block another road. This then protected Limoges from troops moving from the south and there was no indication of troops from the north. Three days were spent in fortifying the city in this manner.

'Hamlet' decided to move with the group to Limoges now. They arrived in time to celebrate the city's liberation. There were 5,000 Maquis in this area equipped with one Bren gun for every four men. They were believed to be the best-armed Maquis in the whole of France. The Germans were heading north from Bordeaux attempting to escape by cutting north of Le Blanc. They succeeded in retaking Châteauroux from the FFI at this time. So the group decided to move to Chazelle and do what they could to hinder this movement. For this they obtained two German fuel trucks and a good supply of petrol. Heretofore, they had been using old French trucks, which had proved very unsatisfactory.

Upon arriving at Chazelle, they found the local Maquis bitter and unwelcoming. This group had never received any supplies from the Allies, which accounted for this feeling. The supplies they had were obtained from containers dropped in the areas evidently by mistake. Hamlet's group remained at Chazelle for two days trying to locate the Germans. When reports were received from various cities of the presence of Germans they would set out, but wherever they went they found no Germans at all. It was evident from this that Maquis intelligence in this area was not always accurate.

Finally, on 27 August, the group moved to La Rochefoucauld and set out for the national highway again. They encountered a great number of Germans including a group of horse-drawn artillery. Then arrived a ten-truck troop convoy and the group decided to attack. The whole convoy was fired on, the first truck being sprayed with gunfire. The Germans returned machine-gun fire and the group was forced to retreat. Another convoy arrived and a column of Germans were sent around to try to cut them off from the rear but the group got away unscathed.

The group remained in the area around the national highway and planned more ambush attacks; on one occasion they were assisted by an American fighter plane which strafed a road before being shot down. The group received orders from London to link up with another group led by Colonel Obolensky but by now the group was exhausted and food and supplies low. While the group was resting Colonel Obolensky received orders from London for the whole group to return. Immediately they proceeded to Le Blanc where they boarded a C–47 which brought them back to England on the morning of 10 September.

The Carpetbaggers had been dispatching their C–47 Dakota at every opportunity. On 9 August Lieutenant Colonel Boone had flown a C–47 to France with 1,800 lb of explosives and eight Joes. This was the first of the C–47 cargo missions, as the others were primarily to carry Joes. Captain Wilmer Stapel was also airborne this night, being instructed to fly to Annecy to pick up a group of evadees and escapees. He recalls:

As we went further into France and crossed the Loire river, the weather deteriorated rapidly. By the time we reached Lyons we were flying by instruments and the navigator informed me that we would have to climb as the Alps were ahead of us.

We climbed out of the clouds just as we skirted Lake Geneva. A quick 180° turn and by flying south we spotted Lake Annecy and the landing site. It was raining very hard and the field was part cut hay and part loose dirt. We touched down and noticed a large tree coming up fast on our landing roll. I attempted to ground loop the airplane but the field was so soggy and slippery that all I could manage was a crab. It was enough to stop us colliding with the tree. After taxi-ing over to where the ground troops guided us, the airplane engines were shut down and the door was opened for unloading the supplies. A loud voice boomed out, 'Hi Willie, you old SOB, what the hell are you doing here?' It was Johnny Mead.

After a brief visit to the town, escorted by Mead, we went back to the aircraft where the evadees and escapees were waiting for their ride to freedom. There were more personnel (thirty) than there were seats and seatbelts and we were at high altitude with a poor field for take-off! I was definitely going to be overloaded if I chose to take them all in one trip. I just couldn't say no to any of them. We all climbed aboard and taxied to the edge of the field for take-off. I lined up with the hypotenuse of the field, revved up the engines and released the brakes. It seemed forever before we started to pick up speed and just about then we hit the dirt spot on the field. We just dropped half flaps, said a prayer and managed to get airborne. As we lifted off, a roar of 'hoorays' echoed throughout the cockpit. The guys were elated to say the least to be on their way back to England. We all arrived back at Harrington, safe and sound.

Meanwhile, operations involving Liberators continued. They were used on the nights of 16/17 and 17/18 August, when thirty-three B–24s were despatched, to deliver 'Lindsey', a group of nineteen men, led by 1/Lieutenant Pierce Earl and 2/Lieutenant James C. Larson, and their bazookas, brens, mortars and ammunition, to France for an initial mission of seizing and holding a hydroelectric plant at La Truyère. This plant was a large switching station which controlled and dispatched electrical current generated from three large dams in the immediate vicinity. This system supplied all of southern France with electric power, which enabled the American and other Allied forces to maintain their communication and make for a more complete and rapid victory in France. Only one Liberator got over the target on 16/17 August, and five men were dropped. Earl and thirteen other men returned because no reception was observed. The next night three Liberators got over the target and fifteen men were dropped at 02.10 hours on the morning of 18 August at Sauvat. Earl broke his ankle in the jump, one of his sergeants broke his shoulder and another strained his back. Despite these, and other minor injuries among the Group, 'Lindsey' set out to take the hydroelectric plant. The group showed themselves at various times so that the Germans would know Americans were in the vicinity. The men wore brassards on their left arms, which could be easily distinguished by the Germans through field glasses. This action was necessary because the Germans were very hesitant about surrendering to the Maquis, who had surrounded a number of Germans in a château in the vicinity of Brommat. The Maquis told the Germans that Americans were in the area and that they should surrender to them by 16.30 hours. They did, but not before they had destroyed their weapons and stocks of ammunition and equipment. About 150 Germans surrendered to Earl's men.

Following this success, 'Lindsey' encountered the enemy fourteen times. Working in conjunction with small bands of the FFI, they harassed the Germans by guerrilla warfare for four weeks. They captured about 300 prisoners and killed numerous others, although always outnumbered by the enemy. On one occasion they captured a complete German hospital unit of 150 men and thirteen vehicles. They also engaged 800 Germans, an advance party of the 20,000 which surrendered at Orléans, and stopped them from getting across the Loire to the escape route through Belfort. 'Lindsey' reported to their Paris headquarters on 17 September and returned to Harrington in a Dakota on the 21st.

An urgent call was received from the Maquis in the Haute-Vienne for the dispatch of a doctor. 'Salesman 21-A', the operation to deliver Captain Fred B. Agee, codenamed 'Antagonist', was scheduled for the night of 13/14 August. Agee and over 50 packages, some containing medical supplies, were loaded aboard a Halifax at Tempsford. The bomber flew to its drop zone at Framboise and Agee parachuted into the night. Out went the packages, including three belonging to Operation 'Percy Pink', which were dropped in error. (Eight men in the 13-strong 'Percy Pink' group parachuted into the Dordogne on the night of the 11/12 August to assist the local Maquis). Agee joined 'Gerbert' who had a headquarters with 'Hamlet' in the Château de la Vialle near Croisille. They were camped in a nearby woods with approximately 25 SAS troops, two Jedburgh teams and 'Faust', all of whom were working under 'Hamlet'. It was decided that during any major 'crisis' with the Germans, Agee would go with the Maquis to a neighbouring village where they were setting up a small hospital in a house and operate there. The north of the department was covered surgically by Major McKenzie, the south by a Russian team. Surgeons were scarce in the Haute-Vienne, but there was adequate care from other doctors.

Agee spent the rest of the week on missions with Gerbert and SAS. They blew a section of the national highway about 35 kilometres south of Limoges, felled trees on a road approaching from both directions and booby-trapped the trees. Possible bypasses were then mined. An approach on the highway from Limoges to St Léonard was also blown. On 21 August General Gleiniger, commanding the German garrison of about 50 troops at Limoges, surrendered to a committee headed by 'Hamlet'. Agee and 'Virgile', a Canadian captain, entered Limoges that evening to supervise the fulfilling of the terms of surrender, 'Gerbert', 'Salesman' and SAS troops remaining in reserve in case of miscarriage of plans until Thursday when they entered Limoges.

On the afternoon of the 27th the Maquis, Salesman troops and the SAS harassed and ambushed small units of German troops in an area west of Limoges. That same day Agee received a wound in the thigh by a Frenchman who accidentally discharged his pistol.

Agee was evacuated to Harrington by Dakota on 3 September and he proceeded to London. (Two more C–47s had been assigned to the Carpetbaggers and on the night of 25/26 August the group had flown its first full-scale Dakota operation.)

The C–47s enabled crews to carry two and three-inch mortars, belted ammunition for Vickers machine-guns, mortar smoke ammunition, Bren guns and ammunition, PIAT guns and shells, bazookas, grenades, rifles, rockets, and even two jeeps. Accompanying each mission were from one to nine Joes, both going in and coming out. During Dakota operations throughout August–September, the C–47s carried a total of seventy-six Joes in and ferried 213 passengers out. They operated out of twelve different landing fields in newly liberated territory and transported approximately 104,000 lbs of badly needed arms and ammunition. Throughout all these missions, thirty-five of which were flown up to and including 18 September, not one enemy aircraft or other enemy activity was experienced. Although all the fields were without facilities and other aids for landing operations, the reception committees did an excellent job, under the circumstances, and considering the equipment available.

An ironic item was reported by Captain Wilmer Stapel, when he returned from a mission on the night of 27/28 August. He reported that on that very afternoon, P–38 Lightnings had strafed a field that he was landing on and that they did a good job of it. Stapel's last mission in a C–47 was flown on the night of 5 September.

When I arrived at the landing site there was a bit of confusion as to what direction the ground party wanted us to land. The navigator had given me the wind coming from the south. The flares on the ground indicated a landing to the north. I elected to land to the north. I realized that we were landing down-wind and seconds after touchdown, a hedgerow appeared in my path. It brought us to a sudden stop. The aircraft almost nosed over and the propellers dug into the ground. The tail came up and for one brief second it just hung there before dropping back to its normal resting position.

We quickly gathered all the classified material and equipment from the aircraft and got out. The Maquis were telling us that the Boche were about 20 kilometres from our landing site. Unknown until I saw it, another C–47 came in about that time for a landing. Colonel McManus was at the controls. There were two aircraft assigned to the mission and I was fortunate enough to be the first in, considering the circumstances my crew were in. We all crawled aboard the Colonel's flight and proceeded to log combat passenger time on the trip back to Harrington. There were many questions to be answered by me as to what happened that night. My explanations were accepted by high headquarters.

Maintenance crews from Harrington, complete with repair equipment, were immediately despatched to France and the Dakota was repaired on the spot. The engines were replaced and the C–47 returned to Harrington on 11 September, only five days later.

In almost every instance the C–47 pilots and crews reported that field lights and receptions were excellent, indicating the eagerness of the committees to receive the supplies and equipment. At nearly every field, a request for petrol was made as each group was in great need of fuel. At one place, the committee requested petrol which they desperately needed because 'The Germans were only 50 miles away and petrol was needed to go after them!'

It will be realized that August proved a very busy month for the Carpetbaggers, who flew a record total of 442 missions. Some 342 of these were successfully completed. The Carpetbaggers dropped over 700 tons of supplies to Resistance groups and 227 agents were ferried across the Channel at a cost of two Liberators. From 19 to 24 August a low pressure system gathered over the British Isles and Western Europe and prevented any Carpetbagger missions from being flown. During the five days of stand down it was reported that the Rumanians wished to seek peace. The news on 23 August that Paris had been liberated by French Forces of the Interior owed much to the support missions flown by the Carpetbaggers and other clandestine units over the preceding eight months. Then, on 25 August, Harrington waved farewell to its commanding officer, Colonel Clifford J. Heflin, who was leaving for a new appointment at the B–29 training facility at Wendover Field, Utah. His new role would involve training the aircrews and the support personnel who would ultimately drop the atomic bombs on Japan. His popular deputy, Lieutenant Colonel Robert W. Fish, assumed command of the Carpetbaggers.

12

FINAL DAYS AT HARRINGTON

Carpetbagger operations in September got off to a bad start when on the night of 1/2 September, of the forty-four Liberators dispatched, thirteen were forced to abort. Results were better on the night of 3/4 September when ten Liberators were used to transport Operational Group 'Christopher', with a complement of 55 men, including 32 members of the NORSO group, Jedburgh team 'Desmond', and all supplies, to Yonne, France. Christopher's primary mission after being dropped near Poitiers in the Vienne départment was to slow down and harass enemy columns moving from the south-west and the Bordeaux area towards Poitiers and Châteauroux. From here the Germans intended to slip through the gap between the Allied armies of the North and South via Dijon to the Belfort gap leading into Germany.

Space had to be found for the Group's twenty-four M–1 rifles, 4 Bren guns, 56 rucksacks, Light Machine-Gun, spares and 20 chests of ammunition for the gun, 500 prepared charges, 170 grenades, 56 gas masks, 11 boxes of ammunition, a box of Gammon grenades, 4 radios, 20 cans of fuel, 2 Very pistols and 14 TSMG pouches, filled. Holsworth's B–24 contained Christopher's commanding officer, Lieutenant Hjeltness, and five of his group. They were followed by B–24s flown by Jackobson, Cunningham, Elmer M. Heaberlin (which contained Lieutenant Apgar, the second in command), Paul Karr, J.W. Fox, Bill Dillon, Bernard A. Sandberg, Curran and John J. Oling. The first seven B–24s carried six soldiers, their rucksacks and packages; Sandberg and Curran's B–24s each carried cargoes of five men and their supplies; and Oling's B–24 carried five soldiers and their rucksacks and the Jedburgh team. Hjeltness and his fellow officers each carried 50,000 French francs and $50, while each enlisted man carried 20,000 French francs and $50. The first Liberator dropped its load at about 23.15 hours, the last, about 01.30 in the early hours of 2 September. Nine of the B–24s dropped on the regular field but after waiting in vain for two hours for Oling's

Liberator to show up, the group went into the village of Avot. (Oling dropped on the auxiliary field.)

The well-organized reception committee was arranged by the Maquis. There were two casualties on the drop. Lieutenant Sather chipped a bone in his ankle and T/Sgt Saunders wrenched his knee. Both men were taken to Avot and cared for by the Maquis medical unit. Of the 120 containers dropped, only six were damaged. All four W/T sets were recovered in working condition. One was given to the Jedburgh team, one to the Maquis, and the other two were used by the group itself. All ten Liberators, meanwhile, returned safely to Harrington and as Christopher got their bearings, further Carpetbagger missions were planned to support them. Large numbers of aircraft were now available to the Carpetbaggers and maintenance crews were working around the clock. On 4/5 September forty Liberators and four C–47s were dispatched. A record thirty-nine successful sorties resulted. The following night, 5/6 September, forty-six B–24s were dispatched, and on the night of 7/8 September a record forty sorties were flown.

On this last date missions were marred by a fatal accident. Lieutenant Lawrence Berkoff and his crew in the 856th Squadron had just taken off from Harrington when Sergeant Alphonse J. Rinz, engineer, noticed that the No. 2 engine was trailing a great length of flame from its exhaust. Not wanting to abort, unless it was absolutely necessary, Berkoff circled the field several times until finally, the flames died and decreased to just a small tongue of flame emerging from the flame damper. After conferring with Rinz, Berkoff decided to pick up course and head for their target. The Liberator flew on over southern England, its No. 2 engine watched all the way by a wary Rinz. He was still not satisfied with its performance. Although the flame damper was preventing the flame from emerging outside the trail exhaust, fumes were still igniting within the exhaust itself giving off a red glow which would make a perfect beacon for enemy night-fighters.

Nearing the south coast, Rinz informed Berkoff that to proceed would be folly under the circumstances and the pilot agreed to turn back. Berkoff brought the Liberator around in a 180° turn and as the aircraft righted itself the oil pressure and mercury pressure gauges on No. 1 engine began dropping alarmingly. Rinz was alerted over the interphone. As he looked at his gauges number one engine stopped cold. Berkoff immediately feathered the propeller on No. 1 engine. At the same time No. 2 engine decided to eject flame again and run very roughly. With one engine dead and the other ineffectual, the B–24 began to lose height quickly. The drag of the two engines caused the ship to turn over onto its side and whenever Berkoff would bring the wing up to level position, which was done several times after tremendous struggling with the controls by both pilots, the ship would nose down and then again the left wing would drop. After repeating the struggle to keep the aircraft on an even keel, it became evident that further flight was impossible and Berkoff gave the order to bale out.

The Liberator had plummeted 1,500 ft to 3,500 ft as the first parachute opened and drifted below. Rinz remained on board to help Berkoff, who was still fighting the controls, while the crew baled out. When the Liberator was down to 1,000 ft, Rinz made his way to the catwalk in the bomb bay. He yelled to Berkoff, 'Come on, let's get the hell out!' Berkoff did not appear to hear, so Rinz yelled again. When he looked back into the cockpit he could still see Berkoff fighting the controls. By this time, Rinz could see the ground and the aircraft suddenly rolled over on its side. Rinz reached overhead and grasping the side of the bomb bay, swung himself out into space. The B–24 continued over into a spin and dived straight down, crashing just below Rinz. The blast from the crashing aircraft and the resultant explosion caught into Rinz's 'chute and blew him upwards. When the force of the blast had subsided, Rinz floated down again, very near the burning ship. As he descended, he narrowly missing being sucked into the flames by the vacuum caused by the blazing wreckage. Berkoff was killed instantly, still at the controls of his aircraft.

In mid-September aircrews of the American and RAF secret squadrons, as well as bomber crews of the 8th Air Force, had to call upon all their experience to fly mercy drops to beleaguered Poles in the ruins of Warsaw. The Polish capital was cut off from the outside world with the Germans on one side and the Russians on the other. Russia had requested General Bor to rise against the German occupiers but had then stood by while the gallant Polish Home Army was gradually being annihilated. Allied airmen in RAF squadrons operating from Italy supplied the Poles in August but then operations had ceased because of the danger to crews. Operations were re-started after Polish protests but it was not until early September that the Russians finally agreed to co-operate and allow Fortresses of the Eighth Air Force to fly on to Russia after the drops.

An attempt by B–17s of the Eighth Air Force to reach Warsaw on 15 September was aborted because of bad weather and it was not until three days later that the 13th Wing was able to fly all the way. Colonel Karl Truesdell of the 95th Bomb Group led the B–17s over Warsaw and the supply drop was made from between 13,000 and 18,000 ft amid limited but accurate flak. The strong American fighter escort was unable to prevent the Luftwaffe attacking the 390th Bomb Group, which was flying as the low group, on the dropping run. One Fortress was shot down and another landed at Brest-Litovsk. However, the remaining aircraft succeeded in reaching their shuttle bases at Mirgorod and Poltava. On 19 September they took off again for now familiar return flight via Italy and France but this time without bombing because all French territory had been overrun.

Meanwhile, on 14 September the Carpetbaggers could afford to dispatch their Liberators in the hours of daylight. Four B–24s took off from Harrington at 09.00 hours for a target in France. They dropped their loads successfully and returned to base at 14.30 hours. However, two days later, with the Allied armies mopping up much of France, the decision was taken to wind up the Carpetbagger project. The OSS detachment received orders to begin leaving Harrington.

On the night of 16/17 September, intended to be the last night of Carpetbagger operations, the 492nd dispatched 32 Liberators and a C–47 to France. One B–24, in the 858th Squadron, flown by Lieutenant James M. McLaughlin and crew, who were on their 35th and final mission, failed to return from their sortie. The weather was very bad and McLaughlin was forced to fly on instruments over the Channel and into France. George F. Bradbury, navigator, called ten minutes to the Initial Point and McLaughlin climbed the aircraft to 4,500 ft over Chartres. At that moment a tremendous flak barrage exploded around them. Tragically, it was fired by Battery A, 115th AA gun Battalion of the US Army which had only just moved into the area that morning. Their orders were to fire at any aircraft not responding with IFF signals. Unfortunately, Carpetbagger crews had orders not to use IFF over the continent.* The Liberator's control surfaces were shot away and the B–24 fell off to the right in a sickening dive. McLaughlin knew that it was hopeless and pressed the bale-out bell. His co-pilot, Carl E. Lee, sat motionless in his seat. Getting no response from him, McLaughlin proceeded to evacuate the aircraft, following close on the heels of Henry Stee, radio operator. The Liberator crashed between

---

* *Carpetbaggers: America's Secret War in Europe* Ben Parnell (Eakin Press, 1987)

Lebeville and Charmes in the Vosges. McLaughlin landed in a tree and next day made contact with soldiers of the US 313th Regimental Headquarters of the 79th Infantry Division. They took him to the crashed Liberator where Lee, Lieutenant Skwara and Sergeants DeVries and Brewer had perished in the crash.

McLaughlin's Liberator was the last 801/492nd Bomb Group B–24 loss while attached to the Carpetbagger project. On 22 September General Joseph Pierre Koenig, commander of the French Forces of the Interior, awarded the *Croix de Guerre* to Colonel Heflin, Lieutenant-Colonel Fish and many of the staff officers and men, at a formal ceremony at Harrington attended by Lieutenant-General Jimmy Doolittle, Major-General Earle Partridge and Brigadier-General Sandford.

With most of France overrun the Maquisards' war against German occupation was almost over. As a result the Allied chiefs of staff reasoned that relatively few Carpetbagger missions would now be needed. The Allied armies were marching relentlessly towards Germany and required petrol for their motorized columns of tanks and transport. To maintain the Allied push through France during late August and early September, the 8th began flying in fuel and supplies to the troops. The bulk of the operation was completed using Liberators, whose cavernous fuselages were ideal for the task, but some Fortresses were also used.

On 28 August three Liberator groups in the Second Bomb Division had been converted to a transportation role and began 'trucking' missions, as they were called. These missions continued until 9 September but when the Allies launched Operation 'Market Garden', using British and American airborne divisions against Dutch towns on the Rhine in mid-September, the Liberators were once again called upon to supplement the troop carriers, which on their own could not carry sufficient supplies.

British troops landed at Arnhem and American forces at Eindhoven and Nijmegen in an attempt to secure a foothold on the east bank of the Rhine. It was planned to cut off the German Army in the Belgian sector and save the bridges and the port of Antwerp for the advancing ground forces. It was also hoped that the operation would draw the Germans away from Aachen. For an operation of this size, the Liberators' involvement was crucial. Fuel for the Allied armour and transport was in short supply. Trucking operations began on 12 September, in which just over 13,000 gallons of fuel was delivered to units in France.

The formerly highly specialized Carpetbagger group took part in the first full-scale trucking operations, which began on 18 September, as Bill Dillon recalls:

> We had to put in some trucking missions. Droppable tanks were installed in and over the bomb bays and back where the Joe holes were. They were filled full of avi-octane gasoline. Even the wing tanks in the 'Baker Two Dozen' were used. We were a flying gas tank! The fumes were very explosive and I believe it was more hazardous than flying Carpetbagger missions over the continent. Fortunately, none of our Libs was lost on trucking missions, which finished on 30 September.

Several crew-members also finished their operational tours with the Carpetbaggers. On completion of the Trucking missions Wilmer Stapel decided he had had enough of combat flying and since he had volunteered for the C–47 missions he was able to return to the USA. Bill Dillon's crew also finished their tour in the autumn of 1944. It was an opportunity to finally let off steam, as Dillon recalls: 'Everyone would save their colours of the day flares for the final mission. Coming in over Harrington we buzzed the airfield and the crew would fire them off. It looked like the Fourth of July. 'Course this was fun for the crew but it was frowned on by everyone else.'

Some Jedburgh teams were also making their last drops. Sergeant Maurice Whittle, a Jedburgh operative who had joined SOE in 1943 as a morse instructor, made his final drop, to the Vesoul area in the Vosges, on the night of 9/10 September 1944:

> We were dropped from a Stirling aircraft in a thickly wooded area near the village of Pont du Bois. Our reception committee was organized by the SAS jeeping operation group, 'Wallace', along with local Resistance members. At the time some eighty containers, four jeeps and two or three personnel were also dropped from four Halifax aircraft. Our main objective was to reach and contact the 1st Regiment de France, made up of Vichy French troops who had deserted from German control and who were believed to be in the area of Bussières, some 50 kilometres to the south-west, the aim being to supply them with arms and equipment. This objective was unfortunately nullified by our inability to reach the area for several days due to the presence of strong German forces. On arrival there,

it was discovered that, following a skirmish with German forces, they had disbanded and dispersed.

As a consequence our immediate task was the collection of information through contact with various Maquis groups about enemy formations and positions for communications to London and the advancing Allied forces. This information was obtained by Maquis reconnaissance patrols, interrogation of captured German prisoners and, fortuitously, the capture of some military maps. One showed the German order of battle along the River Seine. Details were wirelessed to London and the map was taken by Maquis couriers to the nearest advancing Allied unit. After a period of about eight days the team finally established contact with a French armoured unit and transferred all known information to the French Command HQ. We were given instructions to return to London, where we arrived on 21 September.

The next day the 'Christopher' Group arrived back in England.

On 21 September the Carpetbaggers were formally relieved from 8th Air Force Composite Command and assigned to 8th Air Force Fighter Command. At Harrington, only the 856th Squadron was officially retained for Carpetbagger operations. So, it seemed that the Carpetbaggers' clandestine war was largely at an end. At first it was intended that the Carpetbaggers be converted to B–17s for day bombing. Carpetbagger units abroad might also be boosted by an influx of experienced Carpetbagger personnel.

Late in November 1944, plans had been made for members of the 492nd Bomb Group, accompanied by representatives of OSS, to fly to New Delhi, India, to investigate the possibilities and discuss with local OSS officials the feasibility of conducting Carpetbagger operations in the CBI (China–Burma–India) Theatre. On 29 November *Playmate*, piloted by Major Bestow 'Rudy' Rudolph of the 858th Squadron, with crew-members from the 856th Squadron, taxied out from Harrington for the long flight to India. *Playmate* had been selected for the operation because it was one of the oldest Liberators in the group, having flown 89 Carpetbagger missions, and could therefore demonstrate the modifications and general appearance of a typical Carpetbagger aircraft. *Playmate* was actually the second of Rudolph's B–24s to bear the name. (The first *Playmate* had been shot up and had crash-landed at Land's End following an anti-submarine patrol by another crew in 1943.) Rudolph took off without incident and flew to Bovingdon where he was to pick up Lieutenant-Colonels Gable and Chandler of the London OSS, who were going to India to conduct negotiations. *Playmate* then flew on to Naples and then Cairo.

At an OSS headquarters in New Delhi, sessions were held with other members of the OSS to determine the need and practicability of operations in the CBI. The party from England inspected bases and available facilities in North Burma, Calcutta and Dinjan, India in order to obtain a clear all-round picture of the local operations and to determine whether or not the operations could be effectively conducted. Meanwhile, Gable and Chandler spent five days in China before returning to New Delhi. Their work done, Rudolph and his crew departed for England again on 17 January 1945. They encountered exellent flying weather all along the return route and completed the last leg of their 25,000 mile round trip safely.

Conditions in a war zone can change rapidly and during Rudolph's absence from Europe British and American policy had been overtaken by events. On 16 December, von Rundstedt had launched a German Panzer thrust on a wide front with the main axis through the hilly country of the Ardennes. Allied air forces were grounded by bad weather in England and the thrust, aimed at a weak point in the American lines, opened up a salient in the Allied front which became known as 'The Bulge'. It was evident that the war in Europe would not be over by Christmas 1944.

The world was shocked, both by the news of the breakthrough in the Ardennes, and then by the loss of one of the greatest American band leaders of all time. An official news communiqué announced that Glenn Miller was missing. On 15 December he and fellow passenger Colonel Norman Baessell, the Executive Officer at Milton Ernest Hall, had taken off from RAF Twinwoods for a flight to Villacoublay in a Norseman piloted by Flight Officer John Morgan. Miller was *en route* to entertain troops in Paris. Now all three men were missing, presumed killed. Their disappearance is still shrouded in mystery.

13

Spring Will Be a Little Late This Year

Although Miller's demise was a sad loss to music and men and women in the forces and in civilian life, the world barely had time to dwell on his disappearance. Von Rundstedt continued to hold sway, temporarily, in the Ardennes and everyone just had to get on with fighting his or her particular war.

At Harrington on 17 December Colonel Hudson H. Upham arrived to assume command of the 492nd Bomb Group. Upham had spent some years at the military academy at West Point and therefore had no prior combat experience. He was assigned to the Carpetbaggers to accumulate such experience. However, there was little left, on paper at least, for Upham to take charge of.

Two days before his appointment, orders had been received for the 859th Squadron and its CO, Colonel Nate McManus, to be sent on detached service with the 15th Air Force at Brindisi, Italy. In the Mediterranean Theatre McManus's crews formed the second of two squadrons of the 2641 Special Group which carried out Carpetbagger-type operations in support of OSS over northern Italy, Greece and Yugoslavia until the end of the war in Europe.

The 857th and 858th Squadrons were no longer engaged in Carpetbagger work. They had been detached to fly high altitude night bombing missions with 100 Group RAF Bomber Command. The transition had not been easy because the Liberators were unsuitable for night bombing, having been extensively modified for Carpetbagger work. Enough H2X radar-equipped aircraft were needed to equip one squadron so in the end, B–24s had been acquired from bomb groups, such as the 486th Bomb Group at Sudbury, Suffolk, which had re-equipped with B–17s in July 1944.

Missions had begun on 24 December 1944, when eighteen black B–24s were dispatched, in daylight, to coastal defences around Bordeaux. The 492nd returned to the area on the night of 28/29 December when seven B–24s from a force of sixteen dispatched, successfully bombed De La Colibre using H2X. Another notable success was achieved on the night of 4/5 January 1945 when ten B–24s dispatched by the 492nd Bomb Group, again using H2X, successfully bombed the Coubre coastal battery near Bordeaux.

On 20 February 1945, following a period of training with 100 Group, RAF Bomber Command, night bombing missions were resumed with a visit to Neustadt. The RAF issued the orders for each raid, which were flown as a diversion for the actual raids flown by Lancasters of Bomber Command. Although the Liberators were accompanied by RAF night-fighters, there were losses caused by enemy action and the elements. Of six missions flown that month, two Liberators were left on the continent and two battle-damaged B–24s force-landed in England.

Meanwhile, the 856th Squadron had continued to fly Carpetbagger missions in support of OSS. Replacement crews had continued to arrive at Harrington and in January 1945 Douglas D. Walker joined the Carpetbaggers.

After training at Gowen Field, our group of aircrews were shipped to the Boston port of embarkation and we sailed for England. In January 1945 four of the aircrews were assigned to Harrington, including mine, Lieutenant Roger B. McCormick's crew. Upon arrival in England my crew was re-assigned to the CBI Theatre. We drew straws to see who would remain behind at Harrington. I drew the short straw and was ordered to report to Lieutenant Swarts' crew as a Dispatcher. This crew was already a veteran one, with twenty-three Carpetbagger missions under their belt. Their Liberator was also a veteran but it was a tough, durable airplane, aptly named for Carpetbagger operations: *Strange Cargo*.

The first mission Walker made with his new crew involved dropping supplies to the Danish Underground. Walker recalls:

I was a stranger to the rest of the aircrew. This, coupled with the fact that it was my first mission, wasn't very reassuring to me! I didn't know what to expect and, because it wasn't 'macho', I hesitated to ask the other crew-members what we might face!

Looking out of the waist window, I peered into the murky darkness, occasionally getting a dim glimpse of whitecaps on the North Sea below. I shivered. It was very cold in the unheated B–24 bomber. I didn't relish the thought that if we had to ditch in that tossing sea as a result of enemy action, we'd probably freeze to death in a matter of minutes! The co-pilot told me prior to the flight that we would be approaching Denmark at an altitude of 500 ft in order to come in under the Nazi radar and we would then fly at only 1,500 ft all the way across Denmark to our drop zone. As we crossed the coast line, my nervousness increased. I was stationed in the waist of the aircraft all alone and I felt cut off from the rest of the crew. I wondered if the Nazi anti-aircraft gunners would open up on us or if a night-fighter would jump us!

As I looked out of the window at the ground below, the moon suddenly appeared. I could see that we were over a small village. I had a grandstand seat as we flew over streets and houses at 500 ft altitude, so close, I felt as if we were at treetop level. The town was in a total wartime blackout, but I could make out individual houses. It was after midnight and the village looked like a ghost town as it slid by under us. Suddenly, the blackout was shattered by a bright light coming from a house up ahead. As we drew abreast, I saw that it was coming from an upstairs window! The light was flashing on and off rapidly, as if someone were pulling a shade up and down. I suddenly realized what it was. As I looked back, I counted the flashes and their duration – three short and one long – three short and one long! It was the international morse code for the letter 'V'. Of course! The Dane was flashing the 'V for Victory' signal to us! I looked back unbelievingly. That someone, in a hamlet occupied by Nazis, would brave imprisonment or death to cheer us on our way by flashing us the 'V for Victory' sign as we flew over, was remarkable! I admired that person's courage!

We flew on to our drop zone. Spotting the fiery cross lit by our Danish Resistance forces to guide us in, we worked speedily to drop the loaded containers from the bomb bay, as well as large boxes and bales we had to push out of the Joe Hole in the waist of the Liberator.

We flew back to England uneventfully and landed just before sunrise. After de-briefing by S–2, we headed for our bunks and blessed sleep. Just before I dozed off, I thought about that welcome from a brave Dane on my first Carpetbagger mission. I felt embarrassed at my nervousness when I thought of his courage and realized that he, or she, faced danger every day from the Nazi invaders, while I faced it only a few nights each week! I also felt a warm feeling that our efforts to help the Danes overthrow their Nazi oppressors were obviously appreciated.

In January 1945 Swarts' crew carried a Joe. Walker recalls:

I was in the waist of the Liberator preparing for the mission while I awaited the arrival of the Joe. The generator was running, so I had a dim light to work by. I looked up as the Joe stepped into the aircraft. I nodded to him, not paying too much attention, as I was busy arranging the static lines. An OSS colonel stepped in behind the Joe and walked over to me. 'Sergeant,' he said, 'take good care of your Joe tonight – *she* is a special cargo!' I turned to look and she had removed her helmet, unveiling a cascade of blonde hair down to her shoulders! I smiled at her in welcome and told the colonel, 'Don't worry, we'll deliver her in good condition.'

He then told me that she understood only French and German and that her mother and father in France had been killed by the Nazis – the reason she had volunteered to be dropped into Germany. Seems we were dropping her into the Bavarian Alps region to determine if Hitler was really setting up a 'last ditch' stronghold in the so-called mountain redoubt, to hold out against the Allied armies.

After we took off, I made her as comfortable as I could – as comfortable as could be managed in a drafty, unheated bomber on a cold night in January. With my fractured French and her equally disjoined English, it was difficult, but we managed to communicate enough so that I could at least keep her mind occupied until the time came for her to jump into Germany. I'll never forget the sight of that pretty, brave girl, as she sat in the Joe Hole awaiting my signal to jump into the night! Here we were, flying in pitch blackness over enemy territory at 2,000 ft and she had the courage to parachute into enemy skies, not knowing what fate awaited her below! I wished her *'Bonne chance'* as she jumped and she answered with a smile – *'Merci mon ami'*.

The tail gunner, Ralph Schiller, reported that her parachute had opened and we flew back to England and safety – leaving a very brave woman behind in a very unsafe place! We never learned what happened to her, but we were all agreed that she was one of the bravest people we had ever met!

Lieutenant John L. Moore, a navigator in the Carpetbagger outfit, also fondly remembers one female Joe.*

> I briefed the crew, captained by Lieutenant West, which dropped her over south-central France. She was a little thing, 5 feet 2 or 3 inches and about 105 pounds. How many stone would that be? She looked about 19 years old but may have been 22 or so. Beautiful in spite of her 2/Lieutenant uniform. Some of the Joes wore British or American uniform so if caught in their 'chutes they would have a part of a cover story. I doubt if the uniforms helped them live long if caught. Hope she lived through the mess.

During the Second World War thousands of agents were parachuted into occupied Europe and many were female. SOE, for instance, dispatched 10,000 male and 3,200 female agents and operatives into Europe during the war.**

In February Lieutenant Swarts's crew returned to Denmark, to drop a load of munitions and supplies to the Danish underground forces. Douglas Walker recalls:

> As usual Swarts and our navigator had selected the best route possible to avoid all known anti-aircraft flak batteries *en route* to the target area. However, we inadvertently found an enemy flak battery *not* shown on one of the small islands off the west coast of Denmark.
>
> Our black Liberators were normally difficult to spot at night. However, this was clear, moonlight night and we had the misfortune to fly directly over an enemy anti-aircraft gun emplacement, located on one of the small islands off the west coast of Denmark. As was routine on these missions to Denmark and Norway, we approached from the North Sea at a very low altitude to come in under the enemy radar. Therefore, when we crossed that particular island, we presented an easy target to a gun battery on the ground, at 500 ft altitude! We later joked that the Nazi gunner had been cleaning his gun for Saturday inspection for five long years and when he saw us

---

* *Aviation In Northamptonshire* Michael L. Gibson (Northamptonshire Libraries, 1982)
** *A History of the British Secret Service* Richard Deacon (Muller)

silhouetted against the moon at 500 ft, he got off his first shot of WWII in anger and couldn't believe the easy, low-flying target we offered him!

In any event, I was looking out of the right waist window at the ground flashing by in the moonlight, when I saw the gun's muzzle flashes lighting up the darkness. At the same time, I heard metallic, banging sounds in the waist where I was standing. It dawned on me that we were being shot at! Before I could alert the pilot, I felt the plane shudder slightly and fell to the floor as Lieutenant Swarts threw the Liberator into evasive action.

We flew on to our drop zone and parachuted our cargo on the lighted signal of the underground forces and flew back to England without further incident. As soon as the Liberator came to a stop, we jumped out with our flashlights and found, to our amazement, a large hole, about the size of a basketball, just behind the number three engine. We couldn't understand how the shell missed our wing tanks and our hydraulic system! We felt very lucky that night! I jumped back into the plane to see what had caused the metallic banging noise in the waist and found several .50 calibre sized holes in the floor near where I was standing at the time and also found their companion holes in the roof where the bullets had exited. I felt doubly lucky at our near miss! We couldn't help feeling that it was a good thing for some of our 8th Air Force daylight bombing crews that the Nazis were wasting a crack gunner on some Danish backwater island – instead of stationing him around Berlin. On the other hand, who in his right mind would fly over Berlin at 500 ft!

At Harrington Walker and the other enlisted men in Swarts's crew shared their Nissen hut quarters with Lieutenant Hudson's enlisted crew members. Walker had first become friendly with the crew during training at Gowen Field in late 1944, and later at air gunnery school at Harlingen, Texas. At Harrington Walker and his radioman, Bernie Beverley, quickly resumed friendship with them and in between missions enjoyed many laughs together.

Walker recalls:

One evening in February 1945, Lieutenant Hudson came into our quarters with a big smile and handed out cigars to his crewmen and us. 'My wife has just presented me with a baby boy,' he yelled with pride. We all congratulated him. The following night, Hudson's crew and ours took off on a dual mission to drop munitions and supplies to the Norwegian underground forces. Over mountainous Norway we encountered severe fog. After flying on for about thirty minutes, trying various altitudes, the decision was made by Swarts to turn back. We couldn't possibly locate the drop zone, let alone fly low enough to drop our cargo in the dense fog. When we arrived back at Harrington, we waited for Lieutenant Hudson's Liberator to appear, to no avail. We haunted the Operations office for several days, with no answers forthcoming. We hoped for the best. Finally, we learned what had happened to them. The Norwegian Resistance group radioed that Hudson's Liberator had crashed into a mountain in the fog. The underground forces located the plane the next day and buried the eight crewmen in a cave to prevent the Nazis from finding their bodies. We all felt a tragic sense of loss at this bad news.

Two of the men on Lieutenant Hudson's crew were Angelo Santini, the tail gunner, and Jack Spyker, their dispatcher. About two weeks after this tragedy, we were awakened in our quarters about midnight by an apologetic voice asking, 'Angelo, are you here?' We put on the light to see Angelo Santini's brother, in England from a furlough from his infantry outfit in France. To our dismay, he hadn't heard about Angelo's death and had travelled to England for a happy reunion with his brother. He hadn't seen Angelo in over two years.

We broke the bad news to him and gave the grieving man a bed in which to spend the night in fitful sleep. He was naturally desolated by the devastating news we had to give him, but he departed the next day expressing gratitude that the Norwegian underground forces had given his brother a decent burial.

Several months later, when we were getting things ready to fly home, we had another saddened visitor. It was Jack Spyker's father. He had pulled some strings and managed to persuade the Government to allow him to fly to England. He talked with us about Jack's death and explained that he was on his way to Norway to claim Jack's body to return him to America for burial in the family plot. His grief was great. Jack was an only son.

Meanwhile, American night bombing had become a resounding failure. On average, only about a dozen H2X-equipped B–24s were dispatched at night from Harrington. In March 1945, when one B–24 was lost, only seven missions were flown before the Americans' participation came to an abrupt end on the 15th. The cessation in night bombing missions was caused by an order to resume Carpetbagger operations.

On 6 March 1945 General Jimmy Doolittle instructed that the 857th Bomb Squadron would be required for operation of the Scouting Force and Weather and Bomber Relay Flight of the 1st Air Division. The Squadron was disbanded and most of its crew were dispersed among the 856th and 858th Squadrons, now fully committed to Carpetbagger operations. Four C–47s were detached to the Carpetbaggers and were used during the evacuation of Allied PoWs and escaped internees from Switzerland from a central assembly point near Annecy.

In December 1944 several American internees had escaped from internment in Switzerland and travelled to Annecy. Among them was Forrest S. Clark, of the 44th Bomb Group who had been shot down over Augsburg on 12 April 1944. He recalls: 'When I came out, it was a very touchy situation because many Germans were still fighting and there was some confusion in the vicinity of the Swiss border between the Maquis, the Communists and the Allied forces as the countryside was liberated.' Clark and his fellow internees got through safely and were flown home by the Carpetbaggers.

Joseph A. Bodenhamer was on detached service at Annecy and Lyons as 856th Squadron adjutant from January to March 1945. He recalls:

> In mid-February an agreement to exchange military personnel with the Axis was made. The ratio was two German ground personnel to one Allied airman. Our detachment was in charge of a French train that went into Geneva on 17 February. We brought out some 500 Allied airmen and transported them to Marseilles to be flown to England and Italy.
>
> On 13 March the detachment headquarters at the Hotel *Beau Rivage* at Annecy was closed and evacuated as was the *Château Mariex* at Lyons. Our personnel were ordered to join the Dijon mission, our advanced base for flying agents into Germany. [see next chapter.] All but one of the C–47s were returned to the 8th Air Force when Bodenhamer returned to Harrington on 25 March 1945 to resume his duties as squadron adjutant.

With the Allies victorious in France and their armies poised to cross the German border, it seemed that clandestine missions would soon be made redundant. However, von Rundstedt's Ardennes offensive in December 1944 had caught the Allies off-balance and had lengthened the road to eventual victory.

Eisenhower and his senior officers knew that German resistance would stiffen once the Allies crossed into Germany and they therefore needed intelligence on enemy troop movements, morale, her new jet aircraft, 'wonder weapons' and the Redoubt in southern Bavaria, as well as information on the political and economic climate of the Third Reich. All this and other essential information would be needed for the commanders in the field.

This information had to come from within Germany itself. However, the Allies could not call upon resistance from within. The failed attempt on Hitler's life on 20 July 1944 had effectively removed hopes for a fresh impetus in the anti-Nazi movement in Germany. Secret agents and German nationals working for the Allied cause would have to be infiltrated into the Reich from Switzerland and dropped by aircraft operating from behind the Allied lines.

14

THE GERMAN CONNECTION

Plans for the infiltration of Germany by the Intelligence Services had been laid as far back as 1940. German émigrés to America had been carefully screened and a number of potential agents produced. After America's entry into the war more German potential agents were sifted from sources in Britain. In the autumn of 1944 from his offices at 72 Grosvenor Street, London, William J. Casey was placed in charge of Secret Intelligence in Europe with orders to send agents into the Reich. Although OSS would operate quite independently of their British counterparts, ironically, on 2 September 1944, the first German agent to be parachuted onto German soil was dropped from an RAF Halifax of Special Operations. (Starting on 31 December 1944 62 SOE agents were sent to Germany by Hudson aircraft and 161 Squadron's Stirlings, and those of 138 Squadron, are also known to have dropped another 33 agents, most of them into Germany, in the last five war months of 1945.)*

By early 1945 the OSS training programme was beginning to bear fruit and several anti-Nazi agents were ready to be parachuted into their homeland from American aircraft. However, German operations brought their own special problems, not least of which was the need to make air-to-ground contact with the agents once they had landed. In France agents had successfully used the long-established, but weighty, S-phone device. Even so, the agents constantly had to move from one safe house to another to throw the German mobile tracking vans off the scent. In Germany a large and heavy suitcase was highly suspicious and safe houses were few and far between. Another drawback was that the S-phone only had an effective range of up to 10,000 feet, well within reach of the German flak batteries.

---

* *Flight Most Secret* Gibb McCall (William Kimber, 1981)

At OSS, discussions on how to solve the problem of agent contact on the ground in Germany had been going on since late 1944. Stephen H. Simpson, a Texan scientist with the honorary rank of Lieutenant-Commander, promised that given the resources, he could come up with the answer. Simpson did not make the offer lightly. Before the war he had worked for RCA and had been involved in radio-transmission technology for over sixteen years. William J. Casey gave Simpson the go-ahead and within months he had developed, with DeWitt R. Goddard, a transmitter-receiver system so small that it could be easily carried by the agent in the field yet could transmit a radio beam so narrow that it was practically immune to detection by the German 'Gonio' (Radio-goniometry) vans. The new system was named 'Joan-Eleanor' after a major in the WACs and Goddard's wife respectively.

The Joan device, which beamed UHF transmissions and weighed only 4 lbs was carried by the agent. The Eleanor receiver set was housed in the host aircraft and used a wire recorder for capturing the ground-to-air conversations. This method was much simpler and safer than using coded radio messages and as much information could be passed clearly in one twenty-minute contact as could be passed in days by conventional radio. However, doubts were raised in some quarters about the risks involved in flying lone Liberator aircraft at low level deep into Germany. Apart from the threat of interception from enemy night-fighters using radar-controlled guns, the crew would also be highly vulnerable stooging around in the vicinity of the transmitting device. Whereas Simpson considered these risks well worth taking, the Eighth Air Force did not. Simpson was forced to think again.

If the Eleanor device could be modified then it could be installed in a fast, medium bomber. Simpson made the necessary modifications and he was steered in the direction of RAF Watton where the 25th Bomb Group were flying the much-valued de Havilland Mosquito PR XVI. This twin-engined British aircraft, built largely of wood, had a top speed of 400+ mph and a ceiling approaching 30,000 ft. The Mosquito was unequalled at night, save for the Heinkel 219 *Uhu* (Owl), of which the Germans fortunately had very few.

Three Mosquito squadrons were stationed at Watton. Together with B–17s and B–24s of the 652nd Heavy Weather Squadron, they fulfilled a myriad of tasks. The 654th or the 'Light Weather Squadron' flew 'Blue Stocking' or meteorological flights around Britain, the North Sea and the continent, while the 653th, or the 'Special Squadron', was involved in night photographic missions, code-named 'Joker'. During the summer of 1944 the 653rd had performed 'Dilly' daylight reconnaissance missions over the Pas de Calais in search of V–1 sites. Late in 1944 the Light Weather Squadron flew scouting missions ahead of the American bomber streams, and the Mosquito crews who had flown Blue Stocking missions proved best able to send accurate reports back about enemy defences and changes in the weather.

Originally, the Mosquito pilots had come from the 50th Fighter Squadron, equipped with P–38 Lightnings in Iceland, fighter groups in England and ferry squadrons in Scotland. Some had gained previous experience on the Mosquito in RAF and Canadian service.

Personnel in the 8th Combat Camera Squadron at Watton came from a more unusual source. Technical Sergeant Joe Capicotto was one of its original members. He recalls,*

> A volunteer outfit of eight officers and twenty-three enlisted men comprised the squadron. Some of us were combat crew members, others ground crews doing special photographic services. Most of us were AF technician graduates, or washed-out pilot cadets. Those on the combat crew volunteered for special units at Hal Roach Studios in Hollywood, California, where we trained alongside such movie stars making training films as Ronald Reagan (the Administrative Officer), Alan Ladd, Van Heflin, John Carroll and others.
>
> In Hollywood we were known as 1st Motion Picture Unit, then as the 3rd AAF Combat Camera Unit; then shipped to Watton. On temporary duty at 8th Air Force Headquarters, High Wycombe, we lived in tents, but we were never at 'Pinetree' for long periods. Once, I met Colonel Elliot Roosevelt, Commander of 325th Recon Wing, at Pinetree. Some of our secret mission orders were signed by him and it seemed that we were always on 'temporary duty' at various bases with the bomb groups. All our missions were secret and especially selected by Headquarters.

The 8th Combat Camera Squadron Mosquitos photographed actual bombing drops, then returned to the target area subsequently to photograph actual results. Night photography missions from Watton obtained evidence of enemy troop movements, erection of bridges and other military construction, and other events during the night –

* 3rd *SAD Newsletter*

since the Germans tried to conceal activity by avoiding such during daylight. These missions required two runs over the target, one to drop flares (one million candle power each) to light up the night, and another to obtain pictures of the area.

Like many high performance aircraft, the Mossie had certain characteristics which could trap the unwary. Accidents occurred as the American pilots learned to cope with the British aircraft's high landing speed and a tendency to swing on take-off, a new problem for them because they had been used to the P–38's contra-rotating propellers. The Mosquito pilot also had to remember to open the radiator shutters just prior to take-off, to prevent the engines overheating.

PR XVIs used a two-stage, two-speed supercharger that would cut in automatically at altitude. The superchargers were independent on each engine and a small difference in adjustment caused one to change gears hundreds of feet before the other. The resulting 'bang' and surge of power to one engine could wrest control from the unwary pilot and give the impression that the aircraft had been hit by flak.

The 25th Bomb Group at Watton (together with the 7th Photo Group) was part of the 325th Photographic Wing, commanded, since August 1944, by Colonel Elliot Roosevelt. Having a father who was the American President certainly offered many advantages. The 3rd SAD was soon forced to vacate the permanent buildings built for the RAF before the war, and move to less comfortable quarters at a still unfinished site, at Griston, on the south side of the airfield, so that the 25th could take up residence. The photographic group even boasted a Coca-Cola machine in their PX! Commander Simpson too would have the pick of the base. At Watton he shared a room with Captain Roy Ellis-Brown DFC, a 654th Squadron Mosquito pilot. Born of British parents in the USA, Ellis-Brown was a seasoned flier, having flown Stirling heavy bombers in the RAF before transferring to the USAAF.

At first Simpson was given two war-weary Mosquitos, one a former H2X aircraft, the other an ex-night photographic aircraft. These aircraft had the bomb bays fitted with an oxygen system and the compartment was adapted to accommodate the Joan-Eleanor device and an operative. The air force codenamed the operation 'Red Stocking'. It was hoped that German intelligence services would think these were weather missions similar to 'Blue Stocking'. On 22 October the first test flight was made with Steve Simpson and his equipment in the rear fuselage.*

Each Red Stocking Mosquito flew to an established rendezvous point at a pre-set time and commenced circling at 30,000 ft. If everything went according to plan, the Joan Eleanor operator could converse directly with the agent on the ground, recording the entire conversation on the wire recorder. A serious drawback developed if the Joe failed to transmit, either through enemy action of because his or her location had been compromised. In this situation it was impossible to arrange a new location. (For this reason only four Joan-Eleanor teams in Germany made contact, on 22 occasions.) They worked from Weilheim, Bavaria; Landshut, near Munich; a dairy near Regensburg; and from Berlin itself. Some forty-seven other Red Stocking sorties were flown without success.* Later, three more Mosquitos were made available for Joan Eleanor and agent-dropping missions. It was on the latter type of mission that one immediate problem manifested itself during an early training mission. A Joan-Eleanor operator, who took part in a training flight, had not learned to parachute from the small scuttle hole head first. Both engines on the Mosquito quit and the pilot was unable to restart them. The pilot shouted 'Bale out! Bale out!' but the agent became jammed. The pilot had used another escape outlet and left the agent stuck in the doomed aircraft. A few days later the Joan-Eleanor operator appeared back at Watton, knocked about a little, but alive. He had worked himself free of the aircraft and parachuted from a low altitude, falling into a haystack next to a British Women's Auxiliary Corps camp. The young ladies attended to his wounds and got him transportation back to Watton.

On 10 November 1944 the first agent, codenamed 'Bobbie', was dropped from a Mosquito, at Ulrum on the German border with Holland. Bobbie was Anton Schrader, a twenty-seven-year-old Dutch engineer, the son of a Netherlands Governor-General in the Dutch East Indies. An agent was given a line of 100 to 150 miles, anywhere along which he could use his radio. He was never to use it in the same place twice. He should broadcast from a 50 yard clearing in a forest. The spreading frequency waves would be quickly absorbed by trees and shrubbery. The BBC would broadcast an innocuous sentence at a pre-arranged time: 'Mary needs to talk to you Thursday the 10th.' This meant a mission would fly the

---

* Joan-Eleanor operations are detailed in *The Men Who Flew The Mosquito* Martin W. Bowman (PSL, 1995)

line on that date after midnight and call continuously. When the agent responded he was acknowledged and the aircraft continued for 20 miles. The point was then orbited at a radius of 20 miles as the Mosquito flew in a 40 mile circle above 30,000 ft. By using direction finders in the Mosquito, the contact man located the point from which the agent was transmitting. By using synchronized instruments the contact man in the plane could direct the pilot.

Simpson's first two attempts to contact Bobbie failed. Both missions were piloted by Captain Victor S. Doroski and Lieutenant Bill Miskho, navigator. On the first try the Mosquito's elevator controls jammed and control of the aircraft was wrenched from Doroski's hands. On the second effort Bobbie could not be contacted. On 22 November Simpson made a third attempt to make contact. Another Mosquito was used, as the first had been badly damaged on landing after the abortive second trip. As they crossed the Dutch coast Doroski lost height and the Red Stocking Mosquito started circling at 30,000 ft at a pre-set time and at an established rendezvous point to enable Simpson, crouched in the bomb bay, to record the conversation on the wire recorder. There was no response from Bobbie. Simpson ordered Doroski down to 20,000 ft in an effort to pick up the agent's signal, but still there was no response. Below the Mosquito there unfolded a barrage of fireworks. The Mosquito shuddered with each burst. Simpson shouted on intercom, 'We're in a storm, Captain. You'd better get us out of here!'

'Commander, that's no storm. We're being shot at!'

Doroski climbed back up to 30,000 ft and cruised around the area again. At midnight Simpson finally made contact with Bobbie. Through heavy static the agent informed Simpson that he was 'quite all right'. He said that a Panzer regiment was headed towards Arnhem and pinpointed a railway bridge over the Ems Canal at Leeuwarden. If Allied bombers destroyed the bridge, he said, they would paralyse traffic from this key junction into Germany. Bobbie finished abruptly: 'I am standing here near German posts. It is very dangerous.' Simpson said goodbye and told Doroski to head for home. (Doroski was lost on a night photography 'Joker' mission on 8 February 1945.)*

---

* *The Men Who Flew The Mosquito* Martin W. Bowman (PSL, 1995)

On 12 December the seventh mission in contact with Bobbie was flown. Simpson's pilot was Lieutenant Robert 'Paddy' Walker. Captain Bill Miskho flew as navigator. Bobbie told Simpson that the 9th SS Panzer Division was in a rest camp in the area but had been ordered to move in forty-eight hours. He added ominously that 'it is almost impossible as all railroads, cars, trucks and buses have been taken over and are moving troops and supplies. Something big is about to happen.' The message was clear and in English. After receiving and recording the full communication from Bobbie the Mosquito headed for Watton. On arrival the recording wire was transported to London and reported to Secret Intelligence but the significance was not realized. On 16 December Field Marshal Gerd von Rundstedt's Panzer divisions attacked the Allied front line in an area of the Ardennes where American units were in rest and rehabilitation. The German offensive achieved complete surprise and caused widespread confusion and a salient, or 'Bulge' was opened. The Ardennes offensive had proved that the German Army was yet capable and that agents were needed in Germany.

Bobbie was later apprehended by the Abwehr who used him to transmit deceptive intelligence but by a pre-arranged code, OSS knew that he had been 'turned' and contact missions to Bobbie were flown by the 25th BG regularly. The stripped-down Mosquito, however, flew above 45,000 ft to avoid German night-fighters and interceptors. Two months later Bobbie returned to England equipped with a German radio, having persuaded the Abwehr that he would make a good double agent!

Meanwhile, having established that Joan-Eleanor was successful in the field, OSS were now anxious to drop their agents into the capital itself. The Mosquito could easily fly a round trip to the city but its one limitation was the ability to carry only one operative. Paddy Walker recalls:

Steve Simpson convinced the people at Widewing [code-name for 8th Air Force Headquarters, High Wycombe] that we needed two A–26s. After they agreed into letting us have the plane Steve wanted to go back and try for a third A–26. I accompanied him on this trip and then to RAF Bovingdon where we picked up the first A–26. The fact that we didn't know how to get into the plane and the fact that I'd never flown one, didn't faze us. We flew it back to Watton.

The Douglas A–26C Invader was a twin-engined medium bomber with a much larger bomb bay space than the Mosquito's, yet could fly at over 370 mph at 10,000 ft. Careful preparations were immediately put into effect for the first A–26 mission, codenamed 'Hammer'. A hand-picked crew consisting of Paddy Walker, the pilot, two navigators (one visual and one on Loran), a sergeant (to assist the two agents) and a tail gunner, began practising for a drop involving two agents on the outskirts of Berlin.

The A–26C, painted gloss black like the Carpetbagger Liberators, flew two practice sorties to Holland in January 1945. The first, on the night of 3 January, was made without incident. Four nights later an Invader came to grief when it crash-landed on the Watton runway after it had developed hydraulic failure. The A–26C was a very 'hot' aircraft and early tests revealed that an agent could not be dropped safely from the aircraft. Early in February 1945 modifications were made to the Invader and subsequent practice missions proved that agents could bale out safely.

Lieutenant William G. Miskho, the visual navigator on the crew, recalls, 'After studying the original target we decided we could not guarantee to drop the men there. The terrain was such that we could not pinpoint the drop correctly. We notified 8th Air Force Headquarters and a week later they gave us a new target, about ten miles from the city limits of Berlin. They named 1 March the day for the drop.'

Although the Invader possessed a range of 1,800 miles and the round trip to Berlin was only 1,160 miles, Miskho had to take other factors into account which would leave little margin for error and make fuel critical. 'Major John "Nobby" Walsh (the Loran navigator for the mission) and I spent two full weeks on our flight plan. We would have to go over the continent at 500 ft and fly a course to avoid all the thousands of barrage balloons that the Germans put up every night. They changed these positions continually.'

On 1 March 1945 a Blue Stocking Mosquito belonging to the 653rd Squadron taxied in just before midnight to report that the weather over Berlin was clear. Walker warmed up the Invader's engines and taxied to the take-off point. Fuel was critical and bowsers were waiting to top his tanks. When the needles were showing 'Full' again, Walker lined up the A–26, released the brakes and thundered down the rain-lashed runway before climbing into thick overcast.

Despite the foul weather everything went according to plan. Bill Miskho sat in the nose, map-reading:

We managed to avoid the balloons and headed for the drop point. Radar was unable to pick up our blip in time to do any damage, although the tail gunner told us that he did have a little gunfire but nothing very close. *En route* we had to fly over the original target area. It was flooded within 20 miles.

Just soon enough for us to locate our target we slowed our air speed for the drop, made a target run and dropped the agents in the correct field. We did not realize how successful we really were until after the war. Following the drop we headed straight home and landed with barely enough fuel to park.

On 12 March a Red Stocking Mosquito took off from Watton and successfully established contact with one of the agents using the Joan-Eleanor radio device.

Meanwhile, the Carpetbaggers had established a forward air base at Bron Field, Lyons in France for Liberator operations to southern Germany. However, the severe winter of 1944–45 meant that only five missions were dispatched from Lyons during the January–February moon period and only a further six during the February–March moon period. Lieutenant Robert J. Swarts's crew flew missions from Lyons. Douglas Walker, the dispatcher on the crew, recalls:

I'll never forget the first time we flew to Lyons to conduct operations there for several missions. As we approached the airfield, which was used jointly by the American and Free French Air Forces, Swarts dropped the Liberator down into the landing pattern. Entering the final leg of our approach, an A–26 medium bomber zoomed directly across our nose and headed down the runway ahead of us! Swarts swung into evasive action when he spotted the A–26 speeding toward us and saved our skin! He then straightened out the lumbering Liberator and landed us safely. As we walked towards the American Operations office, feeling a bit jumpy from the close brush with the A–26, we passed some French ground crewmen rolling 500 lb bombs off the tailgate of a truck with their feet, allowing them to drop to the concrete with a loud thud! Needless to say, we broke into a run and left the area in a hurry!

Lieutenant Swarts was normally a calm individual. But after our near miss, he stormed into the Operations office and raised hell about the incident. The American colonel in charge managed to calm him down and said, 'Those A–26s are flown by Frenchmen who ignore all landing pattern discipline. They'll cut in front of you with complete abandon, with '*C'est la guerre*' attitude. Just do your best to avoid them and be extremely careful when taking off or landing!' Needless to say, we were glad they weren't flying when we returned, fatigued from our missions, in the early morning hours.

On our first mission from Lyons, Lieutenant Swarts informed us to our surprise that we were given permission to fly over Switzerland on our way to the drop zone in Bavaria. Normally, neither the Allies nor the Nazis were permitted to overfly Swiss territory because the Swiss were neutral. We could only speculate that the Swiss Government could see that the Nazis were losing the war, particularly after the failure of their Ardennes offensive in December 1944, and decided to allow the Allies some special privileges. In any event, by flying from Lyons to southern Germany over Switzerland, we cut the flying time considerably. More importantly, we avoided flying over a considerable portion of enemy territory bristling with anti-aircraft guns and night-fighter pursuit planes.

That night, as we flew over the jagged Swiss Alps, we were all spellbound by the majestic beauty of those lovely peaks glistening in the moonlight under their white mantle of snow and ice. We were all a little nervous about flying over neutral Swizerland, even with their permission! We were concerned that instructions from higher Swiss authority not to fire on us might not trickle down to the Swiss gun crews in time to ensure us a safe overflight. As we flew towards the city of Geneva, we were awed by the sight of the blazing lights of the metropolis, sparkling by the side of Lake Geneva. It was a peacetime scene which we had not seen in some time. We were accustomed to flying over totally blacked-out cities in the rest of war-torn Europe. It was such a drastic change to see brilliantly lit skies over neutral Switzerland's cities.

We were all peering out of the Liberator's windows at this startling scene, when suddenly, the interior of the Liberator illuminated to almost daylight intensity! The Swiss gun batteries around Geneva had thrown several searchlight beams on us! We felt naked and vulnerable as we held our collective breath, waiting for 'friendly' Swiss flak to hit us! However, the word must have filtered down to the gun crews and we flew on without a shot being fired. On the way back to Lyons, after we had dropped our agent in Germany, Lieutenant Swarts carefully avoided the larger Swiss cities, just for added insurance. Needless to say, we were relieved that our Liberator did not get shot full of holes, like Swiss cheese!

While flying operations from Lyons the Carpetbagger crews were billeted in a château on the outskirts of the city. This isolation was necessary to help protect the secret nature of the missions. Douglas Walker recalls:

> In March of 1945 an incident occurred at the château which developed from one of those peculiar coincidences which happen in any war. In order to take care of the aircrews billeted at the château, two French women had been hired to cook and clean and wait on tables.
>
> One evening we were in the dining room eating supper. The pilot and navigator were perusing a large map which covered a section of Germany where we were to fly that night to parachute an agent near a town in the Bavarian region. As the waitress leaned over to place a platter of potatoes on the table, she suddenly screamed and ran out of the room sobbing. Seems that her husband was a prisoner of the Germans and when she leaned over to serve the food, she had inadvertently glanced down where the navigator's finger was pointing on the map and recognized the town as the one where her husband was imprisoned. The French 'locale' knew that we were airmen but guessed, erroneously, that we were bombing air crews engaged in bombing targets in Germany. We, of course, said nothing to dispel this supposition. Naturally, she thought that the town to which the navigator was pointing was to be bombed and she became terrified at the thought that her husband's life was in danger. The pilot found her in the kitchen, sobbing, and managed to calm her down by explaining that the town that the navigator was pointing to was only a checkpoint on the route we were to fly on our 'bombing' mission that night. She immediately became her cheerful self and managed a relieved smile.

Bombing and Carpetbagging sorties were dispatched alternately for several weeks although both types of mission were flown, on occasions, in a single night from Harrington. Douglas Walker recalls a mission to the Norwegian underground forces on a moonless night in March:

> Our mission was to drop a load of munitions and supplies. We had an uneventful flight to Norway over the North Sea. The navigator and the bombardier quickly found our target area and the

underground fighters lit up the usual burning cross on the ground to guide us to the drop zone. We made our first pass over the drop zone and dropped our large containers from the bomb bay. As we made our turn for the second pass to drop our smaller containers from the waist, the tail gunner, Ralph Schiller, reported in on the intercom and said, 'Tail gunner to pilot, bright lights just came on over to our right – it looks like an airport – and there is a plane taking off with its landing lights on.'

We had stirred up a real hornet's nest! The Nazi airfield was only a few miles away and they had obviously sent up a night-fighter pursuit plane to zero in on us! We completed our second pass in a hurry and turned towards the North Sea. When we were over the water a few minutes later, we began to relax, feelign that the night-fighter had missed us. Just then, Ralph spoke again. 'There is a plane directly to our rear. I can see the glow of his exhaust and his faint silhouette!' Instantly, Swarts threw the Liberator into a dive towards the cold waters of the North Sea. When he levelled off the Liberator, we were only a few hundred feet over the water. Swarts then zig-zagged the Lib for about five minutes before climbing back to our cruising altitude. Ralph reported no sign of the night-fighter. We had successfully evaded real trouble thanks to Ralph Schiller's alertness and to Swarts's flying skill – and we had developed a new-found respect for German night-fighter technology.

The handful of Carpetbagger missions continued to Norway, Denmark and Holland. Much to the annoyance of OSS, the 8th Air Force continually refused to send Carpetbagger B–24 crews across the Dutch–German border. And at Lyons they restricted Liberator operations to south-western Germany only. OSS were anxious to dispatch their growing number of anti-Nazi agents to Germany. A clash between the 8th Air Force and OSS was on the cards so negotiations were held in London at the highest level to resolve the matter. The outcome was that the US Strategic and Tactical Air Force ordered the 492nd Bomb Group to extend its B–24 operations to include central Germany and beyond. This meant a change of bases. Lyons had proved unsuitable for Carpetbagger operations so new bases were established at Dijon, France and at Namur, Belgium.

On 16 March 1945 a SHAEF directive to the 492nd Bomb Group said that a 'development unit, which is based at Station 376 [Watton] with A–26s,' would be assigned to the 492nd 'in the near future' and 'may be operated under your control whenever it is deemed most suitable.' This effectively brought the 406th, 856th and 858th Bomb Squadrons under 492nd Bomb Group management at Harrington but operational control would be retained by the 8th. The move resulted in chaos for it coincided with the arrival of B–24 and B–17 night leaflet crews of the 406th Bomb Squadron from Cheddington. No facilities were available at Harrington so most new arrivals found themselves billeted in tents. Aircraft maintenance suffered drastically. Animosity between Upham's group and OSS reached a pitch and no one was too sure who now controlled the agent-dropping operations.

Matters came to a head on the night of 19/20 March, when an A–26, piloted by Lieutenant Oliver Emmel, was scheduled to drop a German agent near Hamm. Major John W. Walsh and Major Ed Tresemer made up the other two members of the crew. All three men were highly experienced but Emmel had still to complete training on the A–26. The weather worsened and the Invader was finally grounded for repair. Despite protests, Colonel Upham decreed that the mission must go ahead. After several postponements the mission finally got under way late that night. Emmel took off in a blinding rainstorm and he and the rest of the crew were never seen again.

Colonel Robert W. Fish recalls:

It was because of Upham's 'gung ho' 'must do' attitude that we lost Ed Tresemer and crew on the first A–26 mission from Harrington. We did not have an adequately trained crew for the mission. I had gone to France to run some operations out of Dijon so I was not at Harrington when the request for the mission came down from Baker Street. Colonel Upham formed an ad-hoc crew of good but inadequately trained people for the job. He reasoned that with senior combat experienced people on board, that would compensate for the lack of team training. He didn't understand that the success of our missions depended on perfect team work. He wasted the mission!

Major Tresemer had been my navigator. He was one of the best. I had also checked him out to be a qualified bombardier and he flew as the bombardier on the mission. We took advantage of every means of navigation we could possibly use. Our bombardiers were in the nose of the aircraft and assisted the navigator by matching the map of the terrain. Tresemer had one habit that may have gotten the A–26 crew in trouble. While map-reading, he was always calling the pilot to fly lower so he could see better. When I got down to about 400 ft I just ignored Tresemer's requests to fly lower. It may be that Emmel, not knowing Tresemer as I did, flew the plane at an extremely low altitude.

Upham was assigned to the 306th Bomb Group at Thurleigh shortly thereafter and Colonel Jack Dickerson assumed command of the new operations. The 306th Bomb Group historian states: 'Although combat flying was nearly over, in his service with the 306th, Colonel Upham established a reputation as a quiet, effective, administrator and a good flyer.'* Upham was later killed in an air crash in Italy.

On 19 March the 492nd flew the first of fifty-four successful operations from Dijon into Germany on behalf of OSS. Missions, for the most part, involved dropping intelligence agents equipped with wireless transmitters into key locations in Germany from where they could transmit vital information to the Allies. Each aircraft that arrived from Harrington to carry out missions from Dijon brought its own crew chief. Living conditions at the French base were somewhat primitive. Staff and combat crews were billeted in tents on the airfield. There were no floors in the tents and no running water on the airfield. However, food was adequate and everyone tried to make the most of the inconveniences. The overflow of personnel was billeted in the town, although a shortage of vehicles created additional difficulties in transportation. The operational cycle at Dijon rarely deviated. OSS telephoned a list of missions daily. A preliminary weather and bombline check determined which mission could be flown that night. Then, Captain Joseph W. Hartley, commanding officer, and S–3, assigned the missions to the crews. A maximum of four crews were maintained for operations at Dijon. At all times an effort was made to combine as many targets as possible for each crew. The number of targets per crew (with a maximum of three) depended on the distribution of enemy airbases, flak defences and aircraft load per target.

After all these arrangements were completed, a teletype was dispatched to the advanced movement officer, giving data on the

* *First Over Germany* Russell A. Strong (Hunter Publishing, 1982)

osed flights. This served as clearance through the Seventh ny and First French Army lines and Allied night-fighter patrols. al pinpoints were referred for approval to Harrington, with the exception that where time was short, radio reception bad and the military situation made a change in pinpoint necessary, Dijon had to assume the initiative of making a change.

In the course of the afternoon, information on the current flak situation was received; changes were seldom more than three days later than flak experience changes in the Luftwaffe order of battle. At 16.30 hours, the crews who would be flying that night were briefed. A final weather briefing was given at the weather office before take off.

Upon their return to base, the crews were interrogated. Weather observations made during the flight were immediately forwarded to the weather officer. The information thus obtained was invaluable to the medium bombers scheduled to take off. Later, the complete interrogations were forwarded to Harrington for S–2. The strictest security, essential to the success of the mission, was successfully maintained throughout the Dijon operations.

Lieutenant Colonel Robert W. Fish was among those who flew missions from Dijon. He recalls:

> We dropped some agents in the foothills of the Alps near Munich. It was a 'hairy do' because the only possible withdrawal manoeuvre was a 'chandel' to avoid slamming into the mountains. A few nights later we were back to the same drop zone with a re-supply drop. We made S-phone contact with the agents on the ground and asked what other supplies they might need. The answer we received was obviously an expression of a wry sense of humour. I quote, 'We want a bunch of bananas and a few packages of condoms!'

Apart from the ever present weather problems, enemy fighter activity and flak defences, there was also another danger. Unfortunately, not all anti-Nazi agents who were to be dropped into their homeland could be trusted, as Douglas Walker recalls:

> One night, while preparing the waist of the B–24 Liberator for the arrival of the Joe, I was beckoned out of the aircraft by an OSS captain. He warned me to be careful that night and to keep my distance from the Joe. Seems that the agent we were to drop was a

former German Army Sergeant PoW who had volunteered to jo
the American OSS and return to Germany as a spy for the US.

'Of course', the Captain said, 'we have no way of knowing if he is
going to spy for us or if he is just looking for a one-way free ticket back
to the "Fatherland". Watch out that he doesn't try to pull you out of
the aircraft when he jumps. You'd be a good prize for him to deliver to
Hitler.'

My concern at this bit of news was further heightened by the actions
of the Joe after we had levelled off and headed for Germany. I felt him
move over to my side of the plane in the darkness. (I had deliberately sat
on the floor opposite him on take-off.) He put his lips close to my ear and
shouted over the roar of the engines in broken English, '*Das* is Liberator
airplane?'

I yelled back, 'Yes, why do you ask?'

He responded, 'My gunnery crew shot down many Liberators in North
Africa!'

I could hear the smile in his voice. This was enough to fuel my
already suspicious concerns.

I pulled away from him, dug out my flashlight and jerked my .45
calibre pistol from its holster. I pointed the weapon at him in the
glare of my flashlight and yelled, 'Move to the other side of the plane
– *Mach Schnell*!' He stopped smiling and moved with alacrity to the
other side of the waist.

For the next few hours, I flashed my light on him every five to ten
minutes, still clutching my pistol in my hand. He didn't move. When
he parachuted out of the plane, I stood five feet away from him when I
yelled the signal for him to jump.

I have often wondered if he was just looking for a way back to
Germany. He certainly said the wrong thing to an American Air
Force man! I must admit, I had to fight down a passing thought
to 'mistakenly' not hook up the static line to his ripcord as a little
revenge for the American flyers he and his gunnery crew killed in
North Africa. He probably wondered the same thing until his 'chute
opened!

Douglas Walker was not the only one to have doubts about the
German Joes they carried in Carpetbagger aircraft. One eighteen-
year-old former member of the Hitler Youth, who had been
unearthed by the French, was suspected of 'working his ticket' by
OSS. Colonel Charles C. Bowman, William Casey's executive officer

...om late March 1945 placed in charge of air operations at
...n, instructed the American agent escort that if he had any
...ubts he was to 'Knock him off'.* On the flight out he could be shot
...s he left the plane. No one would have been any the wiser.

One of the last missions flown from Harrington was carried out
by the 406th Bomb Squadron. Apparently, SOE had several 'war
surplus' homing pigeons they wished to dispose of. Crews were told
that they were to drop them for agents to use. However, SOE really
wanted them dropped with message containers attached, to lead the
Germans to believe that several agents or traitors were on the loose.
Their subsequent investigations, it was hoped, would spread alarm
and suspicion among the civilian population.

Crates containing the pigeons were duly dropped over German
towns in the Ruhr pocket, but the mission did not appear to have the
desired effect. The story is probably apocryphal, but it is said that
one pigeon returned with a message which read, 'I had the sister of
this one for supper. Delicious. Please send us some more!'**

When the final Carpetbagger mission was flown on 16 April
1945, a total of eighty-two agents had been parachuted into
Germany by aircraft of the Dijon Mission, principally Liberators.
It brought to an end an illustrious career by the Carpetbaggers.
Twenty-six aircraft had been destroyed and 208 men had lost their
lives in missions of mercy to aid Belgians, Danes and Dutch men
and women, French and Norwegians, to help free their countries
from Nazi domination.

An incident shortly after the war exemplified how dangerous
the missions had been for the Liberator, Invader and Mosquito
crews of the US special squadrons too. In Paris Roy Ellis-Brown
met Commander Simpson for a drink. The commander showed the
former Red Stocking pilot a Gestapo file on the airman, complete
with instructions for 'special interrogation' if he should ever be
captured. Some parts of Red Stocking had been discovered by the
Nazis and Ellis-Brown was always relieved he never learned just
what 'special interrogation' meant!

On 13 March 1947 in Washington a belated War Department
citation was finally bestowed on the Carpetbaggers. In part it said:

---

* *Piercing The Reich* Joseph Persico (Ballantine Books)
** *Aviation in Northamptonshire* Michael L. Gibson

Despite perilous flying conditions and opposition from close-range enemy ground defences, the 492nd BG (H) dropped by parachute a total of 276 tons of arms, ammunition, demolitions and stores to resistance groups operating behind enemy lines. Conducting operations from a forward base in France, the 492nd BG (H) continued to distinguish itself in special operations involving long flights into enemy territory dropping trained agents.

To this day some of the Carpetbaggers' wartime work remains a closely guarded secret in classified files in American archives in Washington. Subterfuge and false information were factors in many OSS–SOE operations when any manner of covert activity was used to prevent the enemy guessing the next Allied moves.

The world woke on 4 February 1945 to discover that British Prime Minister Winston Churchill, American President Franklin D. Roosevelt, Marshal Stalin and the chiefs of staff were meeting at Yalta in the Crimea to shape the post-war world. It is no coincidence that English locals saw a large man, wearing a bowler hat and puffing on a big fat cigar, step aboard a Liberator at Harrington airfield for the flight to Russia.

15

GLENN MILLER: 'MISSING, PRESUMED MURDERED?'

By June 1945 the last of the Carpetbaggers had departed the shores of England. Much post-war rebuilding work was needed. Rationing continued and Britain looked to the fortitude and resolve of its people. In Bedfordshire, life went on much as it always had, although there remained a few outstanding problems that the wartime occupation had produced, particularly at Milton Ernest Hall.

At the war's end an American unit completely 'cleansed' the hall and the grounds of any vestiges of military occupation. They were so thorough that the task took a month. The bailey bridge was dismantled and huts were removed. Even the conduits to the radio aerials were dug up and taken away. Charles Davies recalls, 'The place suffered a great deal of damage and after the war there was a long legal wrangle as to who was responsible for the damage caused. It ended with the American authorities having to make good the damage when the owner, Captain Starey and his wife, went back there to live.'

To help guide Britain and America through the dark days of the Cold War, rationing and shortages, the old wartime hits continued to be played. Among them were the tunes made popular by Glenn Miller and his orchestra. Although attempts were made, unsuccessfully as it turned out, to prolong the life of his great band, the Glenn Miller magic lived on. No one had time to question the events leading to his death. It was assumed Miller was just another wartime casualty and his Norseman was just another aircraft that had succumbed to the elements. Officially, the aircraft had gone down in the Channel. It was the fortunes of war.

However, many people, like Miller enthusiast Dennis Cottam, believe that perhaps the true reason for his disappearance has been covered up. In 1947, while on leave from the Army, Cottam was invited by some friends to meet in London for a drink at 'Shepherds' in Shepherds' Market. He recalls:

> We discussed several things and the subject got around to Glenn Miller. They said, what do you think happened? I said, 'If it takes me all my life I will find out.'
>
> I was aware that there was a tall gentleman, nicely dressed in a dark suit, leaning over backwards listening to us talking. He suddenly turned around and said, 'Excuse me, I did notice what you said about Glenn Miller. I am glad you appreciate his music and by all means listen to it but don't probe into it if you take my advice.' He was an American and I came to the conclusion he was from the American Embassy, which is just around the corner.

Later, when Dennis Cottam was staying with his sister another odd thing happened:

> A great friend of my sister worked in the library at the BBC. I asked if there were any Miller recordings. She looked, and found all his wartime broadcasts. About six months later I returned and to my utter amazement she said that somebody had taken them and destroyed them all.
>
> I later met a producer who worked for both the BBC and ITV and told him about Miller and the mystery. He was usually a man who got to the bottom of things. A few weeks later he ignored me and told me he had been warned to leave the material alone. He said, 'In fact you have put my whole career in jeopardy over this. I've been sent for by high up.' He refused to say more. Something must have frightened him very much.

In August 1982 Ray Shields, a modern day bandleader who specialized in playing in the Miller style, publicly made astonishing claims of an international cover-up surrounding the death of Glenn Miller and a brain-washing technique which he said the British Government were involved in both during and after the war. Known as subliminal or 'message under the music' technique, it is a method of putting a hidden message through to a person's subconscious without the conscious mind being aware.

Glenn Miller's music was broadcast to the German Army to help undermine morale. Miller and the band were in great demand for propaganda work at the American Broadcasting Station in Europe

(ABSIE) in London. ABSIE was controlled by the Overseas Branch of the Office of War Information, a civilian propaganda outlet for the American Government. ABSIE seduced its overseas listeners with musical programmes and many of the announcements and some of the vocals were in German. Bing Crosby and Dinah Shore, who read from phonetic German scripts, were among the American stars who broadcast. The first recording session was held at the HMV studio, Abbey Road, St John's Wood in London on 30 October 1944. Following its success Glenn Miller and his band recorded a series of transcriptions for half-hour weekly broadcasts beamed at the German Army on the 'Wehrmacht Hour'. The first programme was aired on 8 November 1944. But the 'Wehrmacht Hour' and any 'musical messages' supplied via the airwaves to Allied agents is hardly unconventional. All Miller's musical scores had been written before the war so there was no obvious intent. However, wartime arrangers could have been appointed to convert it for a more sinister purpose, possibly for use by the Psychological Warfare Division. These techniques would certainly have been consistent with the security in force at Milton Ernest. Putting his music to this use would have placed Miller under more pressure than his already overburdened body and mind could take.

Certainly, Glenn Miller was under great stress in the days leading up to that fateful day in December 1944. One man who noticed a great change in the major was the British bandleader, Geraldo. Dennis Cottam interviewed him at his offices in New Bond Street shortly before the bandleader's death in 1975. Cottam recalls:

Geraldo said that a lot of the Americans came to England from very quiet places in the States and were very apprehensive. But as soon as they realized most of the British got on with what they had to do they calmed down. Now Miller was the opposite. He arrived and was rather amazed and upset to find the Doodlebugs and things and he got more and more nervous, more and more depressed.

When they first started working together. Geraldo found Miller a very warm-hearted and a most charming man. Towards the end he found him very difficult, jumpy and very nervous. Miller started missing appointments, something he never normally did. Miller was a stickler for being in the right place at the right time.

Geraldo said that whenever one was talking to Miller about anything other than music he kept saying that he was absolutely convinced in his own mind that he would never see the States again. He gave the signs of a man cracking up. He ate less and less and became more and more irritable and more difficult to deal with. He said he had no doubts the band would go back but he would never see America again. He told Geraldo this many, many times.

Geraldo believed that the whole thing went very, very much deeper. A lot of friends in the music business felt that when it was said that he had died in this aircraft, they didn't quite believe it.

On the evening of 7 November 1944 Miller and the band broadcast from their Bedford studio at 18.30 hours. Next day he was booked on a C-47 shuttle flight from Bovingdon airfield, Hertfordshire to Orly airport in Paris. Miller had orders to attend a conference in Paris with Lieutenant Colonel David Niven and General Ray W. Barker, SHAEF G-1. SHAEF wanted the band beginning on or about 15 December, to make a six-week tour of American bases and field hospitals in France, which would include entertaining the troops on leave in Paris on Christmas Eve and New Year's Eve. Although the conference was scheduled for 15 November, Miller had apparently decided to leave a week early so he could enjoy the delights of Paris first. At Milton Ernest Hall he had become friendly with Lieutenant Colonel Norman Baessell, who was responsible for establishing advanced air deports on the continent. Baessell made frequent flights to France and Belgium and was notorious in Paris for spending money like water, buying drinks all round in restaurants and bars. It was rumoured that he was involved in the Black Market. Baessell had promised to show Miller 'the town' when they were in Paris. The morning of 8 November was cold and frosty. Bovingdon was a tiring 50-mile drive from Bedford so Baessell, who was also leaving for Orly from RAF Twinwoods nearby, offered Miller a 'lift' as far as Bovingdon in his UC-64A Norseman. Miller accepted. Baessell had counted on George Ferguson in Belgium being able to fly a Norseman to Twinwoods but Ferguson's commander had refused him permission. Undeterred, Baessell contacted Flight Officer John Morgan, a pilot in 8th AFSC, at Honington and instructed him to fly his Norseman to Twinwoods to pick them up. Morgan did not obtain flight clearance until noon. While they waited, Miller, Baessell and Haynes had lunch at Milton Ernest Hall. When the three officers arrived at Twinwoods Morgan and the Norseman were waiting. Morgan took off and headed for Bovingdon where Miller left to board the C-47 for Paris. The Norseman continued on to Orly, returning to England on the 18th when Morgan dropped Baessell off at Abbotts Ripton. That same day Miller returned to Bovingdon on the SHAEF shuttle from Paris.

On 25 November Lieutenant Don Haynes flew to Paris to make all the arrangements for the band's visit to the French capital. On Tuesday 12 December 1944 Miller and the band made their last live broadcast in the UK from the Queensbury All Services Club in Old Compton Street in London. That same day an order issued by SHEAF signed 'By command of General Eisenhower' instructed Major Glenn Miller to... 'proceed by military aircraft (ATC) on or about 16 December 1944... to... Supreme HQ, Army AG-TM on the Continent'. The order does not say why Miller needed to proceed to the continent but it seems that Haynes on his trip to France on 25 November, had overlooked how the band would be transported from Orly airfield to Paris. Depending on which account you read, Miller is supposed to have told him that he would fly to France instead of Haynes, who had orders to fly to Paris 'on or about 14 December', and sort this out personally(!) Miller is reputed to have told Haynes to, 'Uncut the orders and have them changed.' In a Haynes diary account for 13 December the 'diarist' (a diary which appeared in the early 1950s, seems to be genuine and a factual account. A second which, surfaced after Haynes' death in 1971, appears to be a work of fiction) says that he 'got Glenn's orders cut to fly to Paris tomorrow.' Why? Even if he had cut the orders afresh they could not have been issued until 16 December and in any event, Eisenhower's order dated 12 December already allowed for any changes to be made!

Miller never showed up in Paris and it was assumed that he and his plane had 'disappeared over the Channel'. According to official nomenclature, on 15 December Miller and Norman Baessell had left Twinwoods in a UC-64 Norseman piloted by John Morgan and it had gone down in the sea off France en route to Villacoublay. Villacoublay is south of Paris. Miller's orders were to 'travel by military aircraft' and Orly could be reached directly, and relatively more safely by C-47 from Bovingdon. In fact on Wednesday 13 December Haynes had booked Miller on a flight from Bovingdon to Orly the next day. It therefore begs the question, why board a single-engined aircraft a day later, on Friday 15 December, and, on a plane which was going to the 'wrong' airfield? The simple answer could be that Miller never did and that the events of 8 November were used to explain away the events of 15 December 1944.

According to diaries in the name of Don Haynes on Tuesday 12 December he walked back to the Mount Royal Hotel with Miller after the Queensbury concert and on the Wednesday evening took Miller's bags to the Old Quebec Street Air Terminal. Then he and John Morgan, who had come down to see the final concert, went to the Milroy Club in Stratton Street, Mayfair, with a girl singer. There they met Squadron Leader Tony Bartley DFC* and Lieutenant Tony Pulitzer and they partied until the early hours. But before midnight Haynes and Morgan left to drive back to Bedford in thick fog. Soon after, Glenn Miller said goodbye to the others and walked away in the fog early Thursday morning towards the Mount Royal Hotel in Marble Arch. In words which could have been written by a Hollywood scriptwriter, 'He was never seen alive again'.

The AEF band played their first concert in France at the Palais de Glace on 21 December but no announcement was made about Glenn Miller being missing. The next two concerts were cancelled but the Christmas Eve broadcast obviously would have to go ahead. The Non-Battle Casualty Report stating that Glenn Miller was "missing" was released on 22 December and in New Jersey Mrs Helen Miller, Glenn's wife, was notified by telegram the following day. No mention was made in either document as to the type of aircraft, departure airfield and destination. The Haynes' diaries give two different airfields Morgan is supposed to have flown from to Twinwoods and neither ties up with Morgan's Form 5 Record of Flight Times. An amended Casualty Report, issued in March 1948, stated that the aircraft 'crashed somewhere in the English Channel while on a mission from Twinwood Field, England to Paris, France...'. The original Casualty Report included the words, 'Was taken to airfield by off. of AAF Band who witnessed takeoff.' In the second version of his diaries Haynes is said to be that officer, having driven Miller and Baessell to Twinwoods to wait for Morgan to arrive! In the entry for 15 December Haynes is asked by Baessell to bring 'Glenn's baggage' – the very same baggage that Haynes had taken to the Old Quebec Street Air Terminal on 13 December!

At 18:00 hours on Christmas Eve, an hour before the scheduled broadcast to America, the news was at last released. Miller's loss was a blow to civilian and troop morale, already low following news that on 16 December von Rundstedt's *Panzers* had cut through the American lines in the Ardennes and opened up a salient which became known as the 'Bulge'. Obviously the war would not now be over by Christmas. Lieutenant Keith Roberts, navigator, was one of many in England at the time who was saddened by Miller's disappearance:

> Emptiness. Loss. The BBC news broadcast announcing that Major Glenn Miller was gone, missing from a flight over the English Channel. Later, at the Rainbow Corner in Paris, after a parachute jump and a journey across France, listening to the great AEF band without Major Glenn Miller, we heard *Moonlight Serenade* as a requiem to a man and his music and as a goodbye to our youth.

In recent years several theories attributing to the loss of Miller's aircraft have appeared in print. However, while authors have pronounced the 'patient' dead, none has diagnosed the cause of the epidemic. Whatever the reason, black marketeering, espionage or blackmail; life may have become too hot for the famous bandleader, now close to complete mental and physical exhaustion with the strain of it all. Matters would have come to a head if Miller, always the perfectionist, had discovered that his music was being used for brain-washing techniques. In seeking confirmation or demanding an end to it, he would have been told bluntly, 'You will play it this way Major Miller, or not at all!' In retaliation, the bandleader may have threatened to 'spill the beans' and 'break the network wide open'.

At this point the American high command would have to retire Miller from the scene and eliminate a potential breach of security without drawing attention to any covert operations still in force. All that was needed was a few days for an agency to come up with the means, and a plausible reason for, his disappearance, be it temporary or otherwise. This would be a fairly simple task but surely, even in wartime, a personality like Glenn Miller would soon be missed, both by his band and the listening public?

While in England, his band knew he was prone to disappearing on one of his 'little escapades' for perhaps five or six days at a time and only a few people would know where he was.* Miller and the band had already recorded such a wealth of material so that after 12 December 1944 (incidentally the date of his last 'live' broadcasting appearance) all the broadcasts put out over the air

---

* Nat Peck in a BBC Radio interview

were pre-recorded. This means that Miller need not have shown his face publicly for at least three days after this date.

The ideal choice for spiriting the major away would have to be OSS. They were past masters at their craft and as we have seen there is evidence that they were involved in, or were linked to, operations at Milton Ernest. It was known in advance that Miller would have to fly to Paris for his forthcoming engagements. OSS would have had some time to put together a plan which would convince everyone that the Major had 'disappeared' *en route*, when in fact he had been secretly flown to the USA aboard a long-range aircraft such as the C–47, which was often used on OSS operations.

However, the best laid plans. . . . Someone may have taken it upon himself to eliminate the Major permanently, over the Channel, or better still, near the Azores, in the deepest part of the Atlantic where the aircraft could never be recovered. A simple shot through the head or through the heart and the assassin could bale out, leaving the twin-engined aircraft to nose dive into the deep Atlantic. OSS could call upon many men trained in the art of assassination without trace. As a former OSS officer had once said about a doubtful operative: 'If you have any doubts, shoot him over the sea and throw him out. No one will ever be the wiser.'

Certainly, some of the documentary material in the US National Archives is contradictory and at worst deliberately misleading. Miller's medical record has never been released and the Norseman which is supposed to have gone down in the Channel with Miller on board has never officially had its engine number released. Also, Eisenhower issued an order on 12 December, instructing 'Major Glenn Miller' to 'proceed by military aircraft (ATC) on or about 16 December 1944 . . . to . . . the Continent. . .'. Curiously, Miller's serial number differs from the one correctly stated on the subsequent MACR (Missing Air Crew Report). It will also be noted that Ike's order instructed Miller to leave on an ATC aircraft, not a US Service Command Norseman which is listed on the MACR.

The MACR had to be compiled in triplicate within forty-eight hours of the time an aircrew member was officially reported missing but it is dated 23 December – a full eight days after the loss of Morgan's aircraft. The delay could have been caused by the need to identify Morgan's passengers. The MACR seems to indicate this as it is typed using two typewriters, with Baessell's and Miller's names added later, and an extract that followed listed all three names in the same type.

On a more sinister note, could the delay have arisen because Morgan's UC–64 conveniently disappeared near the time Miller was 'lost' on another adventure and, to avoid any 'official embarrassment' over Miller, HQ added Baessell's and Miller's names to Morgan's MACR and told the world that all three were on the same flight?

Baessell has become a very effective fall guy as the man who offered Miller what was (especially in view of Eisenhower's order of 12 December) an unauthorized 'lift'. However, some weeks before, in November in fact, Baessell and Miller had already decided how they would fly to Paris. Baessell intended to use Lieutenant (later Lieutenant-Colonel) George W. Ferguson, a test pilot and engineering officer at the Strategic Air Depot at Wattisham. Ferguson first heard of his selection at B.52 in Brussels in November. He recalls:

> Baessell came over with General Goodrich. Baessell mentioned to me that the Miller band would be opening in Paris on Christmas Eve. He and Glenn were coming over a week ahead of time so he could show him Paris. He wanted me to be the pilot. I said I would be pleased to do it but I had to get permission because I had a new commander, Colonel O'Connell. Baessell said Goodrich would approve everything.*

(Early in December Goodrich returned to the USA due to failing health. He died of a heart ailment on 12 July 1945 at the Army Air Force hospital at Maxwell Field, Alabama at the age of only fifty.)

Ferguson, who had served under Baessell in the USA, had already flown him to Paris in August and to the continent on two other occasions. Ferguson recalls:**

> Baessell was a very profane individual; every third or fourth word would be a four-letter word. He was also a braggadocio, a very loud individual who you could hear for blocks; a military bigot. He had been a plantation owner or plantation manager and loved to push blacks around. He didn't speak softly but carried a big stick. Apparently, he came from a money

---

* 1981 Interview with Royal Frey, the then Curator of the Air Force Museum at Wright-Patterson Air Force Base.

** 1981 Interview with Royal Frey, the then Curator of the Air Force Museum at Wright-Patterson Air Force Base.

group because we got talking one time about blacks and he said they had their place. He accused me on many, many occasions with his favourite expression: 'What do you want to do, live for ever?'

Baessell usually sat up front in the co-pilot's seat. On our third flight to the continent I made him wear a Mae West. He hated that. In fact he would loosen the Mae West and parachute but would have it close to him when we crossed the Channel. Over land he would put the Mae West back in the baggage compartment in the tail. This last time crossing the Channel going to England, I suddenly remembered the Mae West and of course nobody could get to them. He looked over and asked what about the Mae West? I said, 'Well I hope we're going to live forever Colonel.'

Lieutenant-Colonel (later Brigadier-General) Richard E. Fisher, Engineer VIII AFSC, who was at Milton Ernest early in December 1944, recalls, 'I spent some time with Glenn Miller at our little Officers' Club at Milton Ernest. He mentioned that he wanted to see Paris and that he might soon have a chance to fly there. He did not say how he intended to do that. If he had, I would have talked him out of having anything to do with the CO of Milton Ernest Station complement [Baessell].'

Early in December, George Ferguson met Glenn Miller and Baessell in the hallway at Milton Ernest. Baessell introduced Ferguson to Miller as the pilot who would be flying them to Paris. However, fate later intervened, as Ferguson recalls:

Baessell called me on the military network in Zaventon, a mile from B58 (now Melsbrôek International) and said 'Copy this Ferguson. I want you over here at such and such a time and so forth.' I said I still hadn't got my commander's approval. Two days later I said it was doubtful. I did get the tacit approval of my commanding officer, Colonel O'Connell. Basically, it would have to be a one-day mission, get them aboard, fly them to Paris and fly back to Brussels. O'Connell didn't want me away any length of time and would not let me go the day before. It had to be all in the one day.

The morning of 15 December dawned shrouded in fog and swirling mist around Milton Ernest Hall. Ferguson recalls that the weather in Brussels was worse.*

---

* 1981 Interview with Royal Frey, the then Curator of the Air Force Museum at Wright-Patterson Air Force Base.

The fog was down around your socks, it was so bad. There was a 1,500 ft ceiling. The weather was still good in England but bad in Villacoublay, Baessell's destination. The continent was more socked in than England. I thought Baessell was aware of the weather situation so he would just be sitting it out. But the field 'phone rang at about 08.30 in the morning.

Baessell said, 'Ferguson, where the Goddamned Hell are you?'

I said, 'I'm in Brussels.'

He told me to 'get my butt over there right away.'

I said we couldn't possibly take off. I asked him what the weather was like over there.

He said, 'Fine.'

I said, 'You know me well enough that as soon as I can take off with an alternate that I can get into I would try to get off.'

He said, 'Hurry up, what do you want to do, live forever?' and hung up.

It was about 0930 hrs when Ferguson received another telephone call from Baessell:

He was getting more profane. I said the weather had not yet broken.

He said, 'What do you want to do, live forever?'

I can remember saying to him, 'Please wait for me. Will you do that please, sir?'

'Well, OK, but you'd better get over here.'

He seemed to want to go that day come hell or high water. Then his final comments were, 'What do you want to do, live forever?' He hung up. It was the last I ever heard from him.

George Ferguson's reluctance to fly over from Belgium and pick up Baessell did not appear to thwart Colonel Baessell's plans to press on to Paris. It was indeed fortuitous that another Norseman was going to Paris. It would appear that Baessell simply 'rustled' up another UC–64 from Abbots Ripton. The pilot was 'Nipper' Morgan, who just happened on 15 December to be flying to Bordeaux via A–42 (Villacoublay, near Paris).

Victor Stillwell recalls, 'Miller left the house between 9 a.m. and 10 a.m. He said to me, "I am going off on a little trip with Colonel Baessell, I may be back tonight. I shall certainly be back tomorrow." He looked quite cheerful. He and Baessell climbed into a jeep and their driver drove them off to Twinwoods.'

Dixie Clerke, a WAAF in the RAF control tower that day, saw Miller board a Norseman and take off with a total of four people in the aircraft. The last contact she had was that the aircraft had landed at Bovingdon, an 8th Air Force Service Command base near London, presumably for customs clearance. One man left the aircraft. Later that evening she telephoned several stations along the route the UC–64 would have taken but no one had heard or seen the aircraft.*

Meanwhile, in Brussels Ferguson waited for news.

> At noon I called Twinwoods airfield and asked to speak to Baessell. The dispatcher said, 'He just left with Major Miller a few moments ago.'
> I said, 'Where did they go, the club?'
> 'No Sir, they took off.'
> 'Who was the pilot?'
> 'Flight Officer Morgan.'
> 'Oh my God.' It really grabbed me. This could not end up good.

Ferguson was alarmed because he knew Morgan's limitations as a pilot, having previously checked him out on the Proctor.**

> Morgan had trained with the RCAF. He ended up as a Flight Sergeant with the RAF and came in as a liaison pilot. He did not fly any of our fighters. He was a rather frail guy and I don't know whether he could reach the rudder pedals. He wore lifts on his heels and needed two cushions behind him. He was a quiet, dapper little guy, mild-mannered, five feet six inches tall and about 135 lb. He was a good VFR pilot but a lousy instrument pilot.

These were hardly the attributes needed for a flight across the Channel in the bad weather conditions on 15 December 1944.

> The balance of the day went by and nothing happened. The following day, at about 8.00, I got a call from 8th AF HQ.

* *Wings of Mystery* by Dale Titler (Dodd Mead)

** 1981 Interview with Royal Frey, the then Curator of the Air Force Museum at Wright-Patterson Air Force Base.

'Where's Miller?'

'Major Glenn Miller?'

'Yes, is he with you?'

'No.'

'Then where in hell is he?'

'I haven't the foggiest idea. As far as I understood he filed for Paris.'

I started getting calls about every hour. 'Where do you think they might be?'

By the end of the second day Ferguson's feeling was that the Norseman undoubtedly went down in the Channel. He put together his thoughts on what might have happened:

The UC–64 had no de-icing equipment. Some models had a prop' de-icer but no wing de-icers. It had mid-frequency radios with little range and no IFF. Morgan was not a good instrument pilot. Neglected to watch his instruments. Forgotten to put on carburettor heat? Panic, engine back fires, lost power, lost altitude – struck water. The UC–64 was a fabric aircraft and when it hit it probably broke up and went in twenty-nine directions.

A Norseman was undoubtedly lost on 15 December but is it the one listed on the MACR? Morgan's UC–64, as we have already learned, was not the only Norseman in the air that day and apparently not the only one at Twinwoods either. (On 14 December a 3rd SAD pilot from Watton had flown a Norseman to Twinwoods with instructions to leave it at the Bedfordshire airfield and return to Watton by road.)

No one can be certain that Miller even left the shores of England on 15 December. Don Haynes, Miller's executive officer, said that the first they realized that Miller was missing was on 18 December when the band landed at Paris. Dennis Cottam recalls, 'If a man goes missing, presumed dead, the next of kin are informed and all the man's belongings are sent to them. In Miller's case there was an enormous delay.' Victor Stillwell adds, 'When it was presumed Miller was dead all his belongings were put in large 4 ft by 2 ft cabin trunks and sealed up by security people at Milton Ernest. They put a stamp on them and after three days they were removed.'

As has already been mentioned, OSS could have been involved in Miller's disappearance. If the MACR report is correct, the addition of Baessell's and Miller's names would seem to indicate that their part in the flight was unofficial. Although Miller boarded the Norseman, he may have had second thoughts before the aircraft departed the coast of England, leaving Baessell and Morgan to go on alone. What if Miller changed aircraft, whether by intent or by force? Under orders from OSS it is quite conceivable that after take-off his aircraft could have alighted on the airstrip beside Milton Ernest Hall. Miller could have been spirited into the hall, leaving Baessell and Morgan to continue their flight. Later, Miller might have been driven out in a car with blacked out windows to another airfield, possibly at night for take-off in a completely different aircraft to an entirely new destination.

Meanwhile, controversy still rages about Baessell, and even Lieutenant-Colonel David Niven's possible involvement in Miller's disappearance. On 15 December the British film star was in Spa, Belgium visiting Army friends, having arrived in France from England one month before. Little has been written about David Niven's mysterious wartime career and details are notable by their absence in his autobiography, *The Moon's a Balloon*. In fact Niven, who could speak fluent German, served in F Squadron GHQ Reconnaissance Regiment (Phantom), a highly secret, fully mobile organization developed during the threat of German invasion of Britain. Phantom did excellent work behind the enemy lines with the SAS after the invasion of Normandy, severely hindering the German effort and pinpointing targets for RAF bombers.*

Dennis Cottam recalls: 'Several people contacted Niven about his association with Miller. He just wrote back to them and said 'Sorry old boy, only met the man twice.' Yet, of the hundreds of documents I received from Washington every order, every movement, is countersigned by David Niven. Also, Miller used to have regular meetings at SHAEF HQ and obviously met Niven time and time again.'

Norman Baessell would have had access to large quantities of scarce wartime commodities and there were always many customers willing to pay for nylons, perfumes, cigarettes, good whiskey and other luxuries, especially in the wartime capitals of Europe. Although Service Command did not stock these items, it was an Aladdin's cave for marketable items such as aircraft spares, stores, foodstuffs and drugs, that could be converted into hard currency or

---

* *The Special Air Service* Philip Warner (Kimber)

expensive goods on the black market. Penicillin for instance, had a street value of about £50 an ounce in 1944. Baessell also had what amounted to his own private airline to run these goods to and from the continent if he so wished.

Certainly, US Postal and FBI investigations were conducted at Milton Ernest Hall and at all the Army postal facilities in the ETO. Their mission was to apprehend and court-martial individuals involved in black marketeering, professional gambling and illegal currency transactions. The safest way for US service personnel to remit dollars to America was by means of US postal money orders. Money orders were purchased for cash with a very low service charge at a postal facility then mailed via APO to recipients in the States. The recipient could redeem them for cash at any US Post Office. It was noted by postal authorities that some individuals were purchasing money orders in amounts far greater than their pay (in some cases thousands of dollars more); hence the investigation.

Black marketeering or blackmail may account for the reason leading to Miller's disappearance and possible murder. If the famous bandleader was involved in psychological warfare to a greater degree than is immediately apparent, OSS may have been involved in a botched attempt to prevent him from revealing the true nature of the techniques involved. But the mystery remains.

Today the few remaining people who were associated with Milton Ernest Hall refuse to talk. Just before his death in 1981 Charles Davies wrote cryptically, 'There was some connection [at Milton Ernest] but I cannot divulge what it was because we were under the strictest security regulations at the time . . .' Others prefer to remain anonymous.

That Miller disappeared there is no doubt. However, all the theories as to why and how are way off course. Legend blurred the issue and was reinforced when in 1954 the Hollywood movie, *The Glenn Miller Story*, starring Jimmy Stewart and June Allyson was released. While most cinema-goers believed the storyline totally and still do, others have their doubts. Brian C. McCulloch was six when he first saw it.

> My dad leaned over to my mother and said; 'They don't have that quite right'. He was referring to the scene where Glenn Miller leaves Twinwoods airfield in Bedfordshire. When we left the theater, I asked my father what he had meant with his comment. He told me that he was Glenn Miller's driver the day Miller disappeared. He added that

the vehicle was a *Dodge* staff car, not a jeep and that he was a Staff Sergeant, not an officer. My mother said she was going to write to Hollywood to set the record straight. Forty-nine years would pass for my dad's role in the story of that day in December 1944, when the Miller legend was born, to become public. More interestingly, my dad remembers the plane that day to more closely resemble a Traveler, a biplane than the currently credited Norseman, a high wing monoplane. As a flight Cadet, he had trained in biplanes. Also, he does not remember a plane as large as the one used in the movie. [The Beech C-43 Traveler served principally in the United States but a few reached the ETO in 1944. Thirty UC-43s were supplied to Britain under Lend-Lease. Interestingly, the Air Attaché operated one at the US Embassy in London!]... Several hours later, the military police and/or intelligence arrived at Milton Ernest Hall. Colonel Early later told my father that they had collected a footlocker and some other personal affects left behind by Major Miller. The Colonel ordered him not to mention Miller's most recent stay at Milton Ernest. He said nothing until he got home.

Another theory that has been proposed is that Glenn Miller's Norseman aircraft was brought down by bombs jettisoned by a RAF Lancaster, which has prompted claims that it 'finally solves the mystery of his disappearance'. Could it have happened? To cross under the Lancasters the UC-64 Norseman would have had to fly west of London. We are led to believe that Morgan could not fly east of the capital because of a prohibited area in the Thames Estuary called the '*Diver* Gun Box', where anti-aircraft batteries were concentrated to shoot down flying-bombs heading for London. In fact Morgan did not need to 'avoid' the *Diver* box. It was inactive. The 137 Lancasters flew through the *Diver* box back to their base at Methwold! Morgan was not an instrument-rated pilot. He would hardly, therefore, choose to fly in bad weather along a longer route to Paris when he could more easily cross the Channel at its shortest point. No pilot, instrument-rated or otherwise, would choose to take this route in winter.

What evidence is there of Glenn Miller even being aboard the 'bombs theory' aircraft in the first place, especially if it did not 'stop off' at Twinwoods Farm or Bovingdon en route to Paris? Morgan was cleared direct from Abbotts Ripton to France and he did not land at Twinwoods or Bovingdon. No record was ever made in the log at the Flying Control at RAF Twinwoods of a Norseman having landed there that 'fateful' day. Lancaster navigator Fred Shaw's 'Norseman surrounded by bomb explosions' was almost certainly another UC-64, which left from Grove, near Wantage, Berkshire, and which was destroyed en route to Creil or Villacoublay, France. Miller's subsequent disappearance, or rather non-appearance – for whatever reason – had to be explained somehow. And the loss of an aircraft – any aircraft – over the Channel was convenient. The only snag in the 'cover plan' story is that on paper, Miller was 'put aboard' the wrong Norseman!

We may never know what became of Glenn Miller but in 1995 there was the first indication that OSS may possibly have been involved in his disappearance. An English OSS researcher in Northamptonshire received word that William E. Colby, who has been described as a 'brave and resourceful OSS officer',* would be returning to the area where he had been based in 1944. Several country estates in Northamptonshire, Bedfordshire and Huntingdonshire were used by SOE and OSS units as headquarters and training facilities and their operatives, agents and guerilla forces. They were flown out of airfields like Harrington, west of Kettering, in black painted Liberators operated by the American Carpetbagger group and parachuted into countries occupied by the Germans. Once on the ground they linked up with underground organizations such as *Maquis* in France and the *Army Secrete* in Belgium to organize sabotage and the disruption of enemy supplies. Hundreds of *Jedburgh* teams, agents and guerrilla forces were dropped into France just prior to and after the Allied invasion of Normandy, 6 June 1944 to disrupt and then harry the retreat of German troops. *Jedburgh* teams consisted of three members, usually English, French and American. On 14 August 1944 Colby was part of a *Jedburgh* team codenamed *'Bruce'* that took off from Harrington and was dropped near Montargis in France.

When the English OSS researcher met his distinguished visitor as arranged at a railway station he assumed that Colby would first want to visit Harrington. (After the war OSS developed into the CIA and in 1950 Colby joined the new organisation. During 1973–November 1975 he was Director of the CIA). Colby however expressed a wish to be taken to Holmewood Hall, an English country

---

* *CIA: A History*, John Ranelagh

mansion on a large estate near Glatton (Conington) airfield near Peterborough. During the war Holmewood Hall was called Area 'H', which included the massive OSS Supply Depot at Holme and a holding area for OSS agents and OGs (Operational Groups) from Area 'E', who were accommodated in the grounds under canvas. Area 'E' was the codename for Brock Hall, an English mansion at Weedon near Daventry, which had been used by the SOE until 1943, when it was turned over to OSS. The OSS used the grounds of Brock Hall to train a Norwegian Special Operations Group called NORSO in guerrilla tactics prior to being dropped behind enemy lines in France in August 1944. After the liberation of France some NORSO personnel were returned to the USA for special training prior to working with OSS units in China. The rest who remained in England would be used behind enemy lines in Norway and they came under the command of Major William E. Colby. Prior to being parachuted into Norway Colby and his NORSO group would have transited through Area 'H' at Holmewood Hall.

The English OSS researcher and Colby walked among the overgrown buildings at Holme packing station, Colby, a man of very few words, paused at the firing range and soliloquized: 'This is where Glenn Miller was executed.'

As incredible as this sounds, Colby then added more fuel to the fire afterwards by saying that Miller's body was later transported to Gaynes Hall, which is a short distance from Holme at Perry village beside Graffam Water (Diddington reservoir). There he was supposedly buried in a field (adjacent to what is now Littlehay Prison) where saplings were planted to cover the several burial plots. Who, if anyone, are in the other plots? In the Second World War Gaynes Hall was a highly secret, heavily guarded SOE facility where captured Nazis and other individuals were reportedly taken for interrogation. Those that proved 'uncooperative' were taken to a large walled 'courtyard' in the grounds of the Hall, blindfolded and strapped to a chair and executed. (Bullet holes can still be seen in the wall). At Holme too Nazis were reportedly executed in woods in the grounds of Area 'H'.

Colby offered no reasons why anyone would want to execute Glenn Miller or why Area 'H' and Gaynes Hall were used. Also, why shoot him at Holmewood and then bury him at Gaynes?

A possible explanation is that during the war Area 'H' was technically 'American soil' and it had been agreed that Holmewood would revert back to private ownership after the war. Though post-war Gaynes Hall was used as a borstal for young offenders it reverted to a private residence, but the field containing the bodies is part of the Littlehay Prison complex.

Less than a year after his visit to Holmewood Hall and Gaynes Hall Colby was found dead at the bottom of a lake near his home in the night. His half-eaten meal was in the house and floating on the surface of the lake was his empty canoe.*

* * * *

A tenuous yet possible scenario for Glenn Miller's demise has been provided by a retired American officer, who at present remains unidentified. The officer claims that he was stationed in England among other places during the Second World War and had strong links with OSS. Remarkably, 'Officer X' as we shall call him, independently stated that Holmewood Hall and Gaynes Hall were the two locations involved in the execution, although he has never met nor had any connection with the OSS researcher who was privy to Colby's assertion. 'Officer X' says that OSS shot Miller for refusing to go along with plans to smuggle some very important looted works of art to America via England. The pieces in question were wall tiles from a Russian palace that were stolen by the SS in 1941 and hidden somewhere in Germany until 1944 when they were moved due to the advancing Allied troops. The location of the pieces was handed over to OSS operatives by a German officer who had been captured and used this information to deal his way out of trouble.

'Apparently,' 'Officer X' claims, 'Miller was involved in this business from early on but it got out of control as soon as the Allies had access to Paris and certain key captured German officers. Up to December 1944 (and until well after the end of the war) a lot of Nazi loot made its way back to the States secretly via UK and USAAF airfields. The location and contact with other Nazi officers came

---

* In *CIA: A History* John Ranelagh says that '... Apart from his temporary assignment to the Phoenix programme in Vietnam in the late 1960s, [Colby] had worked continuously on the clandestine side of the agency... Like many other people, Colby had been affected by the mood of disillusionment and dissent that developed as the Vietnam war progressed and, after the death of his daughter in April 1973, he as thought by colleagues to have become more religious (he was a Catholic) and reflective.'

about via links with the German and British crime syndicates. They in turn were linked with the Mafia, who themselves worked closely with American intelligence on mutually beneficial operations such as Operation Underworld. OSS was up to its neck with the Mafia. Neither could get out of each other's pockets as each knew what the other was up to and because both were making so much profit from the 'liberated' Nazi loot, much of which would never be traceable due to the original owners being Jewish. In the Second World War the smuggling of stolen Nazi loot was an excellent opportunity to make money. Many American officers were willing to take chances to make some big money.

'Officer X' claims that one of the 'arrangers' in the UK was Norman Baessell, the 'so-called passenger on the Miller flight'. Also the profits from some of the loot made a good 'black budget' for the OSS to operate with. Miller wanted to back out because he thought that this shipment was too big in size to be able to move via the usual methods and that they might be caught. 'Officer X' says that Miller did not die in a plane but was shot by OSS and as far as he was aware much of the loot was hidden in stately homes until it could be moved stateside and that there are 'items' remaining at certain houses to this day.

OSS and the Mafia apparently crossed swords over the recovery of European art treasures; upward of twenty per cent of which was looted by the Nazis. During and after the Second World War the United States Government, in part through the Safehaven Program sought to identify, recover and reinstate Nazi-looted assets and expended considerable resources trying to recover looted treasures. Some 823 American airmen in Troop Carrier Command were assigned to the OSS Art Looting Unit for flying this material back and forth. The American Commission for the Protection and Salvage of Artistic and Historic Monuments in War Areas (The Robert Commission), the US Army's intelligence units, and Monuments, Fine Arts, and Archives officers, and State Department Foreign Service officers, among others, were also engaged in efforts to identify, recover and reinstate looted art works. However, many thousands of pieces of art were never recovered by their rightful owners. As late as 1994, 16 of the 40 top paintings were still missing. In 2001 a Jewish family claimed that *Le Grand Pont* a painting by Gustave Courbet, at the Yale University Art Gallery belonged to them and was acquired by a former Nazi Party member after the family fled Germany during the Second World War. The painting was one of forty-eight European artworks on long loan to Yale from Herbert Schaefer, a lawyer living in Spain who said he had bought the painting legally from a dealer in 1938. Eric Weinmann of Washington claimed his mother bought the painting in 1935 from another Jewish family at an auction in Berlin. The Weinmanns fled to England in August 1938, leaving all their possessions behind. In March 1997, Philip Saunders editor of *Trace*, the stolen art register, stated that 'There are at least 100,000 works of art still missing from the Nazi occupation'.

* * * *

Perhaps the mysterious silver-grey-haired old gentleman, who was driven into the grounds of Milton Ernest Hall, during that summer afternoon in July 1980 in the blacked-out limousine, knew the answer to one of the last great secrets of the Second World War. If he did, he has not shared it publicly and unless it is recorded in a top security file in a vault somewhere, he has probably taken his secret with him to the grave.

Meanwhile, one can only speculate.

INDEX

Other titles published by The History Press

SOE's Ultimate Deception

FREDERIC BOYCE

The true story of an incredible deception and the invention of an underground German resistance movement.

£12.99   978 0 7509 4028 3

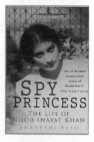

Spy Princess: The Life of Noor Inayat Khan

SHRABANI BASU

Features the story of Noor Inayat Khan, the descendant of an Indian Prince Tipu Sultan, the Tiger of Mysore, who became a British secret agent for SOE during World War II. This book presents the story of Noor's life from her birth in Moscow – where her father was a Sufi preacher – to her capture by the Germans.

£9.99   978 0 7509 5056 5

Poland Alone

JONATHAN WALKER

Jonathan Walker examines whether Britain could have done more to save the Polish people in their crisis year of 1944, dealing with many different aspects such as the actions of the RAF and SOE, the role of Polish Couriers, the failure of British Intelligence and the culpability of the British Press.

£20   978 1 8622 7474 7

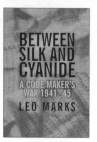

Between Silk and Cyanide

LEO MARKS

Both thrilling and poignant, Leo Marks' account of his time in SOE is truly one of the last great Second World War memoirs. Between Silk and Cyanide tells how he revolutionised the code-making techniques of the Allies and trained some of the famous agents.

£14.99   978 0 7509 4835 7

Visit our website and discover thousands of other History Press books.

www.thehistorypress.co.uk